ADVANCE PRAISE FOR
COMBO PROSPECTING

"In a fad-filled sales world that loves silver bullets, Tony Hughes gut-punches us with what's real and what works. *COMBO Prospecting* addresses the challenges of prospecting with unflinching courage. Sales reps must master prospecting or starve. Companies must embrace prospecting or be run over by competitors who are not afraid to attack the top of the sales funnel. Tony doesn't mince words in these pages. My advice: read it twice and apply its clear lessons daily. Your success will thank you."

—Chris Beall, CEO, ConnectAndSell, Inc.

"This is a manual for dealing with the biggest problem confronting business leaders, entrepreneurs, and salespeople today . . . not enough opportunity pipeline. Yet lack of closable deals is really a symptom of deeper issues, and you must not solely rely on others to generate the leads and opportunities needed for success. Instead, you must take control and step into the hard-core prospecting fight cage yourself . . . you're not really a leader or a serious salesperson unless you do! This book explains how any business-to-business seller can transform results to become a knock-out success. It is filled with practical steps, real examples, and actionable insights. You'll be able to create your own plan worthy of becoming a world champion in your industry."

—Jeb Blount, bestselling author of *Fanatical Prospecting*

"Creating sales pipeline is one of the top issues facing sales organizations today and foundational for sales success. Combining proven sales strategies with modern methods of engagement is a winning combination for prospecting in today's competitive marketplace. Tony's book explains how to intelligently embrace technology to consistently deliver outstanding sales results."

—TIFFANI BOVA, analyst, sales strategist, and growth adviser, Salesforce

"Opening is the new closing because nothing happens with a sale unless you can first get in front of decision makers with the right agenda. Tony's book nails what it takes to cut through all the noise facing executive buyers, and he understands the importance of human connection in a digital world."

—ANTHONY IANNARINO, bestselling author and transformational sales strategist

"Tony Hughes is one of the very few voices I listen to when it comes to pipeline creation and new business development—and you should, too! The sales world needed *COMBO Prospecting* and this book delivers exactly what you need to know and do to succeed creating your own sales opportunities. Read it and implement. Now."

—MIKE WEINBERG, author of the AMACOM bestsellers *New Sales. Simplified.* and *Sales Management. Simplified.*

"Tony Hughes is one of the most respected writers and speakers globally on the topic of business-to-business selling. *COMBO Prospecting* is an absolute must-read for anyone interested in delivering consistently high sales results in the real world of ferocious competition and difficult-to-win clients."

—JONATHAN FARRINGTON, CEO, Top Sales World

COMBO
PROSPECTING

COMBO PROSPECTING

THE POWERFUL ONE-TWO PUNCH THAT FILLS YOUR PIPELINE AND WINS SALES

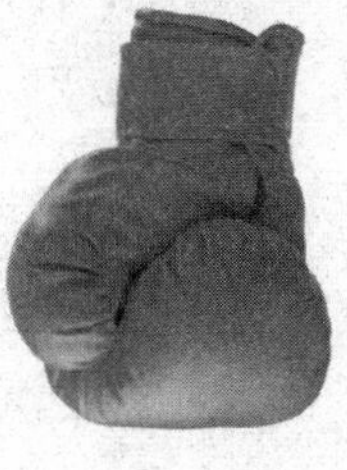

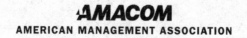

AMACOM
AMERICAN MANAGEMENT ASSOCIATION
NEW YORK • ATLANTA • BRUSSELS • CHICAGO • MEXICO CITY • SAN FRANCISCO
SHANGHAI • TOKYO • TORONTO • WASHINGTON, D.C.

Bulk discounts available. For details visit:
www.amacombooks.org/go/specialsales
Or contact special sales:
Phone: 800-250-5308
Email: specialsls@amanet.org
View all the AMACOM titles at: www.amacombooks.org
American Management Association: www.amanet.org

Library of Congress Cataloging-in-Publication Data

Names: Hughes, Tony J., author.
Title: Combo prospecting : the powerful one-two punch that fills your pipeline and wins sales / Tony J. Hughes.
Description: New York, NY : AMACOM--American Management Association, [2018] | Includes index.
Identifiers: LCCN 2017027802 (print) | LCCN 2017047925 (ebook) | ISBN 9780814439128 (ebook) | ISBN 9780814439111 (pbk.)
Subjects: LCSH: Selling. | Strategic planning. | Customer relations.
Classification: LCC HF5438.25 (ebook) | LCC HF5438.25 .H8657 2018 (print) | DDC 658.8/12--dc23
LC record available at https://lccn.loc.gov/2017027802

About AMA
American Management Association (www.amanet.org) is a world leader in talent development, advancing the skills of individuals to drive business success. Our mission is to support the goals of individuals and organizations through a complete range of products and services, including classroom and virtual seminars, webcasts, webinars, podcasts, conferences, corporate and government solutions, business books, and research. AMA's approach to improving performance combines experiential learning—learning through doing—with opportunities for ongoing professional growth at every step of one's career journey.

20 PC/LSCH 10 9 8 7 6 5 4 3

THANKS AND ACKNOWLEDGMENTS

THE AUTHOR'S JOURNEY DEMANDS CRAZY LEVELS OF COMMITMENT, AND MY creative writing has been done while leading corporate teams and, in more recent years, while supporting my consulting clients. In one seven-month period, I was publishing at least one original long-form blog per day, even while on vacation with my family in Vietnam. Insane, I know. The creation of this book, along with my blogging, occurred during the evenings and on weekends at the expense of time with my family. I am hugely indebted and forever grateful to my wife and children, who have been so accommodating and supportive over the years, as I obsessively wrote while also working to provide for our family.

This book was conceived from my blog and the incredible feedback from my readers. I have read hundreds of books and thousands of blogs over the decades, and I am grateful to the sales leaders around the world who have contributed to my learning. I've asked 100,000+ globally based sellers thousands of questions on every challenging sales topic one could imagine. In many ways, this book is an amalgam of the best sales minds in the world over the last three decades. I've synthesized timeless truths about influence and sales with innovative ways of leveraging technology in the age of the machines, empowered buyers, and naked brands. I've credited every person and source when I knowingly express their concepts; please forgive any unintentional omissions of attribution. If your own unique concepts are included in this book, without acknowledgment, please let me know and I'll promote you in my blog and update future editions.

I thank all of those sales leaders who read the draft of this book and provided feedback, especially Kyle Porter and Chris Beall. Most important, I thank my clients; without their willingness to embrace change and without their courage to lead, this book would not be possible. My love affair with LinkedIn leaps off these pages, and that's because I'm genuinely grateful for the free gift they've given the world in the form of an online profile and publishing platform. Reid Hoffman and Jeff Weiner themselves have had a profound impact on me based on their understanding of networked intelligence and the strength of weak ties.

Last but not least, I send special thanks to Tim Burgard and the AMACOM team in New York for doing more than just editing and publishing this book—they believed in it. They understood the need to focus on generating quality sales pipeline in order to transform the revenue results of businesses.

CONTENTS

Fight Club and Knockout Commitments

"If you set yourself on fire, the world will come to see you burn."
—DON KING

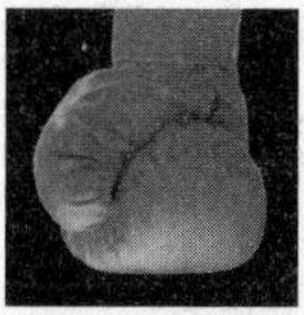

LOOK DOWN AT YOUR HANDS. HANDS OF LOVE BUT ALSO HANDS of steel—make them into fists. If you take just one thing from this book, let it be this: The left is social, the right is the phone—blended together, they are the *social phone*, a term coined by Kenny Madden.[1] In boxing, you jab with your left to offensively keep yourself safe and set them up for a knockout with your right hook or uppercut. For sales, you jab repeatedly with digital outreach via LinkedIn, email, text messages, Twitter, and even Facebook; you are setting up a knockout with the phone. The prospect or customer is not your enemy; rather, you are combating any apathy, walls, or resistance that may surround them.

Anyone who claims that you can succeed with one hand tied behind your back is just plain wrong. Social and digital alone fail. Phone alone fails. Passive attraction strategies alone fail. Intelligent combinations are the only way to win, and this is the essence of COMBO Prospecting.

COMBO refers to this combination, and it is also an acronym for Command Over Maximizing Business Opportunities.

Right now, you may be failing to realize your real potential. There is no question that the Pareto principle applies to sales prospecting. This principle states that 20 percent of the input invested results in 80 percent of the outcome. So how do you stop wasting 80 percent of your time and start landing that 20 percent where the real opportunity is? No matter how passionately you sell, you must still battle the evil forces of competition, commoditization, globalization, disruption, automation, and artificial intelligence (AI) technology—because they all seek to eliminate your very livelihood. Winning requires dramatic changes in how you operate. By embracing technology with real human engagement, you can prosper in the arena of sales. This combination will elevate you and make you hyper-effective in breaking through to engage with the impossible-to-reach people who need your help.

> "The number one issue facing sales professionals, sales leaders, and sales organizations is keeping the pipeline full of high-value propects, and keeping those pipelines moving toward positive outcomes."
>
> **BRANDON BRUCE, CO-FOUNDER, CIRRUS INSIGHT**

This book will show you exactly how to drive higher levels of effective activity and create quality sales pipeline. Right up front, I want you to know that success will only happen if you commit to doing these 10 things:

1. Accept personal responsibility for consistently creating sales pipeline every day.
2. Realize you will need to put in 10 times the activity you are doing now to be remotely successful, and that's past the horizon of comfortable. Fear not; this book will show you how to do it by leveraging strategies and technology.

3. Lead with an insightful business value narrative rather than talking about your company, products, services, and solutions.
4. Create an authentic personal brand showing credibility, curiosity, and positive and aligned values.
5. Actively use LinkedIn Sales Navigator. Even if your boss won't get it for you, buy it yourself because it is an essential tool of trade in the modern age, just like the Bloomberg terminal or a mobile phone.
6. To source email addresses and phone numbers, find a way to gain access to sales intelligence software, such as DiscoverOrg, ZoomInfo, RainKing, Data.com, Lusha, Seamless.ai, or others.
7. Actively use the phone as part of your prospecting strategy. No combination of activities will work unless it includes the phone at the core.
8. Embrace customer relationship management (CRM) and marketing automation to identify and nurture prospects who are not currently ready but who you can follow up with later. Companies that excel at lead nurturing have 9 percent more salespeople making quota.[2] According to The Bridge Group, email automation with tracking remains a key part of any nurturing strategy.[3]
9. Commit to massive consistent action. Relentlessly get into the ring every day, slug it out, be willing to take a beating, and then win by doing what your competition will not.
10. CEOs read dozens of books a year, but most salespeople read none. Rise above the pack by committing to read every book and blog that I reference, and listen to the podcasts I recommend. Especially focus on Mike Weinberg, Anthony Iannarino, Jeb Blount, Mark Hunter, Nic Read, Jim Holden, Jeff Thull, Ben Zoldan, Noah Goldman, Jill Konrath, Trish Bertuzzi, Marylou Tyler, John Smibert, Will Barron, Jeffrey Gitomer, Craig Elias, Tibor Shanto, John Barrows, Jonathan Farrington, Lee Bartlett, Graham Hawkins, Gerhard Gschwandtner, and Tim Hughes.

If you're not up for the challenge or if your success and livelihood is just not that important to you, spare yourself the aggravation of reading on and give this to someone who will actually take the necessary action. If you are serious, commit to actually doing rather than merely trying. I promise you will be very glad that you did.

In this book, I attempt to make the content "eclectically snackable," so feel free to browse and jump around based upon the biggest challenges you face. This book is an in-the-trenches handbook for dealing with the entrepreneur's and salesperson's number-one problem: not enough opportunity pipeline. A lack of closable deals is really just a symptom of deeper issues, and you must not solely rely on others to generate your leads and opportunities. Being successful means taking control over prospecting yourself—you're not really a leader or a salesperson unless you do!

Please understand that it is out of respect that I assume you already have a solid understanding of professional selling. Also note that I cite many technologies but acknowledge that there are hundreds more that could have been included. I mention those with which I am familiar through personal use or the work I've done with clients. I am especially passionate about LinkedIn and Salesforce because they are the leaders in creating business-to-business sales pipeline and end-to-end customer experience to drive sales. Since completing the draft of this book in early 2017, Salesforce became my client.

If you don't understand something I reference, simply Google it or ask me on my LinkedIn blog at www.linkedin.com/today/posts/hughestony. I am deliberately provocative about the things that matter, and my goal is to cattle-prod you into action. All the stories in this book are real, and the use of repetition for key concepts is designed to inspire intelligent action and help you remember what's important. The Jason Bourne–meets–Monty Python writing style is intended to evoke emotion and to interrupt your habitual thinking patterns and mindset.

Finally, if you think I'm full of hot air after reading this book, write to me via LinkedIn, and I'll refund what you paid for it. I could go bankrupt since I only receive a small royalty from the publisher, but I'm passionate about everything you're about to read. I'm putting my money where my mouth is because my hope is that you also put your full effort where your mouth is to realize your real potential as a salesperson, business leader, or entrepreneur.

COMBO Explained and Calls to Put Me in Jail

Jeb Blount is a true sales hero, and his book, *Fanatical Prospecting*, completely changed my attitude toward selling. That's even after being in the field for 30 years in the United States and running entire technology companies in the Asia-Pacific region. Jeb stirred the pot tremendously with this quote that I shared in my LinkedIn profile:

> I closed a $2.5 million deal after leaving the exact same voice mail for a C-level exec every morning for 52 consecutive days. He finally called me back and said, "You're not going to stop are you?" I responded, "Not until you meet with me." The meeting opened a dialogue that, six months later, resulted in my company replacing his incumbent vendor. Persistence is the fuel of winners.

This quote spawned more than 1 million views, more than 5,000 likes, and over 600 comments.

Many missed the fact that I was merely quoting Jeb, and they decided to attack me, thinking I had done this. I wish—it's the stuff of legend! One man said I should be locked up in jail for harassment! Another lady threatened to send two former NFL linebackers to beat me up! The level of emotion was off the charts. The irony is that Jeb did not harass anyone. He simply stayed the course, knowing he could help his customer and staying determined to do so despite the customer's apathy. Customers really can be their own worst enemies, but in this case there are 2.5 million proof points that they ultimately awoke from their slumber and agreed with Jeb. I know that his customers are grateful for his polite and professional persistence. Jeb passionately believes in the value he offers . . . do you believe in yours?

I have become the most-read blogger globally on the topic of buyer-to-buyer (B2B) selling within LinkedIn, and that's where I've researched and tested the concepts within this book. Jeb's quote lit the fuse that ignited a powder-keg realization: Sellers have become too passive, quiet, fearful, and lazy. I discovered the best way to start a fight of mixed martial arts (MMA) proportions, in any sales community, is simply to tell people that they've "gotta pick up the phone and call someone!" Yet fear of rejection and fear of the phone can be transformed and become your best friends if you know the secret to breaking through. Emotion can be harnessed if you have the right thought process.

Again, look down at your hands. The left is social, the right is the phone. Without them both, you can't possibly win the fight for sales success. Their powers together make you unstoppable. Imagine if you can master this right combination? If you grasp this concept alone, you can eventually execute it, and then you can ascend to the top echelons of your company as a sales leader.

Combinations of the right activity, done the right way, with the right people, through the right channels, and at the right time can create world-champion success. This is the heart of COMBO Prospecting. You could also simply see COMBO as the ultimate blended approach for bringing old school and new school together. It is the combination of timeless truths with contemporary engagement that will break through with the maximum prospects. It is the only way to drive sales success in markets where there is increased competition, well-informed buyers, ferocious procurement departments, moats, razor wire, land mines, Barry Manilow music piped to the perimeters, giant walls, and pit bulls preventing any form of seller engagement.

We will cover COMBOs of multichannel outreach where Kenny Madden's social phone is the weapon of choice. We will also address the COMBO for having the right narrative:

- Leading with insight
- Stating why it matters
- Positioning a hypothesis of value

We will cover the COMBO for next steps after you've initially broken through:

- Engage the most senior person
- Be sponsored down
- Build consensus and a compelling business case

Then, we will explore the COMBO for creating a powerful personal platform:

- A strong personal brand
- A network that empowers
- Tools and templates that enable high performance

Next, we will look at the COMBO for knockout success:

- Trigger events
- Referrals
- Customer advocacy

Finally, we will go over the COMBO for closing:

- Setting the right agenda
- Creating trust and confidence
- Demonstrating commitment and leadership

Some COMBOs are a blend of strategies or tools; others have a one-two-three knockout technique or a series of jabs. I have clients that drive six-touch COMBOs that make it impossible for any potential customer to ignore them. My good friend at LinkedIn, Matt Loop, talks about LinkedIn's own combination of systems for execution: system of record (CRM), systems of communication (phone and email), and system of engagement (LinkedIn). Think of these systems as concentric circles, all integrated and overlapping.

Everything you're about to read here has been tested in the real world. Combinations are not new in sales and marketing, with Gary Vaynerchuk and others previously writing on the topic. Research and advisery firm TOPO highlights the power of "the triple touch," and Jeb Blount uses the term "the triple threat." But timeless winning strategies can be refreshed and enhanced to spectacular effect. The concepts and practices here go to the next level of execution and are already driving spectacular results in the United States, Canada, United Kingdom, Australia, Asia, and all over the world. I know this from the global reach of my blog within LinkedIn and the tremendous feedback I've received.

If you believe you've already got it all together, and you just want to know exactly what to do to accelerate sales pipeline creation, skip to Chapter 4, where we take the gloves off and give you everything you need to know for hands-on execution.

I make no apology for getting in your face about what it is really going to take for you to become a sales world champion. But before I do, I want to briefly share my journey into sales, along with some lessons about overconfidence and why a winning attitude needs to be blended with realism and humility.

Misplaced Confidence and My Journey into Sales

Everyone sells and needs to make a living, but you desperately also want to make a difference. Leadership and politics are simply sales and negotiation in a social context. No one can succeed as a leader unless they can positively influence or—put another way—unless they can sell. But few do this masterfully, and even fewer drive the necessary levels of intelligent activity to fill their opportunity pipeline.

This is the true story about confidence and how I landed in a sales career 30 years ago. I had been living in Los Angeles for 18 months, after selling my previous company in Australia, which had dominated the local market. I was confident about my new international business venture and convinced that I was going to be a gazillionaire by the time I was 30.

In hindsight, I should have remembered my flying instructor Peter's words when he sent me solo in a Cessna three years earlier. He asked what I thought being confident meant. I said something about skills and experience. He shook his head soberly, "No. Confidence is the feeling you have . . . just before you understand the real situation. Most dead pilots were wrongly confident. Don't be one of them." He went on to describe the combinations of things that conspire against all pilots. Wasps in instrument tubes, water in fuel, weather, haste, miscommunication—the list was extensive. His advice later saved my life.

Throughout my flying career, I followed his advice and always flew looking for somewhere I could glide to in the event of an engine failure. When

IMAGE I-1. TONY HUGHES PLANE CRASH

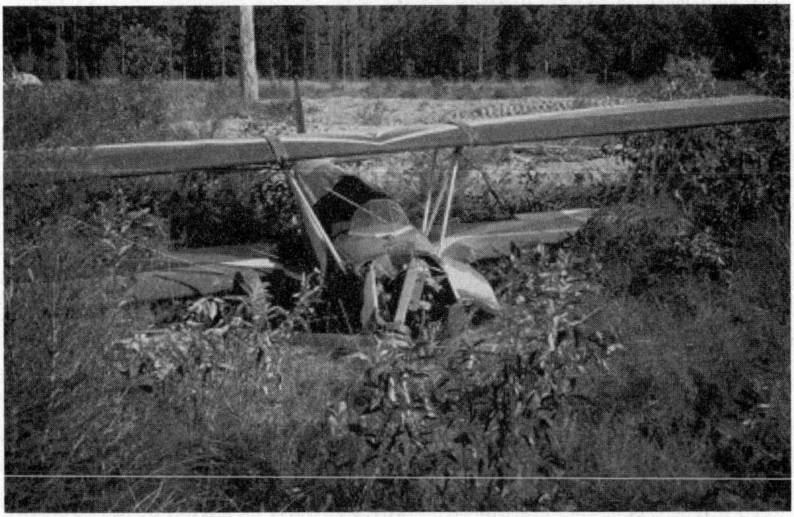

I lost my engine above a pine forest in my aerobatic biplane, I had already identified my landing zone, and that enabled me to walk away alive.

Two years after the plane crash, I was living in Los Angeles. Starting a business from scratch in a foreign country was tough, but I was determined . . . and very naive. It was my 25th birthday when the phone rang. It was my stepdad, and I jumped in, "Thanks for calling to wish me happy birthday!" Silence, then choked words, "I'm sorry mate, your mum is in a bad way. It's liver cancer—there's nothing they can do."

Some believe that bad things come in threes; others may tell you that things can't get any worse. They're dead wrong. My mother died seven weeks later at age 42 in our family home in Sydney. I had returned home to be with her up until the end. Within a week of her death, my sister's relationship with our stepfather, already fractured, broke completely and they would never speak again. Grief-struck and shattered, she imploded and was hospitalized. Our dog was run over and killed. My car was stolen. Then my stepfather went out on his first social outing and got into a fight over something trivial with, of all people, a man who had been at my mother's funeral. They argued, went outside, and as they grappled and fell to the ground my stepfather put him in a headlock and squeezed too hard and for too long. Anger simmers within raw grief, as Johnny Cash knew. My stepdad came home and woke me saying he'd done something bad. The police arrived two hours later and took him away to be interviewed. He was eventually charged with murder. I later testified in court . . . relationship over.

In the weeks that followed, our biggest customer in the United States went bankrupt. Then we discovered a large multinational corporation, a trusted partner, had stolen our designs and was manufacturing a copy of our product in a country where we had no patent protection. They fired their manager who had signed a letter of intent with us and introduced their team of in-house lawyers—17 of them! To cap it off, our joint-venture manufacturer in California filed for bankruptcy protection.

I'd already gone icy cold to cope with my grief and the knocks that followed. My business and family had disintegrated, and my wife decided she'd also had enough. She left me . . . marriage over. I didn't even resist; there was just numbness. My final card to play was my conclusion that God was not worth following—not a good state of mind when you still believe He exists. I was no Job from the Old Testament who steadfastly held to his beliefs, but I was never able to be an atheist like my dad.

With the failure of my U.S. business and the fact that I needed to stay in Sydney to be there for my sister and stepfather, I considered my options for generating an income. The 12-year royalty contract I had signed when we sold the Australian business meant that I could not compete in the same industry during that period, so I needed to do something different. One of the big lessons I learned in America was that you personally had to be able to sell if you wanted to make it as an entrepreneur or businessperson. I confronted the realization that I was not very good. Time for a reboot.

It was in this depressed state that I decided to learn how to sell. WTF! Yes, Wow That's Fantastic! I knew I needed to develop my sales skills if I was to go to the next level as an aspiring entrepreneur, so I secured a job selling radio paging in the mid 80s. Think Twitter on a device the size of a deck of playing cards before cellular phones were available. This was just before the first *Wall Street* movie with Michael Douglas, and you had to phone a call center for someone to type your message into a mainframe. That sounds crazy today, but it was revolutionary at the time.

I'm really not sure why they hired me because I had no real sales experience. Two colleagues bet money on how long it would be before I was fired. I wasn't very good, but I worked harder than anyone else and I had a sales manager who believed in me. Keith rode with me one day a week and resisted the urge to save a sale that I was screwing up with my uncertain language, closed questions, and lack of belief in myself and the value of what we offered. But I improved quickly because I was coachable, reading every book and listening to every recording I could lay my hands on. My only nonnegotiable in pursuing success was my integrity: I promised myself that I'd never sell anyone something that was not in their own best interest.

Although my self-belief was not where it needed to be, I felt I was working for the best service provider in the industry. Most important, I worked harder than any other salesperson, and there were more than 100 in the company. I deliberately treasured my selling time and did administrative work, call reports, and everything else that didn't result in a sale, before and after prime-time hours with prospective clients.

I never allowed myself to become deluded about cold calling and the need to consistently build sales pipeline. For every appointment, I would plan to arrive early and canvass neighboring businesses. "Hi, I'm Tony and I'm early for my meeting next door. Could you tell me who the sales manager (or service manager) is here? Could I have their card so I can mail them some information? I always got the card or the name. Sometimes the sales manager would come out and I'd say, "Hi, I can help you respond to leads faster and get more sales with your team in the field; how many salespeople have you got on the road?" I learned very early not to lead with a pitch about our company or products but instead talk about the results I could help them achieve.

Always lead with what you think you can do for them and their business. No one is interested in your product or service, and no one wants a sales pitch. Initially, they are only interested in why talking to you could be of any benefit to them. Always answer the unasked questions: Why should I care, and what's in it for me?

I thanked every customer for their business and asked them who else they thought could benefit from improving sales or service by being contactable anytime and anywhere (that's what radio paging did). I would phone them two weeks later and ask the same question. A referral is the fastest path to revenue, and being introduced to a potential client by someone they trust creates the highest probability of a sale.

Referrals are your most important source of leads, so it is vitally important that you always deliver for your clients and build an extensive, high-quality network.

I was later promoted to a city territory filled with skyscrapers. Awesome! Prospecting will be much easier and more efficient with high-density white-collar businesses, I thought. Confidence—the feeling you have just before you understand the situation. I learned later that this territory was a graveyard for reps, and no one had ever made their target there. Every building had a sign in the lobby and in the elevators: No hawkers or canvassers! That applied to others—nothing was going to stop me. We had at least one customer in most buildings, so, in my mind, I was not canvassing. I was simply visiting a customer and just dropping in since I was early for my meeting.

I did five months in a row above 200 percent of target and moved up into larger enterprise accounts. But I never forgot the importance of continuously building a sales funnel, always and without excuse every day. It's the only way to avoid the roller-coaster of pipeline versus performance. I became the most successful person in the industry and made the largest-ever deal by selling to IBM at 70 percent higher prices than they were paying the incumbent, who had a bigger network and stronger brand. I even had to convince our own CEO not to drop the price! He was focused on the minimum price we would accept rather than walking in the customer's shoes to determine the highest price they would happily pay for quality service and support. Had I lost the IBM deal, I still would have overachieved my annual target. I later moved into the computer industry, and then into software. The rest is history.

Many times over the years, I've lived the bipolar existence that is professional selling, and I've stared into the abyss of what seemed an impossible revenue target. Most companies have periods of insanity where they thrash around and demand relentless growth. In this pursuit, they hire like crazy, reduce the size of territories, increase the targets, fire up the team with a punchy sales kickoff, and then unleash the flamethrower to blast sellers. They exhort salespeople to step up or face the wrath of blowtorch pressure from stack ranking and performance improvement programs (PIPs) to manage out those who fail. The irony is that many good sellers are chewed up and spat out because of management's inability to analyze the data and provide viable territories and positive reference clients; or its failure to deliver the right tools, such as coaching and support, to enable sales; or its lack of intrinsic value without the right product-to-market fit.

In contrast, the best companies know that nothing good happens unless someone sells something, and they respect and value those on the front line who provide this service. Selling can make a person soar, and I've watched sellers excel as they helped their customers achieve success. Intent is important, and so is work ethic. To succeed, you can't be a snoozer, and you can't be hung up about how others perceive you. Selling is a blue-collar trade dressed up in Wall Street clothing. You must put in an honest day's work, day in and day out, and be able to look yourself in the eye and know that you actually deserve success. No matter how well sales are currently going, no matter how much you feel like it or not, no matter if there is time pressure and others are screaming at you to do non-selling activity, you must prospect every day. You must know that the only thing that creates a consistent sales funnel is consistent prospecting activity.

Just as I've seen the best, I've also seen the worst in people, as they tried to manipulate, lie, cheat, or steal their way to the top. Don't do it—your integrity is everything. Selling is not something you do to someone; it's something you do for someone. Your brand and reputation is your most precious asset. We live in an age where any client or employer can peel back the facade. You must be the real deal and be able to look at yourself in the mirror. Take social media seriously, and invest in creating a strong and authentic personal brand.

Selling, like boxing or MMA, is both scientific and mystical, both art and brutality. Real selling demands that you give yourself completely to what you pursue. You can't make it unless you are actually the person worthy of the success you seek. You must step into the ring and face your fears, passionately speaking up for what you believe. You must be willing to be pummeled and fall to the canvas with everyone watching. Then to get back up, knowing you'll be pounded again.

I've shared a little about the dark times in my own life to let you know that, regardless of the deep hole you may be in, you too can pick yourself up and rise to the top. The best salespeople are heroic, passionate, curious, and driven by positive intent for their customers. But it's never been more difficult to make it in sales, and the majority quietly fail behind their polished online image. Dangerous lies about passive selling and social media distractions are luring people into sales career oblivion. Real success, the kind that makes you a legend in your field, demands masterful skills and the right levels of activity—but you also need to be the hottest one in your business who can win the hottest one in your market.

Why You Need to Be the Hottest One at the Bar

Gisele walks into a bar, and every guy and girl there hits on her—end of story. If I were female, that story would star Brad Pitt or David Beckham. But why is this relevant for sales? The Fortune 1000 is just 1,000 winning companies, the highest revenue generators in the world. Sellers have become so desperate to connect with them that they literally send bottles of fine French champagne to CXOs. Those prospects have become so used to this behavior that they are numb to it—they give away the champagne to their neighbors and complain about it on LinkedIn. Everyone is trying to do a deal with Coca-Cola; everyone is trying to date a 12 out of 10.

So if desired people and companies are like magnets attracting everyone, and you try to do something heroic to generate their interest, you will get two forces that repel. If you reach, they will withdraw. If you sound subservient like everyone else, they'll become bored and lose interest. If you bend over backwards to accommodate their every whim in your sales process, you'll fail. If you send them flowers, chocolates, and roses after one meeting, you'll look weak or desperate.

We all know that the dynamics that play out in interpersonal relationships also govern sales relationships. In fact, InsideSales.com conducted a study that highlighted conclusive evidence from 10 million anonymized sales interactions showing that high-pressure closing tactics, at the end of each quarter, actually cut deal sizes in half and extended sales cycles unnecessarily. Why? Hunger, interest, and neediness cause the opposite polarity: repulsion.

You need to practice something that I call the Law of Principled Disinterest. You need to be present to communicate compelling business value and insight, but you cannot be aggressive like the face-humping alien leaping from the egg in the movie *Alien*. You can't be like a golden retriever running at a Frisbee. You can't be like David Duchovny in *Californication*, and you can't be "winning" like Charlie Sheen.

So how can you do the opposite? You drive pull marketing to catch your prospects upstream. You do this by writing insight-laden content to hook the fish rather than relentlessly hunting them with a spear. The right way to market is with guerrilla activations, truly exclusive events, and "building a garden that attracts the right queen bees."[4]

Create desire, attract attention, and become interesting rather than interested. Radiate confidence, and always be willing to walk away. You don't need the business, and they know that you know it. This is why it's essential for you to have a massive sales pipeline!

How can you get to the hottest one at the bar, aka the profitable business prospect that all your competitors are calling, emailing, InMailing, and trying to get referred to? Here are some questions to ask yourself:

- Have you performed a Google search on the prospect name and clicked on News to find excerpts where they are quoted? Have you sent that quote to them, referenced in an email, InMail, Twitter direct message (DM), or voice mail?
- Have you read the prospect company's annual 10-K report and the CEO's letter to the shareholders? Have you then tied this in to an ROI business case that presents your solution?
- Have you spent the money to appear at the kind of events they attend? This includes holding your own VIP dinner, without any product pitching, at a Michelin Star restaurant with a roomful of CXOs. The event is built by the presence of peers with whom your prospect wishes to rub elbows. Get your tickets to Davos, Switzerland, and TED Monterey. I'm serious!

- Have you had a courier or FedEx deliver a plain manila envelope marked only with the name of your prospect in your best handwritten cursive? Does this VITO envelope contain a super precise value proposition and case study, with a time that you will call to follow up? VITO was created by Anthony Parinello, and the acronym stands for Very Important Top Officer.[5]
- Have you built groundswell with the company's team, demonstrating how much your solution would benefit them if implemented? Have you then had them champion you to the decision-maker internally?
- Have you built a lead-generation engine through native advertising on LinkedIn with vertically targeted white papers to drive form fills (aka opt-in email captures)?
- Have you worked with highly successful lead generators, such as Mike Scher at Frontline Selling or Chris Beall from ConnectAndSell? They can break through the noise and set meetings for you with difficult-to-reach prospects in the Fortune 1000, almost auto-magically.
- Are you running retargeting on Facebook? Are you adding prospects on Facebook, using Facebook Messenger, or sending text messages? Or are you too scared?
- Have you convinced your own CEO to reach out to theirs? Your VCs to reach out to theirs? Your CMO, CFO, CIO, CTO, COO, and other executives to connect with theirs? Have you asked your best customer to be a reference and introduce you (as long as they're not competitive)? Have you used LinkedIn Sales Navigator to find the weak ties between your organization and theirs so that your administration or engineers can connect with theirs?
- Are you running a cadence of touch points across multiple mediums with a system that holds you accountable to your activities

and improves your messaging and timing with analytics? (Kudos, Kyle Porter.)[6]

You must magnetize your prospects to you. Build content, forums, events, and spheres of influence that radiate authority and thought leadership to pull C-levels toward you—for your company and as an individual seller. Educate prospects in a detached fashion before you seek to persuade. Run a 3–5X pipeline, and project confidence that you don't need their business. Read them the riot act when they demand a free pilot because they are actually increasing their own risk by not being committed. Practice nonhunger and leverage strategic disinterest.

You may be wondering how to reconcile this paradox: You must passionately believe in how you can help your customer, but you cannot be desperate in any way.

Think about it like this. If a CEO, president, or even CFO were to authorize investing $1 million in your solution today, how risky would it be for them? And if you had to spend $1 million, how much risk would you feel? Now magnify that that with some slick, fast-talking, people-pleasing yes-man who is telling you everything you want to hear. He's buttering you up, promising the world, and sounding just like the countless other salespeople you've had to deal with in your career. You can see the 7.2-magnitude nature of this problem.

"Mrs. Customer, our product may or may not be a fit, but I'd like to share what some of our similar customers in your industry are doing that might be relevant—it's positively impacting their bottom line. We can go from there; how does that sound?" Disarming, nonhungry, powerful.

Be in the habit of telling prospective customers about things they don't expect to hear, such as flaws in your solution. The truth is powerful. Vulnerability and transparency open magnificent doors and accelerate trust. Honesty, rather than rhetoric, is the best policy—it's how the trusted adviser is born.

Charles H. Green teaches about doing and saying the right things within the process of good business. "Sales and trust rarely inhabit the same sentence. Customers fear being sold because they suspect sellers have only selfish interests at heart. Is this a built-in conflict or can sellers serve the buyer's interests as well as their own? The solution is simple to state, hard to live—and totally worth the effort."[7] The answer is to always act with transparency and integrity.

Reverse psychology drives everything in sales, and David Sandler knew this. The more desperation you project as a seller, the more you repel. Some prefer not to look at it like dating, but it truly is. Are you one of the guys in the bar dressed in glittering Ed Hardy, lining up to buy the same girl a drink? Or perhaps you are the gal flirting with the hunkiest guy who wears an Armani suit? You will both fail. If you're Gisele or David Beckham and many want you, your stock goes up. If you are building sales AI software right now, you are probably one of the hottest at the bar for VC money. Robert Cialdini talked about social proof. This concept dictates that if Coca-Cola is doing it, Pepsi will be interested.

As Dr. Chester Karrass said best, "In business, as in life, we don't get what we want, we get what we negotiate."[8] So how do you become beautiful, exclusive, exotic, and noncommoditized when all the solutions look the same? The answer is not to put on an air of confidence, hit the gym, and go to the tanning salon because this is the same strategy everyone is using. It is not dubious marketing with 3,000 percent ROI case studies. How can a customer actually believe anything good will come from displays of exaggerated confidence?

I recently dealt with an overconfident seller who told me he was the Ferrari of the roadway. He expected me to buy, quoted me an impossibly high price, and then didn't check in for two weeks. This is the wrong way to use the Law of Principled Disinterest. You cannot swagger up to Gisele and brazenly give her your cell number, with Tom Brady standing right next to her, and expect her to call you.

So many enterprise sellers take this tactic when they approach the Fortune 1000. They do not realize that what draws the customer in is a sense of intrigue and exclusivity—the idea that the customer can get in on something special and cutting edge. CMOs, for example, are looking for an edge. They want to find young, hot start-up companies that can reflect well on their business. They like to install them as turbochargers for curb appeal and street cred alongside their current legacy infrastructure. It's not unlike using these companies as arm candy!

Know that what you've got is special. Tell people what you can and cannot do. Underpromise and overdeliver. Put in conservative ROI claims. You don't need to go over the top with your white paper.

Now, how can you be the hottest one at the bar? Here are some simple tips:

- Maintain a polished image. Professionalism, like chivalry, is not dead.
- Be humble and listen more than you talk. This exudes real gravitas.
- When you ask for an on-site, say something like: "Let's brainstorm some ideas, whether it's a fit or not, so that both our teams will get a great deal out of the time together."
- Make your communications to prospects about edutainment and empowerment. Tell them how they'll gain a competitive advantage for their brand. You must educate your nascent market especially if you're promoting a new category.
- Secure the arm candy. In exchange for some smaller paid pilots, push for a case study in your go-to-market strategy. Get somebody like Coca-Cola to agree to trumpet you with some fanfare. You can march into the rest of the target accounts backed with this social proof. Any negotiation should include securing this from the buyer, as it costs them nothing and is hugely valuable for you.

- Give good phone. Ultimately, fewer and fewer salespeople are using their voices. It's all gone passively digital. A relaxed, confident, nonhungry tone is the way in—be helpful like a friend, family member, or someone you actually trust. The sound of this tone soothes the savage beast of fear in the prospective buyer, whether it's on a voice mail, over Skype, or face-to-face.
- Intent. It is a universal law: When one knows they're hot, they're hot. Maybe she's born with it. Maybe it's Maybelline. Beauty radiates from within. Happiness is a decision just as confidence is a decision. You radiate what you feel internally.

What you just read went viral as a blog, and one reader even wrote in declaring that he used the exact principles to "get lucky." Another attested to running an elite management consultancy for 25 years based on its principles. In both cases, it was very eye-opening; the content really struck a chord.

All this is important because you must stand out from the crowd. It's important to maximize the quality of your interaction with buyers, but also the quantity of time with them. But ask yourself these questions: Can you control your pipeline? Can you control your customer, your prospect, your spouse, or your boss? Absolutely not! That's like Siegfried & Roy's tame tigers that inevitably went on the attack. Ultimately, it's not about control. It's about resilience, cunning, and goodwill as you step into the arena of competitive sales. It's about giving everything you've got to win for the sake of your customer and those who depend on your success for their livelihoods or prosperity.

Awful Truths That Can Set You Free

"Everybody has a plan until they get punched in the mouth."
—IRON MIKE TYSON

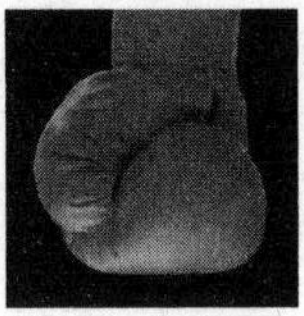

EARLY IN MY LINKEDIN BLOGGING JOURNEY, A TROLL EMERGED and asked this question: "Who are you . . . really? No one can come from nowhere and know all this!" What he failed to realize is that I had taken 35 years to become an "overnight success" and what I shared in my articles was derived through failure and painful experience. I think I've done it all in sales: sold "the dream" in people's homes, cold-called, canvassed for business up and down the street, sold to big corporations, pitched for venture capital, sold with hope and prayer, used Wile E. Coyote cunning, and worked hard like nothing else mattered. I've won and celebrated massive deals but also lost and learned. I've cried out of sheer exhausted frustration, feeling the task was simply beyond me. Even though I've topped the leader boards and been on president's club trips, I know that selling can be a bipolar existence. I've faced impossible sales targets with lunatic bosses who have no empathy and no idea how to support the troops other than halving territories, increasing targets, and applying maximum pressure. Yet all of this has made me who I am today, resilient and wiser, because we're forged in the furnace of life—pressure over time is what creates diamonds. You either implode or you become the honey badger (fiercest mammal on the planet who just doesn't care about its own well-being).

Who we become determines the value of what we pursue, and worthwhile success is never easy. Eventually, I learned to love my team and my customers and to work for their success rather than my own. I've also learned that failure is a better teacher than winning, that you cannot really be successful on your own, and that the passage of time provides the lens through which to measure real success. Being able to look at yourself in the mirror and respect who you see is everything. Selling is not about our own achievements—it's about the success of our customers and our commitment to helping them. Real sales leadership is helping someone achieve a far better state—and doing it with the belief of an evangelist, the passion of a lover, the courage of a warrior, the rigor of an engineer, the thoroughness of a forensic accountant, the diplomacy of a politician, the mindset of a marathon runner, and the discipline and determination of a world-champion martial artist.

Wake Up and Get in the Fight!

We all need "a whack to the side of the head" to snap us out of daydreaming just like Edward de Bono advocated all those years ago. Yet most salespeople are glass-jawed fools because they plan to merely hit their number with spoon-fed leads from marketing, inside sales, or social media activity, sprinkled with a little of their own extra effort.

Wake up! Get off the canvas! Sniff the smelling salts of truth. You're behind on points, so you've gotta find a way to win with a one-two-three knockout combo! Over and over and over again; stick and jab, stick and jab, absorb the knocks; grind it out . . . and then boom! Professional selling is highly competitive, and there is constant pressure as you battle your inner demons, slugging it out against client apathy, barriers to engagement, and desperate competition. It goes 12 rounds, often 14, and it's sometimes the technical knockout that wins when a razor-thin margin separates you from your competitor.

You don't lose sales, competitors outsell you—and the biggest competitor you'll ever face is doing nothing, aka the apathetic status quo. That's Ali, that's Frasier, that's Tyson . . . for those who really know boxing, that's Pacquiao or Roberto Duran. Everyone should watch *Hands of Stone*, about the versatile Panamanian brawler Duran, arguably one of the greatest of all time, who beat Sugar Ray Leonard with strategic combos. Boxing has so many parallels to sales, so any great boxing movie, including *Raging Bull*, can teach the modern seller much. The biggest battles you'll face are from within. The discipline is not to expend too much energy in the first round, to be strategic rather than use brute force, to truly know your competition, and to leverage weaknesses. And these are just some examples.

Beyond sports metaphors and dating psychology, the best takeaways for sellers come from the strategic selling canon. These sales tomes include: *Solution Selling* (Eades and Bosworth), *SPIN Selling* (Neil Rackham), Miller Heiman works, *New Power Base Selling* (Jim Holden), *Diagnostic Business Development* (Jeff Thull), and *The Challenger Sale* (Matt Dixon and Brent Adamson). Many of these books emphasize landing meetings because, as Anthony Iannarino says, "Opening is the new closing!"[1]

"The modern buyer is digitally driven, socially connected, mobile, and empowered,"[2] writes Jill Rowley. You therefore need a superior personal brand and social media savvy to break through or meet expectations. Even with this, clients treat you as a commodity and resist your efforts to engage; all the while, the clock is ticking down and the judges are scoring every move. You're only as good as your last win. Many fail and live lives of quiet desperation behind a professionally smiling facade.

A sales career can be brutal. Delivering revenue is the only thing that protects you, but revenue is an outcome, not an activity.[3] Properly qualified pipeline, and lots of it, is required to generate revenue, and a high level of intelligent activity is what's needed to create pipeline. As a salesperson, the cure of all ills is profitable revenue; lots of revenue is fueled by a big sales pipeline, which also removes the pressure from selling.

"The first commitment to action is to land the first meeting with a dream prospect,"[4] says Anthony Iannarino. Some argue it's harder to earn a second meeting, but this book also addresses that challenge. You can read 10,000 other sales books from any era, but their points will be moot if you can't break through, start a conversation, and then carry the right value narrative. Negotiation—moot. Closing tactics—moot. SPIN selling—moot. So this is a book for solving the fundamental challenge in all sales environments on the planet: getting to the table with the right agenda and narrative. If you open properly, you'll set the tone on value, earn subsequent meetings, and anchor the deal. Beginnings are important, and first impressions count. The greatest forest is contained in a single seed.

COMBO Prospecting focuses on how to break through and engage a prospect: Call, voice mail and email (all in under two minutes), and consider adding a text message, LinkedIn, InMail, and Twitter DM for initial outreach. Craig Rosenberg from TOPO, along with Jeb Blount, refers to the "triple touch." They understand the reality that success depends on persistent outreach. The TOPO Sales Development Benchmark Report published in 2014 revealed that 8–12 touches with individuals, not organizations, were needed in a concentrated period for any campaign to be effective. The report also highlighted the importance of driving outreach over multiple channels, including voice.[5]

If you are a seller who can't land C-level meetings yourself, then you're not where you need to be to survive, let alone prosper. It doesn't matter if you've read 1,000 books and can recite famous quotes and Challenger theories (CEB) from memory. It doesn't matter if you can do Miller Heiman ninja black belt histrionic hand motions with a sheaf of gold and blue sheets bristling from your pocket. Knowledge is not power in sales—the devil is in the details. "It's a paradox of basics,"[6] says Jeb Blount, author of *Fanatical Prospecting,* which is my recommended companion for this book—make it the next one you read.

You could be the best listener, be the best asker of questions, and have the tightest sales process and methodology known to man. Without a prospect in front of you, it's all wasted effort and nothing is going to happen. Reach out and touch someone, preferably with a phone, followed by an email, and then by a LinkedIn InMail or maybe a connection request.

Execution is everything. Bias toward actions, not ideas, will take you the farthest the fastest. Laboring over the perfect email or InMail may seem brilliant, but think of the paradox of relevancy. Michael Jordan spent 10,000 hours shooting three-pointers to become the winningest player ever in the game, and Gretzky's greatness was built the same way. Likewise, Donald Bradman, the greatest cricketer of all time, practiced hitting a golf ball against a corrugated rainwater tank for hours, using a single stump to hone his hand-eye coordination and reflexes.

Abraham Lincoln said: "Give me six hours to chop down a tree and I will spend the first four sharpening the axe." We must "sharpen our sales story"[7] per Mike Weinberg, but once you've got it and understand which customers are analogous to your existing customers, go chop down a forest with massive, masterful action. You will read in more detail how to do this in chapters 3 and 4.

You don't have to overthink it once you have a message that's resonating the right way in a target vertical. A seller who hits 20 prospects with the most perfectly tailored targeted email in one week will never catch a seller who has a sharp template and calls, voice mails, and emails 50 targets every day. To do this, you must hold these concepts about right action in your mind. Analysis paralysis, procrastination, and perfectionism are ineffective. Thinking that there is some magic bullet that you can put in a social selling message that will get you a meeting or deal is just self-delusion.

There have been many research studies citing that it takes 7–12 touches to land a meeting. The issue really is that you can't just spam the same message over and over again to achieve those numbers because you'll be deleted. Enable, educate, and walk your prospect up a ladder of engagement the whole way. Social plays a role but within a holistic strategy. Here is what effective outreach activity looks like: Day 1: COMBO. Day 2: Social engagement. Day 3: White paper. Day 4: A quote by them in social. Day 5: A slideshare. Day 6: A case study.

The essential thing is to absolutely add value to the cadence every time.

You can use software such as SalesLoft Cadence or CRM system tasks to ensure that you are staying organized on your touches. You can also just make a manual spreadsheet and add a column next to the account with the contact name and last touch. If you're only working 50 accounts per quarter, you'll start to remember every contact that you are mining and get a sense for who the ringleader is and how often you've been communicating with them by multiple channels.

What I've created here with COMBO is a way to open effectively and consistently with a high degree of prediction. If you select 100 key accounts, you'll be able to open opportunities with 20 of them in the first two quarters. I've road tested these theories with mentees in multiple global markets from California to New York to London to Singapore to Sydney, with companies selling highly disruptive software.

Opening, rather than closing, is the most important phase of selling because it's binary. It's akin to doing science without Newton's first law or acknowledging gravity. It's like trying to be a fighter but not being able to throw an effective punch. COMBO Prospecting will land a meeting in a down economy, it will land a meeting even if you don't have a solution yet. Just like boxing, a combination of a kidney shot, rib shot, and uppercut is more damaging than a single punch. Sure, Mike Tyson might throw the hardest punch ever and get a knockout—if it's landed. But it's too risky to put all your eggs in one basket. The same goes for prospecting channels because when you pattern-interrupt someone, there's a flurry of designed activity with flashes of brilliance. But in the context of sales, this technique is anything but hostile; it's assertive and in the client's best interest.

Commoditization, increased competition, offshoring, disruption, and the coming of the salesbots mean you must find a way to go to the next level. Professional selling has never been more exciting, yet reaching potential clients has never been more difficult. We live during a time of empowered buyers, distracted audiences, employees who feel entitled, and uncertain economies. Add to this the arrival of the machine age where every industry and every role must be reassessed. They must reexamine how they operate and create the necessary value to fund their very existence.

Professional services roles are especially at risk, and white-collar workers, salespeople included, must upgrade their skills to remain relevant.

Everywhere I go, I see silent sales floors and drone armies of passive millennials checking their smartphones hundreds of times per day as they blast Spotify in their ears like social selling whirling dervishes. And to what end? There's never been a more connected yet disengaged ethos in the history of mankind. Older salespeople struggle as if punch-drunk as they try to embrace the right technologies and automation to drive higher levels of effective activity to save their careers. Many resist customer relationship management systems and sales automation tools when they should embrace both. Few hone the right value narrative and build a strong personal brand that oozes credibility, insight, and value. The old guard often enjoys the support of inside salespeople and loves to use that weekly meeting to school the marketing team on how to build a better value message or marketing program. But truth be told, the most successful senior executives, right up to the CEO herself, will take time out of every day to make targeted outreach calls to critical clients.

I've seen CEOs (especially of start-ups) take this too far, micromanaging, acting as frontline seller and client services head, putting together the slides, flying and doing the pitches, and taking over every facet of the organization under the guise of mentorship. Effective delegation is still critical, but that does not mean as a leader of a business, team, or consultancy that you shouldn't be building out your own targeted lists of prospects. Every CXO should be mining their alumni network and extended contacts and surveying their work history to understand where "six degrees of Kevin Bacon" exists. Wildly, your growth from zero to $10 million and $10 million to $100 million is already living within your social network. If you are a CEO reading this, now's the time to get started on LinkedIn!

Every CEO should personally embrace LinkedIn, not just have their executive assistant (EA) do it on their behalf. Personal brand on social is table stakes for most start-up leaders, but in the Global 2000 it's a competitive advantage. Look at Jack Welch of GE or Howard Schultz of Starbucks—they both allow a direct channel from every employee. Employee advocacy is the most powerful PR engine ever invented. Getting the whole organization buzzing about your solution creates what I call a "bee swarm," causing surround sound for your target. But you can also think about the "thunderclap" technique: one announcement shared by thousands in your company across all social media. The engagement levels are earth-shattering, and your message can go viral.

One of the problems with selling today is that the rise of the silent sales floor is killing business. This book was born to save careers and rescue sales results by creating the right focus, mindset, and culture within the enterprise. Sales is an ancient craft, and it is the engine of every economy. When it comes to personal growth, economic growth, and interpersonal development, quality selling is essential. It's about face-to-face, human-to-human interaction. It's about confronting your fears and raising the priorities of C-levels. It is still the people in power who buy, even if they demand consensus before approving the commitment to buy.

Sellers must become experts on delivering outcomes, managing risks, building the business case, navigating politics, building consensus, aligning products and services, and implementing technology and solutions. But sellers don't get to do any of that unless they can first break through to their customers by harnessing the powers of persuasion and understanding of human psychology. Using these tools intelligently allows sellers to extend their reach and maximize their effectiveness and efficiency.

We've all witnessed those top operatives who seem to have a sixth sense and can read people like a book. How do you think they developed those faculties? By clicking the mouse endlessly like cats watching tennis? No, they built that Gladwellian thin slice in the trenches. They grew by boxing their opponents against the ropes. They learned to live by the sword and die by the ramifications of a single gesture. They developed an unbreakable belief in what they were doing and then had the courage to risk failure, embrace the difficult, and learn by doing. With a whisper, they mastered the art of engineering value and consensus and then closing the deal—all with a genuine desire to help their customer.

You must explore the mindset involved in new business development. Yes, you are helping customers find a better future, but you are also being the hunter, taking the kill back to the cave, and nailing the pelt on the wall. In addition to boxing, selling can be compared to professional sports such as baseball or cricket: In baseball, if you hit 3 pitches out of 10, you look like a genius; in cricket, you wait for the one ball in and over that you can hit to the fence. In new business sales, you must be ready to be rejected dozens of times in a row. You can't take your ego into the office; you need to leave your personal baggage at the door and focus. Successful application of COMBO will include a lot of rejection, and you can't let this deter you. Expect it and know that you are going to push yourself harder than ever before to break through. Imagine how many times Muhammad Ali got punched before he became the world champion.

This is not a book about theory; it's a practical manual born from battling in the marketplace. As such, it poses questions whose answers have been proven in the real world. The first question to ask is why is it important to dramatically change the way you sell?

Behold the Stately Honey Badger Who Never Gets Fired

You have to approach sales like the proverbial honey badger. He goes into the mound of fire ants and feels nothing so he can eat. He lets the spitting cobra bite him with its venom, and he passes out but then gets up and shakes it off. He fearlessly climbs to the top of a high tree and bites the head off a mamba snake for a snack. I knew of a salesperson who never used proposals; he simply did discovery and sent order forms. He was nicknamed The Honey Badger for that reason.

The other thing about honey badgers is that they just don't care and will even attack a pride of lions. Caring too much about closing is anathema in a sale. I've heard it called "commission breath" in the industry because it pushes prospects away. The honey badger is fearless and just keeps going regardless of being bit, stung, and tortured. Be the same; keep going until you get to a real "no" so you can report back to your boss that you know for certain that there is or isn't an opportunity in that account.

You need to hit 10X activity,[8] according to Grant Cardone. This means going harder, deeper, and wider into your targeted list of accounts so you have certainty in the quarter. It's simple: You either go get the honey and larvae and kill the cobra or you don't eat. Cardone was right when he said, "We sell to survive!"[9]

Nick Cummins of Australian Rugby fame earned the nickname The Honey Badger for his fearlessness and full-throttle running and tackling without any regard for his well-being. Some of his famous lines are: "You've gotta be tough as woodpecker lips" and "busier than a one-armed bricklayer in Baghdad" and "When you see an opportunity, you've gotta go after it like a rat up a drainpipe."

Opening new business effectively is the most important skill you'll ever develop. When the efforts of marketing and sales development fail, even if the product-market fit is poor, you can still build pipeline and prove the value of your role and career. It's almost impossible to be fired if you're genuinely showing serious revenue potential. Get all your executive team involved in fixing the product and helping you close the sale. At least you will have the opportunity to do so while your colleagues are on the chopping block with no pipeline and dreaded performance reviews. When revenue is down, all hell breaks loose and fingers get pointed, but the honey badger, stately and valiant, stands triumphantly with the honey pot of 3–5X pipeline. That needs to be you.

Extract Your Head from the Darkness; Facts Don't Lie

All around the world, companies initiate content marketing campaigns and build inside-sales teams for outbound demand generation. Some have even drunk the Kool-Aid and gone full-throttle into social selling, under the mistaken belief that personal marketing on digital platforms is actually selling. They did this with the hope that leads would flood in from the ether. Yes, all salespeople need to market and all marketers need to sell, but the ear-tickling allure of social selling has given many salespeople an excuse for abandoning the fundamental truth of sales performance: You must grab the attention and create meaningful conversations with the people who can actually buy.

The unintended result of social selling for many salespeople is that very little selling is done at all. Likewise, the unintended consequence of account-based marketing (ABM) methods, marketing software, and sales funnel combinations like Marketo is a vast overreliance on marketing to bring qualified inbound leads. ABM is sales plus marketing to drive account-based engagement. Think about C-levels though; they may download a white paper on a Sunday evening, but they probably delegate the insights gleaned to an associate. They probably send in their underlings to research your innovations and watch demos—they simply don't have time. So by and large, inbound marketing attracts influencers but doesn't really pull in people who can buy. It doesn't do much more than cause them to go back to the incumbent supplier to leverage your bid to negotiate more favorable terms.

CSO Insights has written that only 33 percent of a salesperson's time is spent actively selling,[10] and this observation is supported by McKinsey Global Institute data, which shows that salespeople spend "less than half their day selling."[11] In 2016, I conducted a boardroom roundtable for one of the world's leading technology companies. I had a 15-minute presentation to stimulate conversation, and I said I believed the majority of B2B salespeople fail to achieve their sales targets over the course of a full financial year. I then put these statistics from 2014 on-screen:

- Corporate Executive Board research: 40 percent fail to achieve their sales target.
- CSO Insights research: 43 percent fail to achieve their sales target.
- TAS Group research: 66 percent fail to hit their sales target.

I could see the skepticism in the body language of every person in the room. "I can sense that most of you don't believe those numbers," I said and waited for the reprimand about statistics being fake facts. Instead, one CEO cautiously admitted that it was actually worse in her corporation. Another agreed and said their failure rate was 75 percent, and another said there were always a handful of salespeople who did the big enterprise deals but that almost 80 percent missed or barely fell over the line. They all agreed it was getting worse, with average deal sizes shrinking, decision-makers becoming more distrustful, and time frames blowing out as buyers sought broader consensus before going ahead.

The analysts also agree that the trend is negative for B2B sales performance. Research from CSO Insights increased the failure rate of sellers from 43 percent in 2014 to 56 percent in 2016.[12] A 2016 *Harvard Business Review* study cited the number of underperforming salespeople at 63 percent.[13] Objective Management Group reported that three out of four salespeople were failing when they published their findings in the *Huffington Post*.[14] The statistics are sobering, and the reality is that deal sizes are going down while cost of new client acquisition is going up. There is one inevitable result with these trends—fewer expensive field salespeople and greater reliance on designing customer experience that is supported by relevant content publishing and automation. Design thinking has never been more important as market leaders create awesome customer experience across all channels. Salespeople who fail to move to value and make human interaction the key point of difference will become extinct.

Yet every salesperson and leader can evolve. I've been in professional B2B selling for three decades and made tens of thousands of calls. I've consistently ranked in the top 5 percent of performers everywhere I worked, I've won President's Club, and I've set personal and team records that have never been broken. My determination, cunning, and work ethic have always been the foundation of my success, and I've used every ethical tool available to me. The phone remains an integral element of that success, and in the last decade digital platforms have also played an important role.

We must all innovate and adapt. Although it's never been harder to succeed in B2B sales, it's never been easier to research and obtain the contact details of buyers. The information and tools we need to thrive are ubiquitous. I believe in social selling, but it must not be confused with social marketing. YouTube is the second largest search engine on Earth, and its hours watched have surpassed even TV. You can make yourself a media brand through YouTube. I've had clients come to me via Google searches on subjects as diverse as leadership and *The Challenger Sale*, because these searches led to my YouTube channel.

Every engagement channel is important because the world has changed, and buyers are harder to reach, more empowered with information, and increasingly stressed, skeptical, and low on time. There is a new reality that many won't acknowledge—cold-calling alone is a low-yield activity that can destroy morale, annoy potential clients, and even kill a sales career outright. This can be due to overwhelming frustration, rejection, negativity, and day-after-day failure. Chris Beall makes the point that psychologically everyone interprets failure to reach people as rejection—although in truth, it is often nothing more than those people being busy or unavailable. Nevertheless, it takes 18 call attempts to get a business executive on the phone in 2017,[15] which is why sales intelligence and dialing software is essential.

Pounding the phone alone is like charging at the machine guns: It's not noble—it's just plain stupid. In 2012, Keller Research Center, within Baylor University, conducted a study of 50 experienced salespeople who combined made more than 6,000 cold calls on the phone over a two-week period. The result was just 19 qualified appointments, and that equates to less than one-third of 1 percent.[16]

Yet the phone remains the most powerful tool for truly connecting with a potential client, and it is the next best thing to a face-to-face meeting for creating human connection. But how do you dramatically lift the success rate of your phone calls? Social platforms such as LinkedIn play a huge role because a warm introduction with context and relevance is the shortest path to securing a conversation that creates a qualified prospect. The vast majority of CXOs don't take cold calls but will always respond to a referral or introduction from a trusted friend or peer.

Every seller needs three to five times their sales target in qualified pipeline, and if you're not using LinkedIn's Sales Navigator, then you're asleep at the wheel. Sales Navigator can help you broker an introduction in these ways: identify the key players in a target account, determine how you're connected in multiple dimensions, monitor and listen for trigger events, leverage your network for intelligence and warm introductions, and engineer multiple engagement points (someone in your company or network who knows someone in theirs).

In your LinkedIn profile, you can evidence your credentials and set an agenda of value. You can head objections off at the pass by publishing content that shows insight; this can attract and engage those who can help you hit your number. LinkedIn research in 2015, externally validated by C9 Inc., revealed that those who use LinkedIn consistently, as validated by snapshots of their social selling index (SSI) scores over time, achieved the following results:

- They were 500 percent more likely to secure a meeting with the person being targeted.
- They personally had 45 percent more qualified sales pipeline created.
- They were 51 percent more likely to achieve sales targets.

Amazingly, these results included those who used the free version of LinkedIn, but those who used Sales Navigator achieved 7X pipeline growth![17] This was, however, when the free version included the extensive Boolean search feature, which is now available only on the Sales Navigator platform. You should aim for an SSI score in the 80s. Log in to LinkedIn and change the URL to www.linkedin/com/sales/ssi to see yours now.

Creating quality sales pipeline needs to be done intelligently with the seller having context for the outreach. Then the seller needs to provide value in the conversation, rather than seeking to sell value in the form of a product, service, or solution. Research is therefore a key element in targeted prospecting, and the very best use their own CRM system plus Google and LinkedIn for understanding these areas:

- The historical interactions and relationships with marketing, sales, service, and support engagements within the target organization
- The customer's industry trends and drivers to understand the competitive market within which they operate
- The customer's specific drivers, initiatives, and performance, along with their key goals, strategies, and initiatives
- The highest probability paths for introduction and engagement of the most senior people who make decisions and drive change

It's important to know what the status quo looks like, and there are always frenemies—even hostiles—in the account, who are loyal to the current state of play or an incumbent supplier. There is software, such as Datanyze and Ghostery, that you can use to get a glimpse into the software platforms the customer is already using. More about how to work with that technology comes later.

Let's get back to the research numbers, and these may shock you. In 2012, Corporate Executive Board (CEB) published research revealing that 95 percent of buyers expect insight from the seller. It also found that 86 percent of sellers fail to competitively differentiate.[18] Add to this the Forrester research, which revealed that 85 percent of sales interactions fail to meet the expectations of buyers,[19] and you can see that there is a serious problem for the sales community.

Are you awake yet? Ready to lift your game, jump into the ring, and fight for your very livelihood? I'm not saying you need go punch a CEO in the face, but you definitely need to throw a bucket of cold water called insight at the status quo. You need to use "float like a butterfly, sting like a bee" combinations and pattern-interrupts. You're in a marketplace where 999 out of 1,000 do exactly the same thing to reach out to targets with almost an identical message.

How will you stand out and be remembered? It's a war for "one word brand equity,"[20] as David Ogilvy calls it. Mike Bosworth, the godfather of solution selling, says the human mind has about seven slots,[21] so how can you raise priorities, like Jill Konrath encourages, to occupy a slot in the C-level decision-maker's mind? Five to 12 poor-quality touches are just spam. But if you are creating value every time, you will break through. COMBO simply allows you to concentrate the touches with speed and accuracy.

Behold the sequence at the corner of the ring in the 1st round versus the 12th: Call, voice mail, video email, LinkedIn invite with custom message, retweet, Facebook chat message, note card, send a book, Starbucks gift card, voice mail follow-up. You can mix and match all of these as needed as long as the phone is the tent pole of the strategy for multichannel engagement of multiple buyer personas across multiple mediums.

"Wow this salesperson is persistent as all get-out, I better hire her" is what you are likely to hear. Trust me, they'll tell you "no" or offer you a job. That's what the COMBO seller unlocks. You want to be Rudy playing for Notre Dame. Show some gumption, grit, fire, and tenacity—remind the CEO of how they got started. Take no prisoners, display effort, and tailor your message.

The Great Disruption of Your Precious Livelihood

Commoditization, globalization, automation, and disruption impact businesses and their workers. Hundreds of millions have already been displaced by automation, including: elevator operators, toll collectors, farm workers, manufacturers in the automotive sector, back-office and administrative workers, machinery operators in mining and transport, helicopter pilots, and airline flight engineers. And now the "knowledge professions" are in jeopardy, including those in banking, law, accounting, healthcare—and yes, sales.

Some of the brightest minds on the planet, including Elon Musk, Ray Kurzweil, Bill Gates, and Stephen Hawking, believe that the biggest threat to human existence is artificial intelligence (AI). An amalgam of *The Matrix* and *Terminator* is a very real possibility—so much so that Elon Musk and Peter Thiel have launched a nonprofit to ensure that AI is used for social good. For almost half a century, mankind worried it had created the instrument of its own destruction by splitting the atom. We survived the Cold War, but automation and linear computer logic is giving way to genuine self-learning algorithms that will inevitably lead to the Singularity—the moment when AI becomes self-aware. It is projected to occur some time between 2035 and 2050.

What does this mean for sellers? What will happen with the fusion of biology, nanotechnology, and all of human knowledge? Could super-sellers of the future carry chips in their brain with *Minority Report*–style sensors and contact lenses providing real-time data? The question is whether a human will really be needed at all—wouldn't an android be sufficient for many transactions?

At the time of this writing, Mark Cuban has backed a start-up with Falon Fatemi called Node.io. The platform identifies a seller's total addressable market along with the people and company intelligence needed to execute on the right prospects, at the right time, and with the right message. Node acts prescriptively in also recommending the next markets of opportunity for a business, even if they haven't had historical data. The AI scrapers, algorithms, and big data crunching that goes into their secret sauce can only be speculated upon, but imagine the thousands of human hours that are saved.

Other technologies include Everstring, which is achieving good traction in predictively identifying the right leads. Leadtime also addresses these issues and was founded by one of the fathers of marketing automation, David Cummings, who is also founder of Pardot and now part of Salesforce. There has been an explosion in this area.

Arguably, this techno-magical automation can never have the precision to anticipate butterfly wings starting a hurricane, aka the Ripple Effect. This kind of accuracy can't happen even alongside an analog sales team of living, breathing humanoids. Yet I've seen an AI-driven lead-generation engine doing mass B2B personalized emailing to tens of thousands of companies, and it was doing in just weeks what a sales team of 30 took six months to do. Granted, like Siri, it wasn't perfect, but the technology will be honed and quantum leaps will happen. You'd believe that with all these tectonic shifts, sales would close faster—but the information deluge and the procurement super-viruses resistant to any strategic selling have created the perfect storm to make enterprise selling harder than ever. In fact, most corporations are working to thin the herd of vendors from many thousands to just hundreds. They'll bring you in just to run a reverse auction with the incumbent supplier for more favorable terms.

In *Terminator 2*, a future war rips across the screen as AI decides to rid the world of mankind, which is destroying the planet by depleting all the resources with overpopulation and greed. This storyline is not far from the truth. Self-enabled warbots are already in existence, and a Skynet disaster with AI going rogue is not as far-fetched as you imagine.

But make no mistake. Right now and over the next 10 years, the bots will be coming for your job if you allow yourself to be a mere transactor of commodities. You must move beyond low-value relationship-building and instead elevate every conversation by setting the agenda on insight and value. You must aspire to be your customer's trusted adviser and earn that position over time by consistently delivering value in every conversation and always acting in their best interest. But you must also harness technology if you are to survive and prosper in the age of the machines and empowered buyers. Technology may be able to crunch big data and blast massive amounts of tailored offers across myriad channels, but it cannot be creative, generate real insight, or build relationships. These are the things that make you the emotional favorite and trusted adviser, which is how you fend off disruption of your sales career.

What is insight? Is it just statistics, case studies, and a history of customer wins? Unfortunately, that's not enough. In a time when all solutions suffer from the downward pressure of commoditization, and cutthroat vendors undercut the market while touting their spurious ROI claims, skepticism reigns. It is like a *Lord of the Flies* atmosphere, where sellers can't be trusted. CXOs are met with a deafening tsunami of empty promises when they open their email in the morning. They stop reading email and have an EA filter and block you. This EA is now running their LinkedIn profile and InMail account. I've seen employees whose entire job was just to vet vendors, and I know major Fortune 500 companies that turn down any inbound phone call to the switchboard unless the salesperson has the direct line. The common technique, as used by The Gap, is to have a website just for vendors, and that's seemingly the only way in.

Consumers and corporate buyers are bombarded with monotone marketing pabulum passing for insight. They face aggressive hoards competing for their attention with a white wall of noise. Yet the very best sellers cut through to become the signal amid the noise; they are the channels that provide value beyond the generic statistics that are being parroted. These winning sellers go deeper than reading an annual report, studying a tweet storm, or searching cleverly on Google. They go beyond to synthesize and process a wide amalgam of data into a cohesive whole. This helps prospects see their business in new ways, and it redefines their paradigm and disrupts their reality.

Ironically, multiple bestsellers have been published on the topic of insight selling, but garnering an insight is much harder than you would think. The best salespeople bring insight to business leaders even if it does not lead to their own solution. The trusted adviser approaches the target with a way to make or save money, create efficiencies, or foster faster innovation that outflanks competitors. Pain is more pertinent than pleasure in order to drive change from the status quo. Saving money is often far more attractive than schemes to grow revenue.

In my first book, *The Joshua Principle: Leadership Secrets of Selling*, I talked about the three states of business: growth, status quo, or crisis. Sellers approaching tech companies that just raised a war chest of money will often find a business climate of overconfidence. Many companies are plodding along in business-as-usual mode, so they'll just stick with what they've got. The ones in crisis with revenue going down may buy, but then there may be risks associated with credit approval. So all three modes have elaborate challenges to penetrate.

The first state, growth, requires stroking of the ego and showing a path to inflate it even more. The second state requires unlocking latent pain until, as Brent Adamson likes to say, "The pain of same becomes greater than the pain of change."[22] Organizations are laser focused on symptoms, so consultative sellers bring leaders together to triage the underlying problems and mobilize a consensus. If a business is on its way out, make sure you do your research, because you don't want to close a three-year deal with a firm that goes into Chapter 11 (bankruptcy protection) in six months. Did someone say commission claw-back?

Stu Heinecke is a genius, and everyone should read his book, *How to Get a Meeting with Anyone*. His ideas on contact marketing are highly creative; he sends out cartoons featuring the prospect. This is so far out of the box that it lands meetings like nothing else. What can a mere mortal do? You probably don't have time to write blogs, send out cartoons or drones, FedEx printouts with Challenger insights, or hang out in the Atlanta airport hoping to intercept a potential client.

What you can do, right now, is become masterful at using LinkedIn and social platforms for research, monitoring trigger events, and finding the path of highest probability of senior engagement. Smart salespeople leverage their internal CRM and marketing systems and collaborate as genuine team players to maximize the probability of success by focusing on delivering a legendary customer experience. They embrace, rather than resist, technology to assist them with identifying and monitoring trigger events and sourcing referrals.

Research by Craig Elias states that executives new to the job who spent $1 million+ on new initiatives did so within the first 90 days of the job. Therefore, job changes are a key trigger to monitor. There's a new sheriff in town who is looking to bring in what worked in their last company and to shake up the technology stack in play. Who filled their previous role? Where did your predecessor go? There are actually multiple trigger events contained in the silver lining of any job change because of the domino effect. All of this can be mapped leveraging systems such as Avention and InsideView, plus Sales Navigator. Never sell without Navigator; it's a living, breathing prospecting database updated by the targets themselves. Doing anything less is flying blind.

Selling has always been about helping people to see and achieve a better state of affairs. Change management is at the heart of achieving this better state. Leaders crave disruption against the status quo, and they have relied on competent sellers for hundreds of years to help them. As much as technology is changing everything, history is also repeating. You are seeing the golden age of connection via the Internet, and social networks create such a preponderance of information that the world's smartest people are drowning in it. The wild realization is that they're dying to talk with you—you are a strategic partner who can actually communicate value and make a real difference to their results and quality of work life.

Here is the brutal truth. In order to fund your role, you must move to add value for your employer and customer. If all you do is provide a relationship and information to help someone transact, it's not enough! No one worth selling to is lonely and looking for a new friend, nor are they bored and hoping a salesperson will enter their day to tell them about the joys and wonders of a company's products and solutions. Prospects will lie to you to move you off their desk or get you off their calendar. You must press on and press in. You must seek reasons for them to engage and lead with why a conversation matters and what's in it for them.

In *The Joshua Principle: Leadership Secrets of Selling*, I published the value quadrant illustration shown in Figure 1-1. To this, I have now added an overlay of the Forrester Research predictions for changes in the number of salespeople by role through to the year 2020. You can see that the top right quadrant is the only place where there is growth.

The point here is that every seller must move to value if they are to survive and prosper. Even before the salesbots could take your career, inside sales, marketing automation, channels, or customer self-service could be the end of you. You must therefore personally create compelling value

FIGURE 1-1. B2B SALESPERSON VALUE QUADRANT

©Tony Hughes and Andy Hoar at Forrester Research
Death of a (B2B) Salesman, April 2015

in the way you operate. This means engaging at senior levels, being consultative, having an insightful point of view, and talking the language of leaders. It means being relevant in helping the customer build a business case, achieve consensus within their team, and manage the risks of implementation. It also means being accountable for delivering tangible outcomes and earning the status of trusted adviser over time. But no human can achieve all of this on their own at the scale required . . . a cyborgian approach is required.

Cyborg Sellers in the Age of the Machines

The awful truth is that corporations ultimately view us as a unit of production or consumption that must generate a profit for them. Your job is not secure. My opinion is that by 2030, a third of nonretail sales jobs will be gone. The majority of sales development resourcing could be executed by AI algorithms wrapped in cyborg entities. Examples include IBM's Watson, Apple's Siri, Microsoft's Cortana, Samsung's Bixby, Salesforce's Einstein, Nudge.ai, Complexica's Larry, and Node. All of these examples could evolve to contribute to the rapid android explosion. A series of decision trees from natural language queries underpinned by almost unbelievable amounts of data could be retrieved and processed in the blink of an eye. Kyle Porter from SalesLoft believes, "The best AI vendors are the ones who walk a mile in the salesperson's shoes and great AI results in better humanity."

The key here is to become like Iron Man—man with machine—in order to avoid being Terminator career-kill. You are living in a world where Chinese auto assembly lines replace almost all humans, despite those humans being relatively low cost, and achieve compelling efficiency gains and quantum quality improvements.

You are living in a time when automated marketing is replacing salespeople. The most successful car launch in the history of the automobile was the red carpet reveal of the Tesla Model 3 in 2016. Elon Musk livestreamed it, and sent people to his website shopping cart. No showroom salespeople coercing prospects to buy the paint protection package or extended warranty. Just general estimates of range and battery charging times with a promise of order fulfillment starting 15 months in the future. Elon is not even a polished salesman, just an authentic visionary making electric cars cool to own, exhilarating to drive, sustainably powered (the sun or wind charge the batteries). He promises that you can drive it to the SpaceX parking lot for your trip to Mars and that AI will park it when you arrive. The result? Cash deposits of $1,000 paid within 72 hours equating to $14 billion in sales when fulfilled.

Right now, a shopping cart can replace a showroom salesperson, and salesbots are already everywhere when you go online: Amazon, eBay, Google, and even the infamous Ashley Madison website, which allegedly used sexbot algorithms to entice new male members with flirtatious but fictitious women pretending to be interested in an affair. Cheating the cheaters—how ironic.

You may ask, what can I do, I'm just a rep? Well, you have more power than you think. The first thing you must do is realize what is actually happening. To inoculate yourself, you must first think about your own buying behavior. Why would you buy anything sophisticated, complex, or expensive, and what process do you go through to make that decision? Do you feel uneasy, even a sense of fear in the pit of your stomach, with some buying decisions? No robot can take that away. No Svengali AI can mitigate the truth that you're going to spend a million dollars on a home, for example. You research everything, maybe even for 10 years, to get your ducks in a row.

The sellers of the future will be liaisons of the ultra-complex. They will combine the skills of a solutions engineer with the strategic thinking of a CEO. They will write prolifically, speak publicly, have sensational EQ and IQ, and leverage all the available tools. There's no replacing charisma and genuine empathy. The history of the brain's evolution will never be outdone by AI when it comes to the highly analog components of building trust, displaying integrity, and educating and enabling one's quarry for their own good.

The future of high-value selling, the type you must elevate toward, is humans in partnership with machines as everything converges. Customers want insight and value from every interaction. Creating seamless customer experience that delights the consumer is therefore the panacea of sales and marketing, and it must be delivered with a blend of human relationships and easy-to-use technology, anywhere, anytime, and on any device.

Choose to be one of the few people who will be master of the machines, orchestrating a multiplier effect on the modern sales process. They'll set appointments, filter through big data for that wow factor insight to hook the skeptical buyer, propensity score your pipeline using a machine learning algorithm that gets smarter, and provide you with data on a heads-up display from a contact lens—ever so *Minority Report*.

I've been rather pessimistic in the past about automation and AI creating a sales career apocalypse, and I've recently been converted to believe in a far brighter future for those willing to combine old-school value with new-school technology. Humans who embrace working with bots and leverage advanced technology as they engage prospects and customers will unlock the secret to driving sales pipeline. Then they will progress through to accelerated revenue. Here are three real-world examples of how AI is transforming sales results:

1. Einstein from Salesforce is for integrated opportunity coaching in complex sales opportunities. Einstein is a virtual deal coach who provides predictive lead and deal scores along with opportunity insights, including prompts for the best next steps and methods of outreach. Because Salesforce actually enables and integrates best practice sales processes, Einstein has the ability to monitor critical win factors. Factors it monitors include: whether key information has been obtained, whether the right people have been covered, whether the amount of time in a particular deal stage is damaging the probability of a win, whether frequency of deal updates is on track, and whether the number of calls made and received along with emails sent and received shows proof of high-value engagement.

   All of this matters because the level of timely buyer-seller interaction absolutely determines the probability of winning a deal. Unlike a human sales manager, Einstein is always transparently monitoring and providing feedback on which deals need attention and where to prioritize precious sales time. For management, Einstein can deliver the Holy Grail of forecasting accuracy. I've seen it and it's staggeringly accurate.
2. Larry from Complexica is for transactional sales. Servicing a "long tail" of customers with a large SKU range represents a huge challenge for salespeople in terms of investing time in the right areas. Imagine you're a sales rep working in the wine industry. You have

hundreds of licensed premises in your territory, and knowing who is best to call on and what to talk about, beyond your (yawn) specials this month, is a massively difficult thing to figure out. In Australia, the average restaurant or licensed premise has 30 different alcohol salespeople calling every month, along with lots of other suppliers competing for their share of wallet. With 100 or more salespeople banging away at these establishments, no wonder it is so difficult to break through as a salesperson!

Here is the outcome Larry delivers: You are the one and only salesperson the owner looks forward to meeting every month because you provide amazing insights and advice on how they can grow their business and improve the profit! I kid you not. Larry can pull every menu on the Internet from your client's competitors, analyze the meals on the menus and their pricing (including food that is not sold), and identify the fact that restaurants in the same category within a 10-minute drive have food prices averaging 12 percent more than your client. Your insight (the reason to meet) is that your customer could increase prices by 8 percent tomorrow without becoming uncompetitive. Larry can further provide insights about what types of wine (products you do sell) at what prices could be included or adjusted to improve profit.

Larry, the AI analyst, answers big questions for sellers, and his recommendations drive previously unimaginable sales effectiveness for salespeople. Larry answers questions like this:

- In my territory of 300 customers, whom should I prioritize for calls?
- When I meet with them, what insights do I have that help their business?
- In what order should I plan my calls for maximum efficiency?
- Which products should I focus on to maximize our profitability?

The recommendations and call notes from Larry can be pushed automatically into the CRM system. If you operate in a sales environment characterized by frequent transactions with many customers across a large SKU range, and if you've read *The Challenger Sale* and wondered how to generate real insights that actually resonate with the buyer, technology such as Larry could be the answer.

3. Watson from IBM provides natural language dialogue to answer any question as an AI trusted adviser. Natural language is incredibly difficult to deal with for computers, but Watson goes beyond pure logic to cope easily with the nuances, vagaries, and contradictions of the English language. Watson beat the best *Jeopardy* champions easily, and this occurred back in 2013!

   Watson is being applied to medicine to accurately diagnose medical issues, and it is also powering many chatbots. Verbal interaction with truly intelligent computers is a very real part of modern life. Apple's Siri, Amazon's Alexa, Facebook's M, Google's Now, Micosoft's Cortana, and Samsung's Bixby are all examples. You're in trouble if your role in sales is primarily based on answering questions, providing information, and then helping to transact.

Other examples of AI are sales assistants such as Troops.ai with synchronization to Salesforce, and you can even deploy a virtual sales assistant that schedules meetings for you with x.ai. You can leverage big data to crunch all your leads to optimize which ones have the highest propensity to close using Lattice Engines. The rise of "automation of everything," such as Outreach.io, is transforming the way salespeople work, and SalesLoft goes beyond that to incorporate the human element.

Moore's Law is relentless, and imagine how the world will change when the AI Singularity arrives. The question of whether humans will be needed in almost all workplace roles will be answered by societal and political considerations rather than by economics or questions over whether a machine can actually do the task better than a human. Bill Gates is already advocating for machines to be taxed (collected by their corporate employers who fired the humans) to fund the universal wage from government for the vast majority of people who will be forced out of work.

As a side note, many people derive their sense of purpose from the work they do. Depression, suicide, and crime are sure to skyrocket as increasing numbers of people lose their careers to the advances of technology. The implications for society are enormous. Questions of purpose and meaning in life have never been more important.

Man the photon torpedoes, and tune your dilithium crystals because Sales 3.0 or even 4.0 is upon us with AI already making its mark. To avoid losing your job in the coming years, you must make insight and value the reason that customers engage with you and build trusted relationships. You must embrace the very technologies you fear in order to harness their power and achieve new levels of capability, reach, efficiency, and effectiveness.

Go Big, Bust Out, and Break Through

The people you are trying to reach and help are facing a barrage of messages every day they come to work. Their inbox is clogged, their calendar is packed, everyone wants their time, and their boss wants results without excuses.

An average buyer receives 100+ emails a day, opens just 23 percent, and clicks on just 2 percent of those.[23] LinkedIn InMails are increasingly regarded as spam. Office phones usually go to voice mail as people race from one meeting to another. Fifty percent of sales time is wasted on unproductive prospecting.[24] A team of 50 salespeople leaves about 1,277 hours of voice mails per month.[25] Forty percent of emails are opened on mobile first, and the average mobile screen can fit only four to seven words max.[26] Subject lines with more than three words experience a drop in open rate by over 60 percent from shorter subject lines.[27]

It's time to dispel the myths. Social selling alone does not deliver, and cold-calling alone does not yield the necessary level of results. In 2007, it took an average of 3.68 cold-call attempts to reach a prospect, and some claim that it took 8 attempts in 2017,[28] but Chris Beall suspects these statistics include gatekeeper conversations as "reached." His own research, based on more than 50 million dials with ConnectAndSell in 2017, shows that it took 18 attempts per connect for real-world lists. In my experience, salespeople make fewer than three attempts.

So how do you break through? First, ensure that you have the right narrative. Every conversation must provide value for the other person. Focus on the outcomes you can help them achieve, and lead with the value you offer rather than with a pitch or value proposition. Have some humility in your approach, yet project your belief in the difference you can make. You want them to think you are someone worth talking to, who can help them achieve their goals or achieve a better way of operating.

Every communication, whether it is email, InMail, voice mail, text message, or the very words from your mouth (when you are surprised by a live voice on the other end of the phone), needs to be about the customer and the business outcomes you believe you can help them achieve. Note: Buying from you is not a business outcome for them.

Unless you're selling low-value commodities, human-to-human (H2H) engagement is still critically important because people prefer to buy from those they know, like, and trust. The relationships you create are therefore the strongest point of competitive differentiation.

After you have created the right narrative, you need to find the right channels to gain your prospect's attention and secure engagement. But there is a strange inertia to being human. Most people fear public speaking, probably a bit more than death. Somehow, somewhere along the track, cold-calling became high up on the list of loathsome things. Let's review general fears in descending order of magnitude: cold-calling, public speaking, disappointing your lover, being fired, death, and falling.

I know that falling is #6 because so many skydivers hate cold-calling, public speaking, and disappointing their lover! The latter drives trillions of dollars of the global economy!

The phone is important because it involves an act of courage. The more you do it, the warmer it gets, the faster the pre-call research, and the more confident you are in every area of your life—not just sales. Automated sales engagement dialers hold salespeople accountable to the action of calling. The best automated dialer solutions provide news and insights about the target account and individual at the moment of dialing. The best dialers are also systems that enable emailing and social outreach. The call with a local area code can increase call connections by 21 percent, according to a study conducted by SalesLoft that measures the performance of 1 million calls.[29] SalesLoft is a market leader for capturing sentiment and disposition during calls. Most important, automated dialers build courage by shoving you into the fight cage and locking the door from the outside.

Facing your fears is a beautiful thing. Overcoming your fears and your ego is the biggest breakthrough you need to make if you are to truly succeed in sales. There is an amazing liberation that comes from not caring anymore about what people think.

Nevertheless, rejection sucks and so inbound selling systems have become a panacea for the sensitive masses. I'm here to tell you that you want to be a bit extreme as a seller. You want to embrace not just a high volume of activity, but activities that are heavily fear-based that you can turn into an unlimited sword of power.

Be the extreme person on your team who is breaking ice, opening conversations, and doing what's uncomfortable. You can leverage social platforms in this way also, by sticking to the value and going beyond the fluff. Never blast and spam your network with sales messages or publish anything that is inconsistent with your employer's brand.

If you're not in a state of fear when you go sell today, you're not pushing hard enough or taking the actions that will enable you to truly excel and exceed quota. Make no mistake, everything you are doing is to avoid being fired.

Friending everyone and seeking to be a people-pleaser will not make you a trusted adviser. And you shouldn't grasp your way up the ladder via politics because it just makes you a lesser person. You can instead earn credibility by doing what's assertive, hard, and courageous. Fortune will always favor the bold. As Lee Bartlett says, "If you can pick the phone up to 10 C-level execs and chew the fat, nobody is firing you and everyone wants to hire you."[30]

Only the strong will survive, and only those who give their all benefit from the law of reciprocity. I'm encouraging you to hunt. You can't feed the tribe without bringing back the kill and putting the pelts on the wall. You cannot harvest a crop without laboring in the soil and sowing the seed. You cannot achieve greatness with vapor. You must be committed to the hard things. So many salespeople are half-assing, and managers are even worse—literally unwilling to do the prospecting. Are you a CEO or GM or SVP? If so, I'm encouraging you to prospect by phone after doing some research and preparing with the right narrative. The best ones do because they lead by example.

The number-one problem for salespeople across the globe is lack of sales pipeline—yet that's a symptom rather than a root cause. The real problem is an aversion to using the right combinations of intelligent activities that are required for sales success. After you've done quick, pragmatic research, pick up the bloody phone! Call their cell phone, leave them a voice mail, send them an email. Then follow up with a text message and InMail. Jab, jab, jab, jab, jab—two minutes and you're all done. Move on to the next person on your list—the list you researched and created, ready to go, before you left work the previous day.

Anthony Iannarino, Mike Weinberg, and Jeb Blount all advocate the use of time-blocking to maximize efficiency. Lock yourself away for a minimum of one hour at a time to hit the phone in prime time, 7:45 a.m. to 8:45 a.m., before the day consumes your prospects with endless meetings. Leveraging multiple outreach channels rather than using the phone alone will dramatically increase results, but only if you have the right narrative built around insight and value for the buyer, well in advance of them becoming your customer. If you deliver the right message, what will they think as alerts ding away on their cell phone? "Wow, this person is seriously determined." Go beyond social selling, and think digital selling. Harness all the tools available combined with your own value narrative and Wile E. Coyote determination and cunning.

Here is the smartest way to build quality sales pipeline: Interview your most successful customers to find out what happened inside their organization that led them down the path to buying your solution. Dig deep to discover:

- What trigger events should you listen for?
- What problems should you be looking for?
- What does a dream potential client really look like?

Finding alignment is better than evangelism, but to secure high-yield warm introductions you must first do your research. But do it quickly. Whether you're upselling existing clients, securing referrals for warm introductions, turning cold calls into warm calls with pragmatic research and vertical industry relevance, you must create your own authentic combinations of insight, value narrative, techniques, and tools to break through, storm the barricades, cross the moat, and jetpack your way into the ivory tower of the executive buyer's gold-plated private suite. *Yes, that was the longest sentence in the book.*

Seriously, you must find a way to break down the barriers and cut through the stress of your customer's day, and it must be authentic for you. Tools alone are not the answer. Just as with every hit song and movie, there are repeated combinations that are refreshed by producers to make them familiar, interesting, and relevant for their audience. You must stand out in a really cool way, which is why this book discusses the hottest one at the bar analogy.

Winning Combinations of Old and New

Like in metallurgy, the blended steel alloy is the hardest and cuts the sharpest—you must bring the essential elements together with other elements. COMBO Prospecting defies the dismal statistics and gives you double to triple the cut-through when applied. It's simple and works in any market, any vertical. The phone is its tent pole. It's blended prospecting spiked with a new twist—concise combinations that will cause a prospect to instantly remember you and respond. You can get 100 voice mails in a row—it still works. You can never once reach a prospect—it still works. You can feel at peace with your day because meetings will get set at any level in the organization, especially the power base of VPs at the C-level.

The prerequisite for jumping onto the phone or sending an email is to have an authentic narrative nailed, and the next chapter deals with this in detail. Just like a boxer invests thousands of hours practicing the basics—jab, jab, duck, right hook—it must be instinctive. I learned karate and went to the world championships, and I came away with a bronze medal in my division (middle-aged fat men well below black-belt level). In competition, I learned something interesting about my rigid form of martial art. It was high on disciplined katas, which limited you in the real-world heat of battle. It was too predictable with little improvisation. Mash-ups and combinations are what create unique advantage, in sport and life, but only if you can own your form and authentically execute with instinctive passion. Think MMA cage fighting or hapkido.

Leverage timeless truths, but also be innovative in engagement and execution. People still buy from those they know, like, and trust. People desire with emotion and proceed with logic. Successful sales conversations are driven by insight and value creation. The name of the game is human-to-human personalized marketing and outreach done at scale, while also leveraging technology and social platforms. What's amazing to me is the binary nature of the debate—two camps have formed: no tools or all tools. Social or the phone. These are false dichotomies.

Fighters will tell you that courage and skill is just a ticket into the ring or cage. Boxing is a game where strength and speed can only be a competitive advantage when fighting within the usual rules. In the octagon, jiu jitsu upsets this balance. It's a grappling ground game where a frail Gracie could take out a lion of a man three times his size.

There's something to be said for social aikido, which leverages the aggression of one's opponent against them. Similarly, there is a violence to selling. It is a rejection-laden lifestyle, but you will only truly fail if you allow defeat to enter your heart. If you enter the ring thinking about the last uppercut to the jaw you took, it will upset your chi and you will fail desperately. For all of these fighting techniques, winning depends on power, speed, accuracy, and attitude . . . and so does the art of selling.

Success in sales requires a simple, fundamental COMBO that is concise and hard hitting. The human attention span is about seven seconds, very much like that of Dory the fish. Simply call, voice mail, and email—on message and as fast as you can. An entire triple, as this is called, should be performed in less than two minutes. Once you get really good at this, you can do it in 90 seconds. Every day, you should execute a minimum of 30 triples, which can be achieved at scale in less than two hours. You should be carving out at least one two-hour prospecting block every workday, and you need to work 50 target accounts per quarter with three to five contacts per account, with at least two of these being C-levels.

You'll need the right tools to execute this effectively:

- LinkedIn Sales Navigator (make the commitment and buy this)
- Sales data intelligence tools (buy these also, just like the tradesman who buys the best power tools)
- Cadence and dialing software, which enables integrated phone, email, and social engagement (your employer will need to invest in these)
- A bullwhip for your sales manager to use on you if you don't make the calls

After field-testing 30 COMBOs per day all over the world, I know this will create 3X pipeline within two quarters. You may be thinking that you'll drown in your own pipeline . . . fear not! The best prospects will throw you a lifeline by selecting themselves for your attention. You can even compress the ramp to success from 180 days to 90 days by monitoring for trigger events and leveraging referrals in Sales Navigator. This uses the concept that you can tap into your own team's connectivity to the prospect base, and I'll talk more about this in later chapters. Other types of COMBOs include:

- Referrals: You call the connection in common, send them an email, and even go meet them in front of their office. You'll notice the way I stress personal connection.
- Screenshot: You take a screen capture of your LinkedIn InMail and send it as an email with "Mary, your thoughts?" in the subject line. This COMBO is based on the fact that professionals actually check their profiles so infrequently.
- Sheer brute force: This includes increasing the channels and frequency.

Ninety-three percent of converted leads are engaged on the sixth call attempt.[31] I want to storyboard why the COMBO core technique is so powerful. Executives are busier than ever; in fact, I read that the average CMO gets 1,700 emails per month. CXOs have assistants who check their email and shunt many into a black hole to eliminate solicitors. The average worker receives over 200 emails a day, with many siphoned off into a corporate spam filter or junk mail folder. I'll explain how to avoid those filters later, but rule #1 to avoid the spam filter is not to send emails through a marketing automation commercial server. These are recognized and blocked immediately.

So imagine if you're a C-level decision-maker (the one who owns the problem you want to solve) in a Fortune 1000. The phone rings, and you immediately ignore it because the caller is not in your address book. Then you get a notification that the caller has left a voice mail—you ignore it. Then a text message with an intriguing message and an email regarding the call and message they left. Then you see a LinkedIn request that's customized with relevance to you. You think, "My beeper is melting down, Batman!" Do you see how the salesperson is bee swarming or surrounding you? The next day, they might get a referral to you, or they may triple again—call, voice mail, email.

To be prioritized, you must raise the bar, move to the front slot, à la Bosworth, and consistently be the buzzing in their pocket. Most will finally take the meeting out of sheer curiosity, guilt, or—get this—outright respect for how hard you hustled. Displays of sheer grit and tenacity are fleeting in our modern society, and this is why professional athletes are so admired. The world loves the violent determination of UFC, boxing, ice hockey, and full contact sports without the pads like rugby and Aussie Rules football. Why do you think that is? Powerful people pay through the nose for box seats, booths, and exclusivity to see these modern gladiators compete. They know their stats, and they perform the same plays ad infinitum until their COMBOs are precise and uber-powerful.

Every elite athlete, businessperson, and seller is at the top because of their unbelievable levels of commitment and hard work. Talent is just the ticket to compete for a spot on the bench. Your gift of gab is a handicap in sales. Focus on hard work, teachability, and determination. Boxing is a science of training the body to shift weight to hold, block, and respond in ways that aren't natural. By grooving these moves in 10,000 times, they become second nature. When you practice, drill, and rehearse, you can attain an unconscious competence, similar to learning to drive.

If I were to hand you a primer on old-school selling techniques, would you dismiss them or embrace them? Do you truly understand the power of having passionate curiosity about your customer and acting with positive intent? Do you know the importance of politics and how to navigate the competing agendas within organizations? Have you heard of Neil Rackham, Jim Holden, Miller Heiman, Jeff Thull, Keith Eades, or Mike Bosworth? You need to go read every single book by these people to understand that history repeats itself and effective foundations don't change. Technology and access to information can both collapse time in the sales cycle and blow it out as buyers are paralyzed by choice. They can become discombobulated by an overload of information and an inability to achieve consensus within their own teams.

You need to move faster and leverage winning combinations that separate you from your competitors. Anyone can spend three weeks writing the Holy Grail of prospecting emails. But there will still be that rep who outscores you: call, voice mail, call again, call again, message, email, InMail, video email, text message, Twitter DM, social share, social add, retweet.

You only ever have one objective, which is to get that golden "no." Burn out that lead, and celebrate the fact that they won't be wasting any more of your precious time or allowing false hope! You'll be free to focus where there is real potential. If there's any interest, or if the prospect is actually in a buying window, you'll uncover it. If they are a market fit for your product, service, or solution, but the timing is wrong, put them in your CRM so "the machine" can lead-nurture with drip marketing. You'll be prompted to get back in their face again at least 90 days before they will be considering going to market for what you sell.

I'd rather hit 50 accounts and open two or three fully qualified enterprise opportunities than whittle away at 50 accounts just to be left with dust in the pipeline. If you want to rise above the pack, make a commitment to shine bright and treasure your time. You won't have to euthanize your brand—you'll simply keep at it until you get the answer you deserve. You'll put 50 rounds in the chamber and prepare to shoot. Are you ready for full metal jacket, to get rejected hard, to get hung up on, to hear "no"? That's the gig. That's how you'll make over a million bucks a year while a Harvard MBA is schlocking around in five-figure land. Risk = reward.

Now I'm not setting up a *Glengarry Glen Ross* (classic movie about sales) scenario or zero-sum game. I'm making a case that courage is the fuel of champions and one of the most important virtues to cultivate. You've got to be a duck and let all possible negativity slide right off your back. Just like a volley of misplaced punches results in you getting hit back, you'll make mistakes and learn from the pain. Precision will come over time.

Could it be that you need to cold-call like Donald Trump? "Making sales great again!" Ouch, I said it. Legend has it Donald Trump doesn't use email, a port in the storm of a litigious world. He clearly tweets prolifically. I can guarantee you he has a gold-plated rotary phone in the commode where he makes it all happen. I get a real kick out of visualizing him as the SVP of Sales running a cloud SaaS company. Just imagine it: blowtorch in one hand and megaphone in the other, telling everyone in his own unique way that the market potential is "youuuge," and you've gotta deliver results or "you're fired."

But that's enough about The Donald. I want to anchor this playbook with how to open meetings with impossible-to-reach prospects. Yes, the ones you wish you could talk to but never actually do. Here we go.

Blooding Your COMBO Strategy

You are not in control of your customer. The funnel is not linear; it's an infinite loop or a Möbius strip, as Nic Read says. You can, however, control yourself, your own actions, and your emotional responses. COMBO, or Command Over Maximizing Business Opportunities, means you can control your output with smart daily activity. You can control your attitude and responses to the chaos that ensues. You can take furious levels of smart action until, like a tidal wave, you have an abundance of new business opportunities that are so rich and so promising that you can be in command over your role, your company, and your dream customer.

Thirty triples a day keeps the performance improvement plan (PIP) away. Once again, a triple is 1) calling, 2) always leaving a message, and 3) always sending an email—all within two minutes. Blindingly simple! The first time you execute outreach with a new prospect, you could include an InMail, phone text message, and/or direct message in Twitter to make it a quad, pent, or sextet.

Use COMBO with a call to at least 30 people per day. It's paramount that you have direct dials, and you can use RainKing, DiscoverOrg, Data.com, Lusha, Hunter, Rapportive, Discover.ly, Seamless.ai, or others to easily source email addresses and cell phone numbers so you're not snafued in switchboards all day or limited to InMail within LinkedIn.

Never leave the office until you have the next morning all set up with a list of people you're going to call. Time-block two hours every morning, and start calling while your prospects are driving to work. Call cell phone numbers and direct office lines. Senior people get started early. You want to be well into your list before your snoozer colleagues or your boss walks into the office. Be the first salesperson in the office every day!

Pick 50 key target accounts (KTAs) per quarter. If your CRM won't support the process, build a Google spreadsheet you can share with your manager. Select three to five target people per account, and ensure that at least two are C-level.

Go into LinkedIn Sales Navigator (required!), and save these contacts as leads within accounts so you can monitor for trigger events (news they share, job changes, funding, pain, etc.) in the Navigator stream. The best CRM software, such as Salesforce, has integration with Navigator, and this is transformational for sales productivity.

Each day after work, maybe as you travel on public transportation, focus on things such as liking people's status updates in the Navigator mobile app. This is fundamental to never making a cold call again because you become someone familiar when you engage your prospects on social media.

What do you say, live or with a voice mail message, when you make a phone call? Mike Weinberg does a phenomenal job of helping you "sharpen your sales story" in his must-read book, *New Sales. Simplified.* The key is to only talk in terms of business outcomes you've helped others achieve. If you have quantified ROI, that's even better—but be careful with grand claims, as buyers are increasingly skeptical. Each message should be no more than 30 seconds. When sending an email, the subject should be just a few words and the body text should never exceed four sentences—smartphones and executive ADD make this essential! More on crafting your value narrative is covered in the next chapter.

Never forget that a referral is the fastest path to revenue as it leads to the highest probability of a sale. That's because of the timeless power of trust.

Make referrals a priority and something that is always top of mind for you—always ask! Sales Navigator reveals referrals like nothing else, but call the people who can provide an introduction rather than clicking a button online. This is key: If you have a connection in common, don't just send a LinkedIn message. Always, always, always call for the referral, explain why it's relevant, offer to ghostwrite the introduction, and if you can, get the mutual connection to even get your prospect on the phone. This is how you reach the unreachable.

There is a crazy high close rate when using LinkedIn TeamLinks. This is an advanced feature in LinkedIn Sales Navigator where you can understand (at a glance) who in your company knows someone in the prospect company. Again, call your colleague on the phone to ask for the introduction. Some of your greatest TeamLinks, if selling technology to high-tech companies, will be your internal engineering team. Talk about street credibility!

Now I know what most of you may be thinking at this point: What if my managers or the powers that be are Luddites or sticks in the mud? They refuse to bankroll LinkedIn Sales Navigator or "pricey" sales tools. Are you out of luck? No.

You can manually build a list of switchboards that are available and start to write down the appropriate keys to dial by name if they have an automated directory. You can guess email conventions and reverse look-up email addresses with a free browser plug-in, such as Rapportive or Discover.ly.

You can leverage the "neighborhood technique,"[32] where you call an executive assistant from the switchboard. Let her know you're in town the week after next and just want to have a short meeting to discuss trends, use cases, or best practices. Better still, call the target person's cell phone direct, and adopt an assumptive close for the meeting en route. Simply sort your LinkedIn or CRM contacts by city and start executing COMBOs, saying that you'll be in the area. Shoot for coffee and watch how many accept and bring colleagues. Stay the course and email again 48 hours before and then the morning of the meeting to confirm the scheduled time. Relentless follow up will ensure that in a two-day trip, you have five meetings. Now that's pipeline, face-to-face! "Chuck, I'm literally just five minutes away. Why not grab a quick coffee?"

The critical point is that an effective combination of prospecting methods hinges on the phone as much as possible. Frequently, you can send a personalized LinkedIn InMail and then search their "ways to contact" section to pull a cell phone number. You can Google search their name or email address. All of this is currently free, and once you send a bunch of emails over a holiday weekend, you can collect direct cell phone numbers from their out-of-office auto-responses. One of the best tactics is contacting people who left an organization for the direct email and phone numbers of contacts still there.

It's just like golf—there is no point blaming the clubs if you can't master the fundamentals and hit the ball. Equally, even if you have competence, a $400 driver is not going to make you Jason Day. But where there's a will, there's a way. Start to move the needle with calling, and then build a business case for your direct manager to invest in the newfangled tools, starting with Sales Navigator.

Why Savvy Social Sellers Still Call Like Crazy

The year of the sales stack was 2017, and 2018 sees AI sales assistance maturing. If you want to be one of those who thrive rather than fade, then choose to be assisted by AI to engage with prospects and customers with your actual voice, not just your fingers! Find the best combinations to create human-to-human conversation, leveraging your dulcet tones and your alluring insights.

Have you ever noticed that top performers don't see channels or tools? They just connect, whatever it takes and no matter what. They get to the target. They get on-site and in the arena (just like Anthony Iannarino's podcast). The best thing that can happen to you is live human interaction. Everything else is going through the motions—a massive waste of time or something that the salesbots can do.

Amazingly, in some ways, selling hasn't changed a bit in a hundred years, and it won't be much different toward 2020. At least, not for those who succeed at it. Thirteen percent of sellers are generating 87 percent of the business,[33] and you want to be in that camp! It's simple if you follow the harsh advice I'm going to give you.

The achievers will always overcome their fear of rejection, aka picking up the phone, because they know the importance of talking to a live prospect or leaving a real voice message. I've talked to so many about this, and there's really no debate. It's empirically proven by the conclusive feedback I've received from more than 1,000 posts and articles from 2016–2017: The top salespeople are still fearlessly calling—intelligently warm calling.

The best leverage LinkedIn Sales Navigator and their CRM system to assess referrals and targets in their key accounts the night before. They then make direct dials to hit 30 targets every day. What separates the successful seller from the mediocre one is not some elaborate engineering of sales technology stack or social selling mastery to pump out content. Successful sellers just relentlessly and intelligently call! This is getting repetitive here, but are you actually going to do it?

As Jeb Blount so eloquently puts it, "It's a paradox of basics."[34] Or as Lee Bartlett phrases it in his book *The No. 1 Best Seller*, "Get punch drunk on the phone."[35] Mr. Miyagi didn't go right into third-degree black-belt level katas in the first scene in *The Karate Kid*. He started with "wax on, wax off."

This is the paradox of all sales. At the very top level of professional selling, the leaders are picking up phones and, since "brevity is the soul of wit," leaving concise unique value propositions (UVPs) on voice mail or interrupting prime prospects every day. This action is going to work exponentially in your favor as more and more salespeople drink the snake oil of passive social selling.

More and more target prospects have cell phones, and many will own two (as those who adopt the practices in this book increasingly break through to their cell numbers). Millennials: Now is your chance to buck the trend and call cell phones all day. You will advance your career as your snoozer colleagues are replaced by the bots or fired for nonperformance.

We've reached peak social selling, ironically at the precise moment we've reached peak cell phone penetration in the prospect base. The opportunity is vast for the courageous. Be bold! Be a bull breaking fine china! Pick up the phone. Make sure you have the data you need to directly dial. Call prospects that scare you. Call the people that make the decision first. Start high and get sponsored down, rather than going for those in your comfort zone who will become blockers to executive engagement. Don't research all day or overthink it; ensure that you have the right narrative by leading with why the conversation matters, and never mention your product, service, or solution. Go out there and get in front of them, and you will be mystified by how the numbers start to work in your favor.

Here are some muddy statistics that sales cowards hide behind:

- Ninety percent of C-levels don't answer the phone. It's a small survey, and it's wrong. Many CXOs were once sellers and will accept a valiant, professional effort to reach them. Bank on it!
- They are 57–70 percent through the buying process (CEB Research vs. Forrester Research). Yes, they have Google, but they are crazy busy and you can trigger them into a buying window with finessed interruption. Change the goalposts. You've got to uncover latent pain, and I guarantee you that sending smoke signals and passive noise is not going to get a slot. Go and poke the bear!
- 84 percent of new business is being generated by referrals. Again, this statistic is simply not true; in the main, those are internal referrals generated by savvy cold callers who have leveraged social engineering to do the triangulating and targeting. If the CMO flicks your email to the CEO, bingo: internal referral. This data must be debunked!

By the way, if you doubt any of the stats in this book, rest easy because 74 percent of stats are made up, including this one,[36] say Jeffrey Gitomer and Jennifer Gluckow. Seriously though, all of my stats have been obtained from reliable sources. Bogus stats have been torn to shreds by my hundreds of thousands of blog readers and never made it into this book.

I hope this is giving you a lot of hope and causing fists of lightning and fire in your belly. There is a light at the end of the tunnel, and it's called back to basics. Think about how Rocky used to train for boxing matches to become the world champion. Pulling heavy things in the snow, chasing chickens, drinking raw eggs, doing push-ups with a horse cart filled with boulders and children, punching sides of beef in the freezer room . . . you need to do all this to win.

You can do it all with LinkedIn and a phone, plus a few other simple tools. Amp it up by leveraging an intelligent blended approach. If you're cruising along in sales just clicking away at the mouse, then you'll fail. There will never be an easy button on sales success. Social is mainly for quality marketing and brand building; social selling is a crucial component of "whatever it takes," but it's not enough on its own. I hate to burst your bubble, but real A+ selling should strike terror in your heart: You can only win by talking to qualified prospects as often as possible, and you must elevate the conversations.

The Lunacy of Cold-Calling vs. Social Selling

This is a false dichotomy. It's warm-calling *and* social selling—social research, social listening, personal brand building, social collaboration, and social marketing, to be accurate. The term *social selling* is really an oxymoron. I prefer the term *digital selling*. Call it whatever you want; just make sure you combine social and the phone to drive real human conversations.

Salesperson: "Cold-calling doesn't work; it's a really poor use of my time." My response: "You should be warm-calling instead; it's just intelligent cold-calling by another name. If you can't make conversations happen on the phone, then you won't be successful." This was a real exchange.

You need to be a master of new-school and old-school methods to have a fighting chance of success in sales. Let's do some math that The Donald himself would embrace:

1. Out of 100 cold calls, you'll connect with 2 or 3. Dismal. Let's therefore dismiss the phone altogether . . . wrong!
2. Buyers are five times more likely to engage if there is a warm introduction.[37] True, so let's go full bore in social . . . also wrong!
3. COMBO drives two to three times the responses. Behold the triple: call, voice mail, email (in under two minutes) . . . getting warmer. And this is just the beginning!

The bottom line is that channels are never mutually exclusive in their efficacy. Just like combination therapy in skincare or high-intensity training in fitness, a blended approach is required. With the third path above, you're looking conservatively at six to nine connections out of 100 calls, which is much better than number 1.

Now if you get a warm referral from inside the organization on one of those connections, you are five times more likely to close, based on number 2. If you do the math, you have a 40 percent higher likelihood of opening an opportunity on a 100-call prospecting session, which is about a single morning of triples. You're looking at setting one meeting in four hours versus opening one qualified opportunity every day or 48 hours. You need only about three qualified discovery meetings per week to build out 1.5–3X pipeline over two quarters.

So that's the secret math and it's simple. You can fully ramp like this without being at the mercy of someone else to create your leads. Sales development reps (SDRs), also referred to as inside sales reps (ISRs) or lead development reps (LDRs), should themselves be adopting COMBO Prospecting techniques. Focus all your time at work on revenue-producing activities.

You may be reading this and thinking that you need much higher volume, conversion from calls to meetings, and then opportunities converted to hit your number. That's why you need very strict criteria about whom you call. Qualifying systems such as BANT (budget, authority, need, and time frame) or HubSpot's GPCT (goals, plans, challenges, timeline) qualification framework come in handy. More on qualification and discovery later, but it's critical that you get in high and qualify-out correctly based on budget, timeline, compelling event, and success criteria. You must be extremely protective of your time and capture those who are not in the right window into your CRM for high-quality content-based lead nurturing. Be very careful not to allow your future prospects to be blasted with spam from your company!

Spam annoys potential customers, and social selling is also aggravating when they receive friend requests from a stranger. Social networks abound with noise, and buyers don't want any more friends! The majority of people in power are drivers who want to get to the point and engage on the basis that you can actually help them achieve one of their wildly important goals.[38]

If you sell to CIOs, you must acknowledge that only a small minority would probably qualify right now. The vast majority are a) not interested, b) not in the buying window, c) just signed with a competitor, or d) most likely just happy to do nothing (status quo). The reason triples work is that you're "qualifying the buying window,"[39] as Jeb Blount states. If you're selling SaaS, chances are you're being commoditized and facing stiff competition. You need to move exceptionally fast to a "no" to even understand if there is a need or if you should create one upstream of the buying process.

Pattern-interrupt is one of the reasons COMBO Prospecting works. The majority of sellers follow up by email just twice. If you show up knocking on the CXO's door, chatting up multiple EAs, sending over several white papers and YouTube videos, building a quantified ROI-based business case, and touching their organization a dozen times a week in relevant, customized ways, then you're going to rattle the tree and the forbidden fruit will fall off.

The decision-makers who can buy your products and services are starving for insight, and you must be the signal in the noise for them. They're bombarded constantly by inanity, so the first person to pattern-interrupt and knock some sense into them—laser focused on how they'll actually make or save money—will be a refreshing change and will even be prioritized.

The COMBO of social and the phone is game changing. Special thanks to Steve Jobs—may he rest in peace—for creating the first genuinely mobile COMBO tool. But an amateur with expensive tools is still ineffective; you must become a masterful tradesperson.

Blended prospecting approaches are nothing new; they are just rare. But they have been previously highlighted extraordinarily well by Jeb Blount, Mike Weinberg, Anthony Iannarino, and others. Lee Bartlett, from London, used these combination techniques when seeking a meeting with the highly influential Jeffrey Hayzlett from New York. Lee saw a tweet from Jeffrey saying he had landed at Heathrow Airport (trigger event) and immediately tweeted a public reply, followed by a personal message offering to meet anywhere. As soon as Jeffrey responded, Lee called. Within 24 hours, they were face-to-face talking business over breakfast.

Social selling gurus have recoiled in horror at me pushing the phone, but the truth is that we're embracing their methods, too. I'm just making the argument that the previous techniques are just as relevant as ever. The human voice must be central. Mixed martial arts provides the best analogy. It's a ground game of grappling if you take away strength and speed. It's a game of social aikido or tai chi where one can use the opponent's own energy and weight against them. Metaphorically, your competitors are actually making your job easier, creating a layup for someone who's actually delivering real strategic value.

Selling is a full-contact sport and really only gains traction with human conversation where there is insight and rapport. Success happens face-to-face, even if it's video conferencing with GoToMeeting, Skype, BlueJeans, appear.in, Zoom, or something else. You've got to learn effective "smart calling" with Art Sobsczak and how to sharpen your "sales story" with Mike Weinberg before you go and apply these same communication tactics on other mediums. Without a value proposition delivered to an ideal client profile (ICP), you're dead in the water no matter what the channel.

Why Being Beat Up Is Good for the Soul

Intelligent calling to generate business is good for the soul. It's humbling, scary, and highly rewarding. Sales is about real communication, and I believe we need a massive return to innocence. Why call? Literally, face your fears and call a stranger. When is the best time? Right now! Any day that ends in *y* is good for calling, and any time that they are not with their family is good for calling. People obsess over making the perfect scripted call at the perfect time of day to the perfect prospect as if they're about to get in an elevator with Mark Cuban and get 10 seconds to pitch. Mark Cuban ran a college bar, and if he had to start all over, he would be the master of . . . wait for it . . . cold-calling!

If you just master that one skill of cold-calling, and then add pragmatic research and COMBOs to warm the calls beforehand, your entire career will be transformed from the inside out. Focus all your energy on developing this one mental muscle for six months, even if you talk to only 2 in 100 people. Watch your self-esteem, income, and influence take off like a rocket ship! You'll develop the COMBO Prospecting habit for life.

If you're serious about calling, you could utilize ConnectAndSell and get those contact rates through the roof. Just ask Chris Beall, who lives life at 1,000 dials a day. I've affectionately nicknamed Chris Bruce Wayne because he is the Dark Knight of our social selling–crazed digital age. Chris drives 40 live prospect conversations per day, per salesperson. Like Batman, Chris Beall is cleaning up Gotham of charlatan jokers who push their social selling schlock to the masses by fear-mongering and who are petrified to be human and authentically communicate. There has been a vast trend, which borders on obsession, of checking mobile devices hundreds of times a day. Being a screen jockey is an introverted activity and not natural or healthy for the human brain or body. You see couples at fine dining restaurants immersed, heads down on Facebook (always Facebook) or Instagram. You see it on the train—the endless swiping of meaningless magazine drivel, living vicariously through some celebrity's shallow excuse for an existence.

What is sales really? What defines success? Sales is about communicating with others and making a positive difference in their lives. It is about saving people from failure and helping them see, and then achieve, a better state of affairs so they can soar. It goes beyond fear of the phone. Maybe you fear something deeper—like someone discovering you're full of hot air. This fear is endemic to a virtual society of isolation where no one knows anyone anymore. Our whole waking lives are constructed with the selfie-stick and the humble brag, a Jenga game of polished glass ready to shatter at the sound of a human voice.

The purpose of social media like Facebook and LinkedIn was always to connect. This is a call to arms for everyone to just be real and move from being connected to being truly engaged. When I'm reaching out to people, I reach out to the ones I truly believe I can help. My positive intent and my belief in what I offer is a port in the storm of rejection. This rain of rejection slides off me like water off a duck's back as I paddle like crazy under the surface to get my activity up to the point that I can break through. I don't use wooden scripts or canned responses: I intend to break through by being real, and so I do.

We are spirits in a material world on a quest to drive value by actually interacting. We need to break down the barriers and really get to know each other; break bread and show vulnerability; and release fears, bias, and divisions to build a better society and world. I think that the real dinosaur concept is the idea that you can sit in front of a computer screen, clicking away passively, and call it sales. Used in this way, social becomes a misnomer. In sales, social is like a fleeting meme that has passed us by.

Many say that managers of millennials should not push them to get on the front foot. But that's just like bad, permissive parenting, where your kid loves you and then goes to join a street gang at the tender age of 13. Millennials would rather have a smartphone than a car. They should take the car and go meet other millennials for a hike in the wilderness. Sales roles should be 70 percent real human interaction on the phone or in the field. You could easily dismiss me as a Luddite or iconoclast, but this is just level one: wax on, wax off. The power tools are for the big boys and girls. Social media is an added privilege, a dessert after the main course—the phone!

I can teach you everything you need to know about strategic sales, social selling, and how to close million-dollar deals. But first, you must address mindset and preparedness because these are the price of entry. Do you love people? Would you love to help a customer? Do you truly believe in your product or service? Do you respect yourself? It all starts with heart. Selling is a people business. You must go forth and wander out of the shadows of the shire. The most modern technology I can impart to you is the oldest of all: love of others and infinite curiosity!

Earning the Right to Win

"I fear not the man who has practiced 10,000 kicks once, but I fear the man who has practiced one kick 10,000 times."

—BRUCE LEE

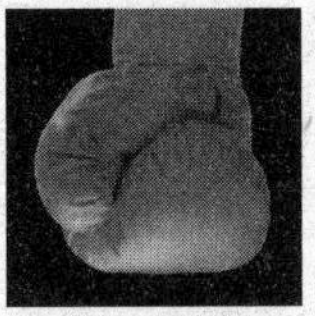

ARE YOU REALLY THE PERSON WORTHY OF THE SUCCESS YOU seek? Go stare in the mirror—look deep inside your soul. Truth be told, most people in leadership roles secretly worry about being found out. The real deal is rare, and most salespeople are full of crap, projecting a persona of clichéd social bravado and wearing a suit of confidence. What's really there when people or circumstances scratch past the surface? Do you really have the right values? Is it all about your client and your team, rather than yourself?

I was managing director for the Asia-Pacific region of a North American multinational, and we won a massive contract. It meant paying my salesperson half a million dollars in commission and paying each of the five people on the pre-sales team the equivalent of their annual salaries in a single bonus. It was one of the biggest worldwide deals in the company's history, and my commission was also substantial. We got the contract signed, and we all celebrated. But then I got a phone call from my boss overseas. "They don't want to pay that much commission to anyone. There is a clause in the compensation plan about out-of-the-ordinary 'bluebird' business opportunities being exempt." They offered to pay me all of what I was owed if I could negotiate the amount of commission down for those who worked for me, especially the sales rep. My instant response was "no."

We had been pursuing this opportunity for years. There was nothing out of blue about it at all. We were an enterprise software company, and the deal had been in the CRM right from the beginning. We had been tracking it in the pipeline and forecast reports for over 15 months. Long story short, I talked with the CFO and rather than treating him as the enemy, I treated the situation as the problem. I listened and sought to understand the root cause of our problem. It was the "out of whack" levels of commission (due to accelerators on our deal) being paid in a single quarter compared with global revenue. If we could defer the payments, it would smooth the problem into downstream quarters. I called the salesperson and explained the dilemma. I said, "If I wait nine months, will you wait six months? Then we can pay all the pre-sales team their full commission this quarter." He agreed without hesitation, saying, "They worked the hardest on this, so they deserve to get paid first." We both deferred and eventually received our money. It was gratifying to take the pre-sales team to lunch and watch them receive their checks.

Values are everything. So are attitude and commitment. What happens once you've danced around in your corner before the opening bell for round one? Will you hold to your values and do what is right regardless of the temptations or obstacles? After all the bravado and trash talk, once you get punched in the head, can you keep moving forward to go toe-to-toe in the ring as a genuine heavyweight contender? The personal foundation you build will determine the platform on which you will perform.

Foundations of Executive Engagement

C-level executives are drivers. They want to drive straight to the point. They're not interested in chitchat, and they're usually just dying to see their family. But even the leader of the free world will be stopped in their tracks by a relevant data point or insight. Successful people got there with an insatiable hunger to know, to learn, to improve, and to master interdisciplinary skills.

Your first step in accessing the CXO in the corner office is to think from their viewpoint—by using empathy. What are they primarily concerned about with their business? If it's a publicly traded company, this is usually revealed in the annual letter to the shareholders or quarterly call. You can also find some financially savvy friends or colleagues to help you go through their balance sheet and financials. Jonathan Farrington says it best: "Most important of all, you have to identify where or how you can make a significant contribution in helping them achieve their overall goals this year. How can you help them save, gain, reduce, increase or improve? These are the five magic words that grab C-suite residents."

Boiling this down, it's generally going to be efficiency (cutting costs) or revenue (increasing top line), and then more efficiency—doing things to get higher outputs that accrue to the bottom line. This includes staffing up, staffing down, retrofitting existing processes with lean Six Sigma, or changing the business-unit structure. It may include piecemealing together disparate technology systems or sending the whole pile to the scrap heap for a new unified system.

Organizations must still be pursued from top down, with a unified message that has one singular theme—not a pastiche or more white noise. In the old days, this was called selling to VITO (Very Important Top Officer), and Anthony Parinello trademarked processes for getting in high. Authority and hierarchy have not changed much in the Fortune 1000, and even start-ups are pretty insular and autocratic when you break it down. That means that if some junior person has the most ingenious idea to collaborate on with a vendor, they'll usually get neutralized in a heartbeat to cut costs. You need authority to sanction the conversation and smoke out the committee, whether permanent or temporary, for a deal cycle.

Executives are protected by a bulletproof glass shield that is their executive assistant. Don't be fooled, the EA is likely one smart cookie. It's a mistake to think this person isn't running the CEO's life. They are. So pitch to the EA as a deputy or proxy to the C-level you're looking for. Good leaders and senior executives are not vain or narcissistic, but they are extremely selective with their time. When you see one quoted in a magazine article, online trade journal, or any excerpt from an event, you've literally struck gold. They are men and women of few words. If you reference specifics from their quotes in the press and tie this back to the value of your solution, you'll land meetings left and right. You've got to be thoughtful about it, just like when you reference details from their annual reports.

The most important thing is to respect the C-level's time and get to the point by starting at the end. They want to know what you want from them and why it is important. The conversation could go like this: "I believe there's a real opportunity to [insert tangible business benefit here], and once we've met, I'd like you to sponsor an engagement with [insert the names of leaders in the business areas you will positively impact]. We will invest time together to create a business case we can bring back to you." Then provide some additional detail. The C-level person now knows why they're investing time in the conversation and what you want from them.

The Language of Leaders and Relevance Challenge

The problem for those aspiring to leadership, and for those in sales, is that you're delegated down to those you sound like. For example, if you start talking technology, they will respond with: "You need to talk with our IT department." Strategic selling, by definition, means engaging with the person who owns the problem or opportunity that you seek to address. They may not even have the word *chief* in their title, but every time you identify the buyer or person who owns the budget and can approve or veto a decision, think of them as the "CEO of the problem." The CEO and their inner circle of CXOs and domain leaders are the ones you must delightfully surprise as you spring from the bushes and wow them with how you engage.

But if you are to elevate how you influence and sell, and to engage at the CEO or CXO level, you need to speak the language of leadership. This includes two important points:

1. Discuss how you can deliver business outcomes and manage their risks.
2. Talk about the numbers and the business case, plus how success will be measured.

This is the essence of leading with why the conversation matters, and it focuses on the business outcomes they care about. That's really what leaders want. If you can also learn to speak the language of numbers, then you can start to become a trusted adviser. This allows you to work with your client in partnership, rather than being perceived as someone who's merely attempting to sell. Every seller needs to do these three things:

1. Lead with insight and engage by having a perspective on the client's world.
2. Build trust beyond mere rapport, with relentless positive intent and business literacy.
3. Create value in every conversation, backed up with real evidence.

These three together are the foundation on which the seller earns the right to gain understanding, propose solutions, and ask for the business as a trusted adviser. Beyond this foundation, strategic selling is first and foremost defined by early engagement at the most senior level possible. You may not need to engage the CEO of the organization, but you do need to sell to the person who actually owns the problem or opportunity. This is the person who is on the hook for delivering the result, the one who controls the funding and authorizes the decision—this is whom you need to engage. Everyone else is a mere influencer, recommender, or blocker.

How do you actually engage effectively at the CXO level? What do

CXOs typically care about? Beyond mere results, the very best leaders focus on making a difference, treasuring time, building up people, and leaving a legacy. Here are 10 rules to honor on your quest to engage successfully:

1. Be a person of value, a domain expert who can help make things happen. No one likes being sold to, but people do value relevant information, insight, and perspective from someone with humble wisdom, a strong network, and the gravitas to carry the conversation.
2. Start at the end and lead with *why*. Get to the point and be concise. Genuine insights are rare and never clichéd, so do your homework and understand why the conversation is important. Only once you've anchored the conversation should you talk about the what, how, who, and when.
3. Open powerfully by not talking about yourself; make it all about them. Show that you've done your homework and that you understand how you can help deliver their agenda, solve their problems, or realize their opportunities—both personally and professionally.
4. Speak the language of leadership: finding positive outcomes and managing risk.
5. Speak the language of business: delivering financial results and achieving KPIs.
6. Speak the language of legacy: enacting sustainable change that makes a difference in the lives of customers, staff, and the community.
7. No faking it and no bullshit. Know the industry and have evidence to support your assertions. Be masterful at telling powerful, true stories, but be conservative in your claims. Also be honest and transparent. If you don't know, then say so.
8. Always be early, have an agenda, respect time, and follow up in writing. In short, be a professional.
9. Let them be in control. Simply ask them what they want to see

happen after the meeting and what the next steps should be to create progress. But when they sponsor you down, always maintain your direct relationship and the right to contact them whenever necessary. People are best motivated by reasons they themselves discover. Never preach, sell, or lecture. Instead, ask insightful open questions that cause them self-reflection.

10. Always deliver on every promise, have integrity, and be rock-solid reliable.

All of this is relatively straightforward, but there is something else that dramatically elevates the way you engage at the CXO level.

Paradox of Nonhunger and Genuine Curiosity

The power of nonhunger has been explored in "the hottest one at the bar" story. It is also known as the Law of Principled Disinterest. This comes with a paradox: You can come across as arrogant or uninterested. Conversely, the more interest you show in closing a deal, the more repulsed the prospect will be. Jeb Blount calls this the "universal law of need." It's the idea that when you need a deal so badly, you're going to have sales breath—a repellent to prospects.

How do you manage the paradox between nonhunger and engagement? Ali could "float like a butterfly and sting like a bee." The best salespeople are not desperate but genuinely curious. They seek to be interested rather than needy. They have no desire to pitch anything until the buyer is in the zone.

Genuinely curious people ask the best questions because they are not seeking to manipulate or steer the conversation in a predetermined direction. The genuinely curious have an advantage when prospecting because questioning is in their DNA, and they don't have to fake it. Barry Rhein advocates selling through curiosity, and he is famous for being paid equity on future revenue performance by his customers.

The egomaniac blabbermouth never gets to the root cause, so they can't ever really propose the right solution. However, curious people with the right values go through hell and high water to understand another person's business. They actively listen to cultivate curiosity on both sides, and this is fundamentally important to COMBO strategies.

A big fat sales pipeline, nonhunger and curiosity, combined with a love of customers and enjoyment in making a difference, prevents sales burnout. You can afford to focus on alignment rather than pressure for a close. These values beat negative attempts at Machiavellian manipulation or brute force tactics. Hunting big game is going to take an extremely sharp spear and a willingness to walk away, exhibit gravitas, and stay dead calm while operating at the highest echelons. You cannot lose your cool, nor can you become hungry, needy, or pushy. It's crucial at all times to be creating value in conversations, listening proactively, and remaining detached from the outcome of the deal.

By filling your pipeline with 3–5X the qualified opportunities that you need to hit your number, you gain the confidence you need. On the phone, tone is 86 percent of our communication.[1] Other research revealed that words account for just 7 percent of received communication.[2] Whether it is 7 percent or 14 percent, words alone account for a minor portion of influence.

The whole point of this book is for you to consistently build a pipeline that takes almost all the pressure out of selling, where you focus on alignment rather than persuasion and the business case rather than the pitch. To do this, you must lead with value rather than relationship.

Friending and Relationship Selling

All sellers need relationships with buyers, but the last thing a buyer wants in their busy day is a salesperson seeking to "friend them" on social or on the phone. No one worth selling to is lonely and bored and looking for a new friend or a salesperson to come and tell them about the joys and wonders of their products. Leading with a relationship sell or a pitch is therefore a giant mistake. Instead, lead with insight and value in the very first conversation, and build a meaningful relationship of trust over time.

Executives like to put salespeople to the test. They put the fake family photos on their desk, a big stuffed marlin or trout on the wall, and some trophies on the bookcase. But the joke is on the seller because the punch-line is that it's a test. The average salesperson will come in and start talking about fishing or their family to try to build rapport. Savvy executives are so sick of this that they literally play practical jokes on sellers.

One senior executive told the story of when he received a magnum of Veuve Cliquot, and then posted on LinkedIn offering to give it away to the person with the best comment. He did this to highlight just how disingenuous it felt for him to get buttered up with free gifts.

The book *The Challenger Sale* was pivotal in revealing the profile of those who are most likely to succeed in securing the C-suite. "Challengers account for nearly 40% of all high performers while Relationship Builders come in dead last at only 7% of high performers."[3] Ironically, relationships are essential and not to be undervalued.

For eons, it seems, sales executives were encouraged to either blaze a trail as the lone wolf or focus all effort on being likable with rapport-building skills. From "smiling and dialing" to golfing, this was the nature of the beast in the 1980s and 90s. Get out your pink Izods and *Miami Vice* white blazer, and get ready to go deep-sea fishing or occupy your private box at the game with beer and shrimp cocktails.

What's wild now with the Cambrian-style explosion of the Information Age is that buyers can easily source all the information they want. They only seek to talk to experts who share best practices, trends, and true insights that give them an edge against the competition. Blunt practitioners of value, who deliver insight immediately, become the trusted advisers at light speed. While the CFO has free football tickets delivered to their desk by their executive assistant, you're actually in the meeting pitching to them. This is because you're showing them how to hit their roadmap targets six months earlier by implementing a business process management system in the cloud that lowers their overhead by 30 percent.

You can meet powerful people at networking events, charity galas, and celebrity golf and poker tournaments, and you can shoot the breeze all day.

But these relationship socials never beat an engineer of value, who FedExes to the CXO's desk a plain manila envelope containing pearls of wisdom for accelerating profit. This document contains information on how to see around the curve and deliver important outcomes while managing risk.

Rather than leading with a relationship and providing value with what you sell, lead instead with insight and value in every meeting and document. Value is the reason people will initially engage, and it builds a relationship of trust over time. In new business development, lead with value and then build a relationship—never seek to reverse the order, even with a referral.

The Truth About Trust and Value

People have always done business with those they know, like, and trust. In fact, all business is done at "the speed of trust," as Stephen Covey says, and it's almost impossible to win a new client without the presence of trust. I think you can see that trust is an essential prerequisite for sales success and almost everything else that is worthwhile in life. This is why having positive reference clients and a strong personal brand is so important.

Don't focus on analyst reports that place your company or solution in some kind of magic quadrant. Customers don't really believe those slides because all of your competitors march in with similar claims of market leadership or superiority. Never allow your confidence cup to runneth over so much that you appear arrogant. Instead, always have empathy and humility, and never say that you "dominate the market." Instead, use the phrase "we lead the market," and talk about how you've helped other relevant customers achieve real business results.

Make no mistake, your online reputation, corporate and individual, is critically important because professional buyers and executives do their research before deciding to engage and meet face-to-face. If a sales lead has come to you, then the customer is normally well advanced in their process and your online presence and credentials will have been pivotal in being included on their list. Creating a strong personal brand will be covered

FIGURE 2-1. FORMULA FOR BUILDING TRUST

$$\text{Trust} = \frac{(\text{Understanding} + \text{Shared Values}) \times (\text{Capability} + \text{Reputation})}{\text{Perform Consistently Over Time}}$$

later. Here, we will focus on how to create trust with the buyer. Figure 2-1 shows my formula for how to build trust with individuals and teams.

Most salespeople spend way too much time on the back end of the formula by talking about their capability and reputation. This part of the formula is the easy area for salespeople to talk about because it's in their comfort zone. Your company, products, and solutions may be what you know most about and what your marketing department has invested a fortune in honing. But it's a huge mistake to lead with these things. The customer instead cares about what you can do for them and whether you have the right level of understanding and aligned values.

Evidencing capability and reputation is important but only to support the customer's decision to buy, which occurs much later in the relationship. The vast majority of buyers will research you before you get to have a meeting, so use your LinkedIn profile, website, and social media presence to tick that box. When you actually engage in a conversation with a customer, make it all about them by focusing on the front end of the formula: Genuinely understand their needs, constraints, problems, and opportunities. Show them that you are someone who listens, asks intelligent questions, values their time, understands their culture, respects their processes, delivers results, and will work as an extended member of their team. Having aligned values is hugely powerful.

The best sales professionals focus on understanding and insight rather than pushing features and benefits. They frame what they have to say as thoughtful open questions. They are committed to working in the best interests of the customer and avoid trust-destroying rhetorical questions that are usually perceived as manipulative or redundant.

Plan every sales call and meeting. Lead with insight and strive to talk no more than one-third of the time. The reason this is so important is because listening is the most powerful form of influence, and you learn nothing while talking. Listening and asking intelligent open questions are the keys to gaining understanding and building trust in every situation, especially in selling, negotiation, and conflict resolution situations.

Building trust requires a substantial investment of time and energy in gaining, and then demonstrating, an understanding of the customer's industry and business. Anthony Iannarino describes this as "situational awareness," and it includes having an understanding of the customer's economic and market conditions, internal politics and power base, problems and opportunities, and, most important, biggest challenges they face with their own customers. Nic Dennis says, "Invest extra time in preparing and practicing great questions because that's how you will be remembered and invited back again."[4]

But hang on, you may be thinking, COMBO is about rapid levels of effective activity, so how can I generate insights for my conversations quickly and on the fly? You are right; unless you are targeting large enterprises, you don't have the luxury of time for deep research when prospecting. That's why it is so important to work in industry verticals or with a specialized domain area or set of business problems. It is also why you must position your insights in terms of a humble hypothesis of value, rather than act like a Challenger bull in the china shop.

By specializing, you can understand the typical value levers that apply to your prospective customers and markets. Although you can set a vision with the customer for a potential future state, it's important to remember that the customer, not you, determines value. Any business case must quantify the costs and risks associated with staying in the current state before positioning the benefits of a future state. Only the customer is qualified to assess value for money and the positive impact on their economic metrics and business drivers. Nevertheless, everything you sell must help customers improve revenue and/or margin; or reduce cost, time, or effort; or reduce serious risks.

The basic equation for value (shown in Figure 2-2) is: Business Value = Benefit minus Cost, and this is why it's so important to ensure that all benefits are expressed in monetized form wherever possible. Yes, it's true

FIGURE 2-2. FORMULA FOR BUSINESS VALUE

Business Value = Benefit - Cost

that not all benefits save or make money for the customer. For example, less stress, improved productivity, or less risk in noncritical areas can all be difficult to justify in financial terms. The language of business is numbers, not words, so always ask yourself: How does this benefit drop to their bottom line or improve their balance sheet?

When prospecting and engaging in initial conversations, you must lead with value as defined by the customer. To be clear, they see no value in having another business friend or supplier relationship to manage, nor do they see any benefit in buying from you. According to Graham Hawkins, vendor rationalization (doing more business with fewer vendors) means that buyers are not permitted to purchase your product even if they wanted to. Some procurement organizations have policies in place to block off-panel purchases. They do, however, typically see value in the insights a third party can provide concerning what their competitors or relevant peers are doing. Qualify early concerning their ability to buy from you, and ask them to explain how the process works if they want to become a customer.

People are most open to these conversations when there has been change or some form of trigger event. Craig Elias and Tibor Shanto wrote about trigger events for pipeline creation in their excellent book *Shift!* There is a window after a job change where CXOs deploy a million dollars in capital on innovation and change initiatives, which sellers can tap into. In this scenario, someone has just been promoted or switched companies, and the weight of the world is upon their shoulders to overachieve in the first 90 days. This is where a savvy seller can come in, collaborate on a business case based on relevant similar clients, and do a six- or seven-figure deal. This can happen when the "pain of same is greater than the pain of change." This comes back to "speed to trust," as Stephen Covey put it, because the more relevant the need or stronger the pain, the sooner you can diagnose it, solve it, and help your customer to be a hero.

Value is often intrinsic, but it can be extrinsic in the sense that there can be political value to the win. The right technology can help a decision-maker gain the corner office or revolutionize a division. This is why Jim Holden's seminal work, *Power Base Selling*, is important for all salespeople to read. As the buying committee balloons to seven people,[5] you start to see nontraditional power structures build. Jim Holden nails this concept with the "situational fox" in his book *The New Power Base Selling*, and Miller Heiman expresses this as a champion or coach in the account.

From the perspective of COMBO, you're trying to flush out these people and their allies early, set meetings in parallel by multi-threading (generating multiple communication avenues to multiple stakeholders), and then bring the committees together to form consensus around value. In the book *The Challenger Customer*, this idea of consensus is debunked—it says by challenging the many fiefdoms, you typically bring on even more dysfunction and gridlock. In order to win, the book posits, one must break down the group's mental model and help it construct a new one.

Again, the inherent flaw in all the closing methodologies is that there's no point in mastering the flying of an Airbus A380 if you can't even get it off the ground. That's just as crazy as never learning to land it, which we'll get into later. So while all this is relevant once you have a major opportunity in play, I include it here because the way you open is more important than how you close. Strategic selling is defined by engaging early at the most senior levels and then setting an agenda of unique value that creates disadvantage to, or even excludes, all competition.

All sellers need deep understanding of complex enterprise selling, but when it comes to building pipeline and driving high levels of proactive outreach, you just have to get on with it and have a bias toward intelligent action! You need to know only enough to secure the meeting, so don't try to boil the ocean with research. Again, if you are selling into a particular industry vertical, then there are common problems every player is facing. Take the time to go deep on these issues because they will apply in every engagement. But when it comes to individual companies and buyer personas, you must be pragmatic in rapidly executing research.

The Art of Pragmatic Research

The world's biggest and most powerful business directory is LinkedIn. But it goes beyond that to also provide amazing insights into what potential clients are thinking, who they know, where they were educated, where they've worked, what interests them most, who can provide you with coaching or an introduction, and more. That's why Microsoft paid a staggering $26.2 billion for the company in 2016. I will provide details later on how to use Sales Navigator to rapidly source insights about the power base of individuals within the enterprise you are targeting. But first, let's explore how to rapidly research your target client's industry.

Sourcing insight and data points that are relevant to the prospect's world is about synthesis of a broad swath of data. That's why social platforms are so powerful. If you followed 30 omni-channel retail CMOs and started to piece together that patchwork quilt into a sensible amalgam of insights, you'd have data points to bring back to each one of them. They are often blind to these insights because they are on the inside looking out—they can't see past their hermetically sealed box of a system.

The basic search information you use is the name of the company and the name of the prospect popped into Google. Then you click on News. You can sort the results by last month through to last year. This is basic, but if you're using the "show them you know them" technique, you're already ahead of 90 percent of other sellers. This is because most of your competition is lazy or unimaginative—their approach may sound something like: "I read your profile and see that you love the Chicago Bears." Again, this is a losing approach of relationship selling, and it provides no value in helping the client drive business forward, reduce costs, or make money.

Beware the dangers of shallow clichés. Jill Konrath gives an entire list of buzzwords to be avoided in her book *SNAP Selling*. Talk like a real human being, and leave the jargon behind. You get delegated down to whom you sound like, so it's crucial that you speak like a leader and use real-world customer examples of outcomes. It is incredibly powerful to view your target client's world through the eyes of their customers—they are the CEO's real boss.

Part of researching a target account is to first locate who can make the decision. This is often as simple as doing advanced searches on the role responsibilities in LinkedIn's Sales Navigator through Lead Builder. If you are selling mobile, search the 10,000-person bank for any profiles that have the word *mobile* in the title. Perhaps it's *ERP* or *HR software*—then do an advanced search for profiles within the highly matrixed organization that mention that acronym on the page.

You can search 100,000 profiles in a nanosecond. I've even seen extremely rare classifications, skills, programming languages, and code-base requirements uncovered like a needle in a haystack in near real time by using this research technique. The best recruitment consultants are masterful at Boolean searching. They can find the people who are not being found by their lazy or ignorant competitors who don't know how to scratch past the surface of a rudimentary search.

If you claim to be a sales professional, then you should know how to construct a Boolean search within any search engine and LinkedIn. Google it and also watch YouTube tutorials to educate yourself about it. Find a recruiter and ask them to show you how they find people within LinkedIn—you'll be amazed. This is a fundamental skill you need to master.

Leading with Insight and Why a Conversation Matters

Our conversations need to anchor senior engagement so that they agree later to sponsor us to their team for the purpose of discovery, consensus building, and business case development. The reality is that you have only 20 to 40 seconds to create the right impression and hook the interest of the person with whom you are seeking to engage. This is especially true in the age of social media, sound bites, and executive ADD. Buyers and decision-makers have never had less time.

To succeed, you must focus on why a conversation matters rather than lead with what you do and how you do it. The what and how are irrelevant until they first know why they should invest time in talking with you. By focusing on why a conversations matters, we overcome the worst competitor—the option of merely doing nothing. If we establish a compelling reason why change is necessary, then we overcome client apathy and earn the right to help them build a strong, compelling business case for going ahead with transformation. This approach feeds into talking about business outcomes and the business case for investing and taking on risk.

As you prepare your own narrative, ask yourself this important question: What's the business problem I can solve for the client, and why should that be a priority for them? Then ask: How do I create compelling business case value better than anybody else? And finally: How can I lead with insight to create value in a conversation? The answer to this last question is especially important because leading with insight is how you earn the right to have a conversation with a senior person. Think about this fact validated by CEB Research: The way we sell (engage) is more important than what we sell (our product, service, or solution). CEB Research surveyed 5,000 buyers and discovered that 53 percent of a competitive selection is based upon the experience the seller creates for the buyer. Price or value contribute a mere 9 percent to the buying decision, and brand, product, and service capabilities together contribute 38 percent.[6]

Here is how I teach my students to open after briefly introducing themselves with some context (common connection, trigger event, etc.). "The reason I'm calling is that I work with others in your industry and I've done some research on your company. I think you may have the opportunity to achieve [nominate a specific business outcome you typically deliver]. I think it's important because [cite industry trend], and I'd like to share some of my findings with you and discuss how you could potentially improve results. How is Thursday of next week?"

This narrative answers questions in the mind of the potential customer. It's important because "leaping out of the bushes" with your initial outreach must quickly explain who you are, why you want their time, and how they will benefit from the conversation. No friending, no pitching—just brief context and then a request for their time to discuss your insights about their industry and competition and the trends that matter to them.

Become masterful at opening because it sets the agenda and begins the process of building trust and credibility. Once you've anchored a customer initiative with purpose (the why), you can be an engineer of value rather than just a warrior of persuasion.

Creating Your Own Value Narrative

In the eyes of the buyer, all sellers look pretty much the same. It's a brutal truth that sales and marketing leaders need to confront. The way most companies seek to overcome this is by creating a beautiful and engaging "customer experience." This is designed to support the buyer's journey as they research, evaluate, decide, approve, purchase, renew, and then advocate.

Marketing departments seek to differentiate customer experience strategies, leveraging content, tools, and platforms that attract and engage buyers on the web, on social, and on mobile devices. Salespeople also need to differentiate. The compelling point of difference for salespeople is their domain expertise and insightful value narrative, evidenced and supported by their personal brand and network within LinkedIn. This is my simple framework for creating your own value narrative that sets you apart from your competition and engages senior buyers and decision-makers:

1. Provide context through a trigger event or referral.
2. Lead with a genuine insight or relevant point of view about their industry or business.
3. State the opportunity for them or (less ideal) the consequences of inaction.
4. Bridge with why it's important, and (only if needed) have evidence to back up your claim.
5. Explain the specific business outcomes you can help them achieve (do not mention your products, services, or solutions), and ask for their time with an appointment. If you secure an appointment,

stop, thank them, and send a LinkedIn connection request, confirmation email with an agenda, and also a calendar invitation.

6. Ask open questions that lead to your business value, and create the reason to engage.
7. Have powerful true stories that evidence your claims.
8. Ask for their time with an appointment. Send a LinkedIn connection request, confirmation email with an agenda, and also a calendar invitation.

One of my clients is the New Zealand government's international business development agency, New Zealand Trade and Enterprise (NZTE). Its purpose is to grow companies internationally—bigger, better, and faster—for the benefit of New Zealand. As part of my work with NZTE, I helped its own business development managers and management teams elevate the narrative they were using to engage companies that were candidates for NZTE's services.

Before my workshops, NZTE was approached by CEOs considering overseas expansion, the pitch was typically: "New Zealand Trade and Enterprise has offices in 40 international locations, and we offer services for companies that are either exporting or looking to set up an office overseas. We can help with. . . ." The person would then start going through the list of services offered hoping that something would resonate with the CEO or owner of the business.

We transformed that approach to be in line with my framework, and used the COMBO of phone calls, voice mails, and supporting emails and messages. The new approach looked like this: "Hi [client name]. I'm [your name], from New Zealand Trade and Enterprise. [Open with context of trigger event or referral]. We work with others in your industry, and based on my research I think you could accelerate your push into international markets and also minimize risk. The reason that's important is that companies in our portfolio typically achieve nearly double the growth of those not working with us. The common traits for those who succeed are a clear understanding of the target market, a strong value proposition, and the right local partnerships. How is your calendar next week?"

The above incorporates points 1 through 5 of the framework, and if the person wants more information before committing, then you ask questions like this: "What are you doing now to manage the risks of entering the market? What's your strategy in leveraging local partnerships?"

Regardless of their responses, you then say, "Great. To maximize the likelihood of success, you can leverage the experience of others who've done this before. We've helped many companies avoid wasting time and money and instead achieve their goals. How is your calendar next week?"

Then you tag it with this last question, which helps determine the strength of the business case for engaging: "What are your revenue growth expectations in the first three years, and how are you tracking?"

Then ask again for the meeting. "We can help you develop the right plan through market intelligence, strategic planning, relationships, resources, and focus. It definitely makes sense for us to talk; what day works best for you next week?"

For yourself right now, take this framework and craft your own value narrative for a target vertical or market and with a specific buyer persona in mind. This will be the most senior person you can engage with who makes or approves the buying decision. Invest in creating the right narrative. There is no point in getting busy with prospecting and outreach if you're like a deer in the headlights when someone asks why you've called them. Here is a template for you to use:

- Brief introduction for context and then: "I'm calling because your industry is . . ."
- "I've been working with others in your sector and based on my research of your company, I think there's an opportunity for you to . . ."
- "I'd like 40 minutes to meet, and I think it's important because . . ."
- "I've been able to help ABC company achieve XYZ, and I don't know yet whether you could get the same kind of results, but

that's why I want to meet."

- "What time is best for you on . . ."
- "I thought you'd have questions; let's cover those when we meet. How is your calendar?"
- Create three open questions that lead to your business value.
- Your true relevant customer stories/case studies with emotional resonance.

Seriously, commit to doing this very challenging piece of work, and honestly answer these questions: If you were a CEO, would you buy from someone like you? Can you really carry the conversation at senior levels? Do you have genuine insight about the customer's industry and issues? Do you focus on the business outcomes you can deliver for them? Can you have a conversation without mentioning your products or services?

There is no point hammering away with high levels of activity if you're doing it the wrong way! You must be both effective and efficient if you are to create the success you deserve. "A fool with a tool is just a busier fool,"[7] as Jill Rowley says. Having the right narrative also requires the ability to ask the right questions, so let's explore how to create these and ask them in the most powerful way.

Questions That Qualify and Set the Agenda

Explaining facts or pushing a value proposition often repels the other person. Rather than leading with a pitch, you must instead lead *to* the business value you offer. This is important because people are best motivated for reasons that they themselves discover.

Questions are how you guide a conversation. In my workshops and training courses, I often do an exercise where people team up with a partner and take turns asking each other only open questions for two minutes. It amazes me how few can execute the task successfully. An open question forces the other person to engage in meaningful conversation. Here are some examples of open versus closed questions:

Closed: Is that a serious problem for you?

Open: How does that impact the business and you personally?

Closed: When can you sign the paperwork?

Open: What's your timing and process for being able to go ahead with this?

Closed: If we could do that, would you buy from us?

Open: If we could do that, how would that change things for you?

One of the negative byproducts of asking closed questions is that the prospect can feel manipulated and raise objections. Objections reduce the probability of a sale by damaging trust and momentum and usually occur when the seller seeks progression before the buyer is ready. Objections can be avoided if the seller ensures understanding before seeking commitment, and this is why asking insightful open questions is so important.

Almost all questions should be asked in the open format, and closed, manipulative questions are to be avoided. True story: A life insurance person once asked me if I loved my wife and children, and then whether I wanted the very best for them. I just smiled at him, and I'm sure he thought, Game over! He was right. I showed him the door.

You have created your value narrative and a few questions that lead to value so that you can secure the first commitment from the buyer—their precious time. Once you have that appointment and get yourself on-site, you will need to go deeper. There are two types of questions that all sellers need to ask if they are to build quality sales pipeline. These are qualification questions and discovery questions.

Qualifying is not just about eliminating time-wasters, and the seller should avoid asking clumsy closed questions, as they execute the process. Instead of asking: "Are you the decision-maker?" you could ask: "If the business case was strong, who else would you need to involve before going ahead with this?

Just because some of the answers to qualification questions are negative does not necessarily mean you should walk away. If the buyer does not have committed funding (different from having a budget) that does not mean you qualify out. You could instead explore whether it makes sense to invest together in building their business case. This is how you strategically influence their requirements and the way they will go to market for a solution.

The best salespeople combine qualification and discovery to build understanding and trust, and also to create progression. No one likes being just qualified, so you need to nuance your approach by asking open questions that uncover the truth and your priorities. Here are some open questions for digging deeper in a way that encourages the prospective client to engage with you to build mutual trust and understanding:

- I've done my homework, but there are some questions I think only you can answer—may we cover a few of these now?
- What's really driving the need to make this kind of investment?
- You're very busy and have lots of people seeking meetings with you, so why did you agree to meet with me today?
- What has to be delivered in terms of business outcomes?
- Where do you see the risks?
- What is your process and timing for having a solution in place?
- What other options are you considering? Why are these attractive?
- What happened inside your organization that caused you to look at investing in this area?
- What's the business case for making the investment and changing the way things currently operate?
- Who's impacted internally and who else needs to be onboard before you can go ahead?
- How is the project being funded and, beyond a budget, what sort of funding is already secured?
- When does this need to be implemented and delivering results? Why is that date important and what happens if it slips?

These questions enable the seller to focus on how they can help deliver the necessary outcome and manage the buyer's risks. The questions lead to understanding about budget, decision authority, timing, and whether the buying decision is really a priority.

The most important qualification factor is not any of the qualification questions, but instead whether the buyer will engage in a conversation, then provide information, insight, and access to their team. Be worried if the lion's share of activity is from the selling organization because a passive buyer who just sucks you dry of information is unlikely to transact anything, except maybe validate your parking.

Many qualified opportunities in CRM systems are lost to client apathy—in other words, they are doing nothing and maintaining the status quo. A 2016 study of 675 selling organizations revealed that 24 percent of qualified opportunities are in fact lost to nondecision with the potential customer failing to buy anything at all.[8]

Every salesperson must therefore be able to answer the following three questions:

1. Why will this customer buy anything at all?
2. Why will this customer buy from us?
3. What's our strategy to provide best value and lowest risk in the eyes of the buyer?

Access to those with decision authority and economic power is the most important common mandatory requirement. At a more granular level, these are the various qualification frameworks that help you decide whether to invest in an opportunity pursuit:

- ANUM: Authority, Need, Urgency, Money
- BANT: Budget, Authority, Need, Time frame
- BMANTRR: Budget, Method, Authority, Need, Timing, Risks, Roadblocks
- FAINT: Funding, Authority, Interest, Need, Time frame

- GPCT: Goals, Plans, Challenges, Timeline (Hubspot)
- MANDACCT: Money, Authority, Need, Decision criteria, Ability to deliver, Competition, Coach, Timescale
- MEDDICC: Metrics for ROI, Economic buyer, Decision process, Decision criteria, Identify pain, Champion coach, Compelling event
- NUTCASE: Need, Unique, Timing, Cash, Authority, Solution, Enemies
- RSVPselling: right Relationships, winning Strategy, unique compelling Value, strong Process alignment
- SCOTSMAN: Situation, Competition, basis Of decision, Timescale, Solution, Money, Authority, Need
- TAS: Target Account Selling 20 questions

Beyond qualification, you are looking for potential clients who are either in rapid growth or crisis mode. Organizations in steady state are notoriously prone to moving at a glacial pace or simply doing nothing. Every CRM system should have a field for organization mode, as it impacts the probability of closing.

If, despite your efforts to elevate the conversation, the buyer seems intent on keeping you at arm's length and obsessively focuses on features, functions, and price, then it's a safe bet to politely qualify out. There is no shortage of prospective clients out there, just a shortage of hours in the day for you to execute. Qualifying an opportunity properly has never been more important, and it is a giant mistake to pursue business you cannot win. Beyond your personal integrity, treasure your time above everything else.

The Power of Truly Listening

Listening is the most powerful form of influence. It draws the other person toward you, it shows them you believe they are the most important person in the conversation, it builds empathy, it demonstrates your values and positive intent, it earns you the right to ask questions, and it helps them believe that you understand them and what they need.

You learn nothing while you're speaking. Worse still, pushing your message creates resistance. Whether you are online on social platforms or face-to-face, you should adopt an attract-and-engage strategy rather than trying to project your message. Everyone should seek to understand before expecting to be understood.

Professor Neil Rackham did the first genuinely sound academic research into professional selling back in the 1980s. He was transparent in the way his team gathered data in the field and also in how the results were assessed. Never before or since has there been research with this level of integrity. Every salesperson should read the initial book published as a result, *SPIN Selling*. Dozens of researchers observed more than 35,000 face-to-face sales calls spanning 12 years. SPIN is an acronym for Situation, Problem, Implication, and Value or Benefit. SPIV or SPIB did not seem to roll of the tongue so Neil went with Need-Payoff. It's not a sales methodology but rather a timelessly brilliant questioning framework.

There were many insights published from the analysis, but this stands out above everything else: The top 10 percent of performers spoke only one-third as much as the bottom 90 percent. This means that high performers in sales and business are excellent listeners. But in the same way that there are modes of questioning (open or closed) and different types of questions (fact-based, problem-based, implication-based, and benefit-based), there are also different modes of listening:

- Selective (husbands are renowned for this)
- Passive (think of teenagers grunting in reply while clicking away on social media)
- Responsive (providing detached feedback like a counselor or psychologist)
- Active (fully engaged and invested with empathy and emotion)

Active listening is the best mode for sales and naturally opens the door for asking open questions where issues are explored and understanding is confirmed. Skilled listeners communicate sincere interest through positive eye contact, and they avoid distracting the other person with fidgeting or interrupting except with clarifying questions.

Bill Clinton is legendary in his ability to make a person feel valued by holding eye contact, nodding, and asking questions. He knows how to make the other person feel like the most important person in the room. Many loved him for it and voted accordingly.

Strategic Selling in the Real World

In my first book, I focused on how to win large complex opportunities, selling to the enterprise. It explained my RSVPselling methodology, which has been used to win hundreds of millions of dollars in business by understanding and managing the four key elements for winning a deal: Relationships with the right people, Strategy for navigating the politics and overcoming competition, creating Value as defined by the customer, and Process alignment to ensure that the evaluation, selection, and procurement processes work in your favor.

The RSVP framework simply requires you to ask yourself these questions:

- **Relationships:** Do you have the right relationships? Followed by: Are you selling at the right level, and does your target have real political and economic power? Do your relationships provide differentiating intelligence, insight, and genuine influence?
- **Strategy:** Do you have an effective strategy for managing relationships and competitive threats? Followed by: Do you understand the power base, and have you identified the competition (external and internal, including the risk of them doing nothing)? What's your strategy for winning while engineering a positive bias in the customer's requirements toward you?
- **Value:** Are you leading with insight and uniquely creating compelling business value in the eyes of the customer? Followed by: Why will they buy anything at all, and is there a risk of the status

quo prevailing? How are you differentiating and evidencing our credentials as lowest risk and best value?

- **Process:** Are you aligned and do you truly understand the customer's process for evaluation, selection, approval, and procurement? Followed by: Do you understand how they define and assess risk with suppliers and solutions? Do you have a close plan validated by the customer?

Excellence in execution underpins the four RSVP elements with pragmatic tools for qualifying, closing, and understanding the players in the buyer organization. Ideally, all of this resides within your CRM.

The most important element in strategic selling is to find the puppet master, the orchestrator of change, the pinnacle of the power base. This is essential because you must have a strong personal relationship with the person who can successfully drive change within the customer organization. Doing this is the foundation of strategic selling. Be wary of investing in long sales cycles if you are denied access to power.

Although this book focuses on how to build top-of-funnel sales pipeline, the RSVP principles remain relevant even at the earliest phases of engaging with a potential customer. This is because the initial entry point into an account and the value narrative you use to set the agenda have a huge bearing on the eventual size of the opportunity and probability of success. Engaging strategically demands understanding of the customer's value drivers. It demands that you bring your own hypothesis of value, which is a relevant perspective that you take to the customer that causes them to rethink their situation.

Operating strategically is defined by being proactive, researching, targeting, planning, and engaging at the right levels (see Figure 2-3); it involves going through the right channels at the right time based upon trigger events or contextual relevance. The best sellers seek alignment with the ideal prospective customers rather than attempting to raise the dead through evangelism. The way they achieve this is by focusing on win reviews with their best customers to identify the triggers that caused the customers to invest in

FIGURE 2-3. STRATEGIC SELLING DEFINED

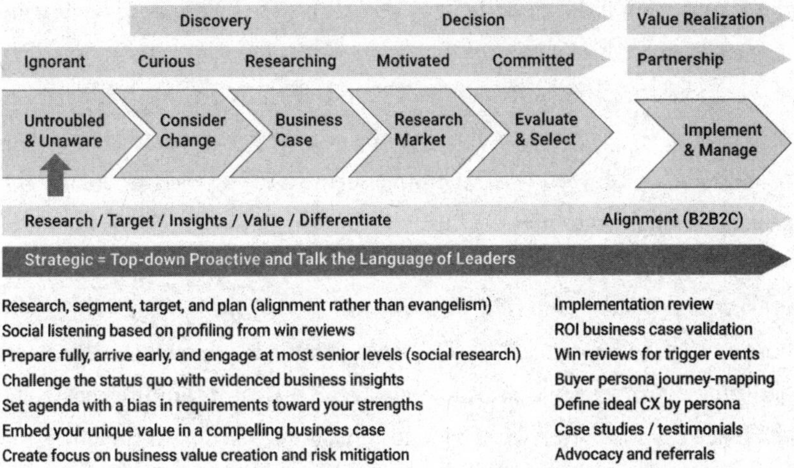

a solution (kudos Craig Elias, Tibor Shanto, and Cian McLoughlin). There is a very important distinction here: It is not about discovering why a customer bought from you over the competition; it's instead about identifying trigger events that caused them to decide they had a serious problem or opportunity that started them on their journey of discovery about who to invest with.

Salespeople are wired to behave as if closing the sale is the end of what matters, but for the customer, it's where the risk begins. Buyers want a supplier who cares about delivering the outcomes they are seeking. Customer experience (CX) is the new sales model for driving sustainable competitive advantage. Sellers who take the time to do post-implementation reviews with ROI validation are the ones who generate the most powerful case studies and testimonials. They also use that process to identify trigger events and profile the ideal new dream client.

But there is another magical approach to creating ultimate buyer empathy, insight, and alignment—it's the power of thinking about your customer's customer. Business to business to customer (B2B2C) is what you need to focus on. If it's possible for you to actually become a customer, then you should do that and document the experience. The sellers who think deeply and care greatly about their client's challenges and opportunities earn the right conversations because they can discuss how to help reduce costs, gain market share, reduce customer churn, improve customer satisfaction, and more. These are the sellers who change the rules on the competition through the way they sell. It demands that you go vertically deep in industry segments, and it requires substantial investment—this is where insight selling, or Challenger ideas, occur.

Real differentiation happens in the way that selling occurs rather than in what is actually being sold. The way you sell has always been more important than what you sell, and CEB Research has proven this. The very best prepare fully, arrive early, and engage at the most senior levels. They challenge the status quo with evidenced business insights while setting an agenda with an inbuilt bias toward their strengths. Finally, they embed their unique value in a compelling business case to overcome apathy and the status quo. They use risk as a weapon and fear as a positive motivator to find best value. They create a strong focus on business value creation and risk mitigation while aligning with those who have genuine power within the political power base structure.

You can tell whether a salesperson is selling strategically by the type of conversations they have with the buyer (see Figure 2-3). If the focus is on product, price, features, functions, or competition, then the seller is engaging at the wrong level. Those things are usually used to exclude the seller from the game; they are rarely the reasons that the customer buys.

In addition to all of this, you need to combine old school with new school by embracing the best of the social selling concepts, especially leveraging the power of LinkedIn. The term *social selling* can be a misnomer because in the context of B2B sales, most of the activity is actually social monitoring, social research, and social marketing. The smart operators avoid digital spamming and instead use proven old-school methods accelerated by new-school social platforms to deliver improved leverage, scale, and reach. Here are the most important aspects of strategic social selling, which culminates in using the phone to actually call. All social selling supports the phone call because social and the phone together are supremely powerful.

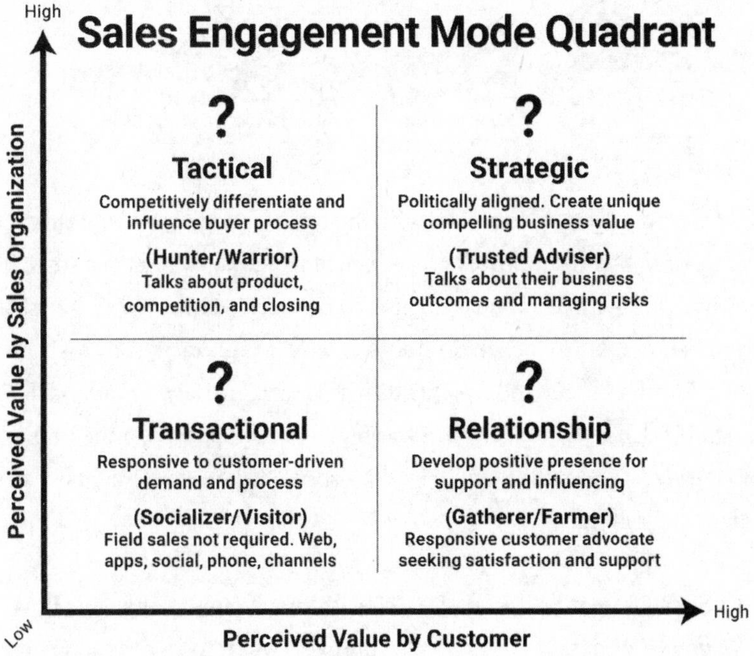

Social Selling Framework Defined

You could easily form the view that I am against social selling, but the opposite is the case. I have been a huge proponent of a modernized approach and have been exhorting old dogs learning new tricks for years. I jumped on the social selling bandwagon with evangelical enthusiasm back in 2013, but I became horrified once I saw sellers using it as an excuse to become insanely passive and avoid the phone.

Here is my definition of social selling, published back in early 2014: "The strategy and process of building quality networks online to attract clients and accelerate the speed of business and efficiency of selling. It is achieved with personal human engagement through social listening, social publishing, social research, social engagement, and social collaboration."

In my definition, technology is merely an enabler but can be leveraged

FIGURE 2-5. STRATEGIC SOCIAL SELLING

to create truly incredible results with the right strategies. Social initiatives may be driven and supported by the use of technology and platforms, but they have always been about real human connection and interaction. This is what actually provides memorable value through insight or assistance with relevant content and conversations. The big mistake I made with the infographic shown in Figure 2-5 was having no emphasis on the phone—the original social selling tool! Here is a summary of the elements of strategic social selling.

- Social Research: Social research with social monitoring will allow you to understand the precise moment when to strike. Passively monitoring the leads in the top accounts in your territory will bear fruit. You'll start to notice patterns in what your prospects are posting that will influence the insights you can share. You'll start to notice a near unanimous consensus about challenges and strategic objectives. The differentiators in your suite of solutions will emerge.
- Social Listening/Monitoring: The most powerful trigger events to monitor are changes and transitions. Are you segmenting and targeting your ideal buyers and putting feelers out to filter their signals from the noise? This can be done with tools such as HootSuite and TweetDeck. I'm surprised at how few sellers are creating basic Twitter Lists, which allow you to listen by segments to 25 individuals or fewer who are actually practical to track. You must first open your ears, heart, and mind. Be present and make sure that you have a dashboard set up to glean every aspect of what your dream prospects are putting out into the social ether: press re-

leases, white papers, reflections on the annual report, interviews, YouTube videos (subscribe to their channel), tweets, Facebook shares, Google+ updates, LinkedIn Sales Navigator updates, Pinterest boards, Instagram pictures, and SlideShare. You can also set up Google Alerts.

- Social Publishing: What you write and what you share shows people who you are, what you believe, and what you value. Few people write well, and this is of itself a huge opportunity for you to differentiate. Take the plunge on LinkedIn Publisher/Pulse by publishing articles that show your insights and your values. In nonselling time, share your subject-matter expertise and thought leadership. The second huge way to amp up your social publishing is to get in front of as many qualified buyers as you can to understand the issues and insights most important to them. Start to compile a list of links as you peruse the Internet so that you can reference and link to them in your posts.

  Becoming a social publisher is more about overcoming fear than anything else. If you got into a career in sales because brevity is your strong suit and you love picking up the phone and talking with clients—well, you're probably already a top producer. I would suggest writing in LinkedIn as if you're writing a letter to your biggest client to explain how your solution solves their challenge. You'll notice you write volumes of emails every day sharing your hard-won expertise and insight. Carry that intensity and authentic voice into social publishing. The fastest way to build compelling posts is with mash-ups or hijacking current events ("newsjack" is the term used by David Meerman Scott). Pick a current event or a sport you know about and mix it with some business rules: For example, write an intriguing post based on your real-world experience with bingo. Do this in your own time at night or on weekends. More on this later when I discuss building your platform.

- Social Engagement: This is all about subtlety. Blasting updates with your Twitter handle can and will hurt you. Poorly worded connection requests or InMails will cause a crickets response. Engagement has to be meaningful for your prospects, not just formulaic and self-serving for you. You must move away from interesting and toward interested to move up the ladder of engagement. It's best to slowly warm up prospects from a simmer to a roaring boil. Then the phone becomes the tip of the arrow for engagement that hits the mark! It is also important to be where your buyers are online. Thoughtfully like, comment, and share their content, but never jump in and sell. Simply become known so that you can make a warm call with the right context.

- Social Collaboration: This is all about efficiency in working with your team, ecosystem, and customer. It's amazing what happens once you start to form digital bonds with a super network that can enable your success. This applies within your own organization and out in the marketplace. Actively use tools such as Salesforce Chatter, Yammer, or others within your CRM. Also, attract thought leaders and bloggers in vertical industries, and join mastermind groups. Participate in your target market's social hangouts as you build a virtual network to brainstorm and become a mastermind yourself.

Your social selling efforts need to focus on monitoring your targets and finding a way to make warm calls. Personal brand is also essential—more on this later. Let's now explore why opening with business case value is so important.

Building a Winning Business Case

Opening the door, landing on the beach, securing that initial meeting. These are musts; but no one is going to buy something substantial without having a business case. Never forget that your decision-makers, the people in real power, are constantly wondering:

- Why should we change when what we're doing still works?
- Why should we invest money in this area compared with other priorities?
- What is the cost of current state, and does it really outweigh the cost of change?
- What are the risks, and how will they be managed?
- Can we really trust this person to deliver for us?

Your role as a salesperson is to inspire someone to see a better future and change state. But for them to secure agreement and approval internally means they must achieve consensus and have a compelling business case. The language of business is numbers, and every leader wants tangible, measurable results. They also want someone "on the hook" for managing the risks and successfully delivering.

Before we dive into the elements of a business case, let's be crystal clear about the most important factor. You must show exactly how any benefit will monetize and drop to their bottom line. Avoid the fluff and compliance arguments as drivers of a business case. Things such as improved staff morale, better brand recognition, or adherence to standards are as weak as water. Instead, lead with screamingly strong financial results that will be achieved and have proof of why the numbers are valid, how progress will be measured, and how risks will be managed. The enemy is their apathy, so lead with your knockout punch rather than dancing around, poking and prodding, hoping for a reaction.

Commercial enterprises are driven by profit, which is achieved with a combination of margin and volume. Margin is the result of deducting costs from the selling price. Volume is a function of market size and market share. There is room for only a limited number of generalists in any sector, and that is why most companies specialize. Successful companies therefore have business models focused on either low volume with high margin or high volume with low margin. Think about Coca-Cola (high volume) compared with Boeing (high margin) as simplistic examples.

If a business is seeking to improve margins, then it increases its selling price or reduces its costs (COGS: cost of goods sold). If, on the other hand, a business is seeking to increase volume, then this is achieved by gaining more market share or accessing new markets. You must therefore help customers to reduce costs or increase prices through value, or you must help them increase market share or gain access to previously untapped markets. Cost-cutting is a tactic, not a strategy, and no organization can cost-cut its way to long-term success. A final consideration is the cost of acquiring new customers, and it is far more cost-effective to invest in retaining existing clients than replacing those lost due to poor service or failure to provide adequate value or great customer experience. When you seek to sell at the very top in a commercial environment, you must align your value with their focus and business drivers.

In addition to business drivers, you also need to consider an organization's level of urgency and motivation to solve problems or realize opportunities. Organizations in either high growth or crisis/survival mode will make decisions quickly, but if an organization is in business-as-usual mode, decisions will be slow. Any business in survival mode is desperate to reduce costs and improve cash flow (not to be confused with profit). A business experiencing high growth, on the other hand, will be driven to increase profit and achieve greater efficiencies. The problem with selling to a business that is maintaining the status quo (business as usual) is that it can easily do nothing and defer investment decisions. Although it wants improved profitability, through greater efficiency and reduced costs, it struggles with investing and can move so slowly that decision momentum is lost completely through endless analysis.

The lesson in all this is that you need serious problems or opportunities in order to create compelling value for the client. Seek organizations that are growing or, depending on what you offer, are in crisis. Beware of prospective clients who are comfortable and have the option of simply doing nothing.

Government and charitable organizations are not driven by profit. Instead, they are focused on achieving outcomes. These not-for-profit organizations either want to improve service value (efficiency and service levels) or to increase service volume (the number of people or organizations utilizing their products or services). When you seek to sell at the very top in government or charitable environments, you must also align your value with their drivers and metrics for performance measurement.

You must help them increase efficiency and improve productivity or you must help them to cost-effectively increase the reach (or capability) and utilization of their services. In essence, the drivers are almost always to improve compliance and service levels or to operate more efficiently. Beware of any government employee, however, telling you that their business case is compliance alone. The very top people see compliance as a relatively low-level "tick in the box" issue and will not allocate serious funding in isolation. Compliance may be a driver for some, but it is never a business case alone. Compliance outcomes must be the by-product of investing in improved efficiency and service levels. This is not to say that return on investment (ROI) cannot exist in nonmonetary terms, but treat these things as a bonus of the financial business case—a cherry on the top.

The concept of COMBO applies to building a business case because there are different types of return on investment and every industry has its own metrics that drive the way they manage. In retail businesses, for example, they care about how many times they can turn stock on the shelves in a month to improve return on working capital. Services businesses care about the utilization of their billable people as a measure of profitability per person. SaaS businesses care about renewals and churn to build their compounding recurring revenue, which is critical for company valuation. These are examples of compelling business case drivers that feed directly into bottom-line profit:

- Increased revenue
- Increased market share
- Improved margins
- Improved efficiencies (more output with the same resources)

- Improved staff retention
- Reduced costs
- Reduced customer churn (better client retention)

"Second order," or less quantifiable, benefits are important as they create strong emotional connections to drive change and can include:

- Improved customer satisfaction
- Improved staff engagement
- Greater compliance
- Improved brand
- Improved investor relationships
- Better community engagement

These two categories of benefits could be characterized as targeting the head versus the heart. Every organization is a collective of uniquely different people who have their own personal needs, priorities, and agendas. Ideally, these should be aligned with the organization, but this is not always the case. Internal politics, restructuring, takeovers, retrenchments, and career changes are common. These are all trigger events you must become masterful at monitoring using social!

Honoring the law of self-interest is also important. A person in the buying center or power base of an organization may be in either a negative/conservative mode or in a positive/ambitious mode. The motivations of individuals are either positive or negative, depending on their personal situation within the enterprise. Their motivations may include:

- Seeking to protect their position or reputation versus wanting to look good and being a leader or hero
- Avoiding mistakes and maintaining control versus receiving recognition or earning a promotion
- Avoiding conflict and stress versus being an agent for change

- Saving money and reducing costs versus driving revenues and productivity

Your approach when prospecting needs to be sensitive to all of these factors, and this is why you need humility and inquisitiveness as you position your hypothesis of value. An individual does not function in a vacuum; they are part of an organization that will have certain business drivers that influence all decisions. People drive agendas and decisions, and they always have an emotional favorite they would like to see win their business. It is essential therefore to understand and align with both personal agendas and corporate drivers so that you are the emotional favorite.

Every commercial enterprise is driven by a need to increase profit, and most government organizations are driven by a desire to improve service through efficiency and effectiveness. Ideally, these outcomes are achieved without increasing costs or exposure to unacceptable risk. In essence, there is a universal desire to achieve more with less, and any value narrative, proposal, or business case should focus on greater output (or more revenue) from existing resources (achieving greater productivity) or less cost or effort (resulting in better efficiency).

The pace of business, decision urgency, and how you are prioritized is determined by the organization's operating mode and individual priorities. It is vitally important to understand which business mode and personal agendas are in play when seeking to drive a sale. This is why social research, social listening, and trigger events are critically important as you decide where to invest your precious time in pipeline-building activities. Alignment is key, and the mix of variables can be quite complex. But there is another element of complexity—politics operate in every organization, and consensus needs to be achieved before implementing change.

Engineering Consensus

The best salespeople are engineers of value rather than mere warriors of persuasion. They know how to engage leaders. The reality today is that most executives in the customer's organization are not secure. Behind their well-groomed smiling facade of power, they all secretly lay awake at night worrying if they will be found out, blindsided by a scandal, damaged by market forces they cannot control, or executed from above on the notion that they've reached their use-by date. Politics abound as people smile up and push the crap down.

The result is that even if the boss can autocratically pronounce a sweeping change for the organization, they're smart enough not to do it. They know that they need consensus and must take their team and the greater organization on the journey. If they fail to do so, then the initiative can be scuttled, stillborn, or white-anted all the way to failure. As you target an organization for your pipeline-building activities, you must start at the highest practical level. This will be the person who truly owns the problem or opportunity at a profit and loss (P & L) level, and they will have the power to say "no" to any proposal that affects their area. You must start there, with the CEO of the problem, and then be sponsored down and across to engineer consensus and a compelling business case.

Traditional wisdom has been for salespeople to hunt down the influencers, recommenders, and decision-makers to tailor their value pitch based on role and agenda. That's a valid approach, but increasingly today it is not enough because of organizational politics, competing agendas, and misaligned priorities within the buying organization. The problem of decision commitment is that as you add more and more people to the evaluation, selection, and procurement process, the probability of stalemate increases.

According to CEB Research, the number of buyers needed to achieve consensus for a decision is approximately seven (I highly recommend that you read *The Challenger Sale* and *The Challenger Customer*).[9] But the problem is even worse than it looks because instead of dealing with seven people, you are increasingly dealing with seven groups of people! These groups can include evaluation committees, project boards, and steering committees, not to mention those who lead the areas of economic, user experience, technical, financial, and line of business.

The cost of sale in targeting enterprise and government is going up at the same time that savvy buyers are commoditizing the seller's offering to drive prices and margins down. This is why it is critically important to open with the right value narrative and make sure the conversation is with exactly the right person who can sponsor and secure consensus for change.

Creating alignment around the need for change, which is supported by a compelling business case, is the key to sales success. Our prospecting dialogue needs to anchor this right from the very beginning. Here is another example of an effective opening: The executive prospect asks, "What do you want from meeting with me?" You reply, "If you believe what we discuss is worth exploring further, then I'll need you to introduce me to your teams so I can work with them to build a business case. Both our teams will need to invest some time as the next step from there."

Engineering consensus happens when you are sponsored into the organization by the leader. Then you can begin to understand all the issues and collaboratively build a business case with their team that documents and evidences the cost of inaction versus the tangible benefits of change. The focus of the seller is not to make a sale but to help the buying team identify potential value and build the case for change with implementation plans that manage any risks. The opening focus should not be about your product but rather about their business case—even if it is not yet conceived, you can be the twinkle in their eye.

Opening Is the New Closing

"Opening is the new closing," says Anthony Iannarino. I often ask senior executives what they think the biggest weakness is within their sales team. A common answer is that their salespeople need to be better closers. But here is the thing I've learned from three decades in the trenches: The perceived problem is rarely the real problem—inability to close is usually a symptom of deeper issues. The way you open a relationship has greater bearing on success than how you close the deal.

In both complex enterprise selling and simple (or transactional) selling (lower value and usually a single decision-maker), there is a universal truth that must be embraced if you are to improve results: Opening is far more important than closing because it is where the agenda is set, trust is established, and understanding is created. The way you initiate and build the relationship, along with your understanding, largely determines the likelihood of success.

The critical issues in opening are:

- Selecting the correct role to engage within the customer organization
- Creating a conversation that provides value (through insights) for that person
- Finding a way to positively break through their barriers

A common mistake in selling is to engage with the people you feel would be easiest to access and with whom you could carry the conversation. Outsourced lead generation providers and inside sales SDRs also suffer from the tendency to operate at mid-levels of the buying organization. Inbound leads are even worse because they often come from recommenders and researchers who act for others. These people are keen to obtain information but can quickly become blockers who seek to deny you access to real decision-makers. You must carefully select the right entry point into every account and opportunity, knowing the person will be difficult to reach . . . but that's where COMBO comes into its own.

As a sidenote, if you are already engaged at the wrong level and struggling to elevate your conversations in an account, these questions can earn you the right to go higher:

- What's the business outcome this initiative has to deliver within the business case?
- What are the biggest risks in this project and what's your strategy to manage them?
- What's your approach to ensure stakeholder buy-in and manage change?

These questions also set the right agenda when engaging a real decision-maker because leaders care about delivering results and managing risk. The business case and change management issues always figure highly in their thinking once they're interested in the future-state vision that has been set.

We have previously discussed creating conversations of value and insight for the targeted CXO, but just in case you are tempted to lapse: No senior leader worth engaging is initially interested in you, your company, or your products, services, and solutions. They instead care about their own results, stakeholders, and career. Although you are wired to talk about yourself, you must instead lead with why a conversation should matter to the other person. You can create conversations of insight and value by truly understanding your best customers and the disruptive market trends that are relevant to your new potential clients.

If you are seeking to engage the CXO in an existing client, simply call them and say that you are not happy with the level of value they are getting for the relationship with your company. Go on and say that you know they are seeking to drive greater value from fewer suppliers, and you have some ideas on how they could do that very thing. This absolutely works—make the call now!

Open in a way that separates you from everyone else, and be positively memorable in how you engage. If you can be the one who obsessively focuses on business outcomes and delivering results for the client, you'll be invited into the C-suite and become their emotional favorite. They'll open up and allow you to help with their business case and design the process for evaluating and selecting the right solution and managing change internally. It can happen—sellers really can become trusted advisers. As part of earning that right, build a strong personal brand evidencing credibility, insight, influence, value, and integrity.

Building Your Platform

"I hated every minute of training, but I said, 'Don't quit. Suffer now and live the rest of your life as a champion.'"
—MUHAMMAD ALI

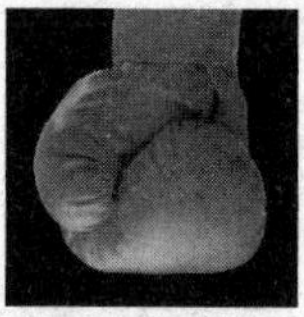

NO ATHLETE WINS AT THE ELITE LEVEL WITHOUT THOUSANDS OF hours of pain, suffering, blood, sweat, and tears. As a cyclist, I know you must build a base of fitness or you'll suffer like a dog and fail when the time comes to deliver a marathon performance in the searing heat. I've bonked on a bike (no sex involved), and it was brutal. Bonking is the sudden fatigue and loss of energy caused by the depletion of the body's glycogen. You just have nothing left except a tortured vacant stare, and it's caused by getting behind the nutrition and hydration curve in extreme sport. You suffer knowing there will be no quick recovery, no matter what you do.

I've also competed in karate and seen people freeze and fail because they did not invest the necessary hours sparring with gusto when there was no crowd watching. As a sport aircraft pilot, I practiced forced landing by turning my engine off at 500 feet above the airfield to perfect emergency landings. Every overnight success spent many years in quiet discipline to be ready for their moment in the spotlight. When I won my first President's Club working for BellSouth, I knew I'd earned it.

You must build the platform on which you can achieve success. The previous chapter was about earning the right to engage. Once you have understood your buyer and built a value narrative to carry a conversation at senior levels, you then need a brand and network that empowers you. In addition to this, you need massive leverage created from using the right tools and scripted content to choreograph every move. Only birds and amateurs wing it. The very best salespeople instead execute repeatable winning combinations.

Beyond COMBOs of multichannel outreach where the social phone is the weapon of choice, we've addressed the COMBO for having the right narrative: 1) leading with insight, 2) stating why it matters, and 3) positioning a hypothesis of value. We've also talked about the COMBO once you've initially broken through: 1) engaging the most senior person, 2) being sponsored down, and 3) building consensus and a compelling business case.

Here, we will explore the COMBO for creating a powerful personal platform, which is: 1) a strong personal brand, 2) a network that empowers, and 3) tools and templates that enable high performance. Later, we will cover the COMBO for knockout success with: 1) trigger events, 2) referrals, and 3) customer advocacy. Finally, we will cover the COMBO for the close, which is: 1) setting the right agenda, 2) creating trust and confidence, and 3) devoting yourself to commitment and leadership.

Let's now focus on your brand. Study the work of Michael Hyatt, who wrote the book *Platform*. Every salesperson needs to become a micro-marketer, so also read the book *The New Rules of Marketing and PR* by David Meerman Scott. Essentially, your personal brand as a thought leader on social, especially LinkedIn, can start the process of building trust and setting the agenda on value before your utter a single word. This is because the majority of people who consider responding to your outreach, whether via voice mail, email, InMail, video mail, text message, Twitter, or a personal note or message, will Google you or look at your LinkedIn profile. This is where you evidence your credentials of insight and value and where you show your personal values and the quality of your professional network.

Building a strong platform will accelerate and compress a sales process because it establishes you as someone worthy of trust who solves real business challenges for similar clients. Ninety-eight percent of salespeople with 5,000+ LinkedIn connections achieve quota,[1] but it can take a seller up to five years to build a LinkedIn network with that many connections. Rome wasn't built in a day, and you can't just grab 300 business cards at a conference or blitz LinkedIn connections and think you're done.

Creating Your Online Brand

Your social media pages are yours, but never write, post, or upload anything that is not consistent with your employer's brand or your professional profile. As John Smibert says, "It takes a lifetime to build your brand but just a moment to destroy your reputation." Treat everything you publish online as if it will be there forever, and only publish content that you would be happy for your next potential customer or mother to read.

If you're a leader or salesperson, you must transform the way you use LinkedIn. Stop treating it as an online CV for securing your next job, and stop using it as a marketing page for your company. Instead, make your LinkedIn profile shine as your personal brand website where the value you provide and the values by which you operate are front and center.

At the time of writing this, there were well over 500 million LinkedIn members, with 2 people joining every second of every day. The overwhelming majority of people you need in order to be successful in your professional life are all there. According to IDC Research, 75 percent of buyers use social media to research sellers before engaging.[2] Add to this the research from both Forrester and Corporate Visions that revealed that 74 percent of buyers choose the seller who first provides insight and value.[3] This begs the question: What do potential customers see when they find you online? Do they see a Porsche driving, quota crushing, transactional, pushy salesperson with a profile aimed at their next potential employer; or do they see a warm and friendly professional offering insight and value relevant to them and their industry?

No one wants to be sold to, but we all value assistance in making the right buying decision—we all want to manage our risk and ensure best value. Here are the essential things you need to do with your LinkedIn profile to create a credible digital personal brand that paves the way ahead to accelerate engagement.

First, settings: Go into LinkedIn settings, and disable notifications to your network. Do this after logging in by navigating to account/settings and privacy/privacy/sharing profile edits/select "no." This is important because you will be making many changes within your profile, and you don't want to bombard your network or give the wrong impression that you are updating your profile because you are looking for another job!

Second, photo: Ensure that your photo is a professionally friendly head and shoulders close-up. It needs to be in focus and well lit. Always avoid high-contrast bright backgrounds. Also avoid the Zoolander Blue Steel look, glamour shots, power pics, wedding shots, mug shots, sporting shots, trophy shots, and pictures taken more than five years ago. People form an opinion within a second, and your photo and headline is what will most influence them.

Do you appear to be credible or arrogant, friendly or cocky, approachable or unprofessional? Make sure your photo has the right background, which means there should be a soft image behind. Not your cubicle, which makes you look like you don't deserve to meet with a CEO, and certainly not a stark wall that looks like it was taken at the police station. Never hide your photo from people viewing your profile: Check LinkedIn settings under Account/Settings and privacy/Basics/Showing profile photos/select Everyone.

Third, headline: Instead of your title and company, have a headline under your name that describes what you do for customers or those whom you serve. What is the difference you make for clients? Avoid passive words such as helping, seeking, enabling, etc. Instead, make a positive statement such as "Transforming customer experience for retailers" or "Delivering process efficiency for the mining industry" or "Placing customers at the heart of strategy and systems" or "Creating memorable events that deliver results." Your headline should describe the results you create for your customers, but not in a way that makes you look like a complete tool. Avoid clichés, acronyms, and over-the-top phrases.

Fourth, URL: Personalize and shorten your LinkedIn link (the URL that takes people to your profile). View your profile page by clicking on the small thumbnail of your photo in the upper right, then on the right side of the screen as you begin to scroll down, select Contact and personal info, then click on the small pencil icon, then click again on your LinkedIn URL (maybe LinkedIn will have made this easier by the time you read this!). Then change to something that is not already taken by another member with your name. Don't forget to save, and this link should be included in your email signature.

Fifth, contact details: Complete your contact details. If you are in sales, forget privacy, and instead make it easy for people to contact you. Whenever you change employers, always remember to update the website links. View your profile page by clicking on the small thumbnail of your photo in the upper right, then on the right side on the screen as you begin to scroll down select Contact and personal info, then update details as appropriate.

Sixth, summary panel: Create a summary that describes the business value you deliver and the values by which you operate. Write it in the first person, and neither be too over-the-top nor hide your light under a bushel. This is where people can get a sense of what you believe and how you operate. This starts to create trust and set the agenda on value even before a single word has been spoken. Your summary can potentially start with "I believe . . ." and then go on to talk about your vision for your customers. One of my clients, Emma, gave me permission to showcase her summary on LinkedIn. We designed it to support her outreach with the heads of government health departments, and it worked. We also changed her "expressive" LinkedIn photo with an office cubicle background to one of her dressed as the senior manager she is and standing in front of her CEO's high-rise office window with a harbor view. We took the photo with my iPhone, so don't use the absence of a professional photographer as an excuse.

Her summary reads:

> The healthcare sector is modernising the way services are delivered with technology and consumer expectations transforming the delivery of both public and private sector healthcare. I work with government, health and peak body organisations to achieve better outcomes through digital transformation. I help them translate their policy initiatives into business strategies, and build evidence-based business cases that make the best use of health sector funding.
>
> I am passionate and committed to deliver for my healthcare sector clients, and I have two decades of experience in senior government, not-for-profit, and private sector roles. With a diploma of health science, 10 years' experience as a registered nurse, and a bachelor of business, I have both understanding and empathy for the challenges facing the healthcare sector. My extensive experience in human services, and the quality and reach of my professional network, enables me to provide positive influence with a wide range of senior stakeholders within government and industry.

This worked along with personal coaching. Emma was immediately taken more seriously and began securing meetings with senior executives who had previously ignored her. She was also promoted within her company seven weeks after the makeover. By changing your LinkedIn profile to be a mini personal branding site, you enhance the way you sell but without any downside for a future career change with potential new employers. They will be attracted by the way you intelligently use LinkedIn to engage prospective clients.

Seventh, references: Getting recommendations from people who have engaged you in current and past roles is a way to powerfully build trust. These recommendations are ideally from loyal customers or partners and evidence your positive values and the results you deliver for them. Simply use the request feature within LinkedIn to ask trusted relationships to make a recommendation. You will have the opportunity to review it before adding it to your profile. LinkedIn Recommendations are far more powerful than Skills and Endorsements within your profile, and they focus on listing those skills that are valued by your customers.

Eighth, education, qualifications, volunteer experience, and accomplishments: Within your LinkedIn profile, provide details about your credentials but avoid bragging or coming across as a "quota crusher," as Jill Rowley famously says. It is especially important to show credibility in your ability to deliver for customers and to list any philanthropic activities that evidence your positive personal values. If you achieved number-one performer status, then you could provide a description like this: "Highest performer of the year. I achieved this by working closely with my customers in the manufacturing industry to enable them to benefit from substantial improvements in supply chain efficiency."

Again, the focus with your LinkedIn profile is to speak to customers rather than potential employers. Create an authentic narrative that shows how you can help customers deliver results through your insights, experience, positive track record, personal network, and credentials. Make sure you convey the fact that you can do something worthwhile for them, rather than being a salesperson seeking to sell something to them.

Beyond first impressions and everything above, publishing content is a big differentiator for salespeople as they build strong personal brands. But how do you publish content without detracting from selling time or from the essential COMBOs that drive pipeline creation and sales success?

Publishing Insights That Set the Agenda

Let's face an awful truth: Very few salespeople are good writers. Add to this the imperative that sellers go all-in with COMBOs for prospecting during prime time, and you can see we have a problem.

I do not advocate that salespeople write content during business hours; they should instead pick up the phone and dial prospects and customers. All sellers should, however, self-educate and do research. Then they should create their own insights, which enables them to carry the right conversations with senior people in their target marketplace. As a result of this activity, there are two types of content that can be created within your LinkedIn profile:

1. Posts (updates) are short and often for the purpose of sharing other people's content, which is relevant to your audience or customers. This is where you need to subscribe to a content-sharing tool such as Buffer, which has a plug-in for your web browser. It makes the process of capturing content and scheduling it for publication on your social media extremely easy.
2. Original articles (blogs) may be shared. They are typically more than 400 words and embedded with images or videos.

Let's cover posts first because anyone can do this, even if you have poor writing skills. Anytime you come across content that will be appreciated by your customers, simply click the Twitter share button on that content's page or the Buffer icon in your browser . . . bingo! It is queued and ready to go without you needing to give it another thought. Sign up for the free version of Buffer, and install the web browser plug-in.

But where do you find this content? Every professional stays current by reading the latest articles, journals, blogs, and publications relevant to them and their patients or clients. The best salespeople do this, and those who struggle with reading listen to podcasts. If you sell into an industry vertical, or if your market is defined by a particular demographic, or if your buyer is a particular role or persona, then you can identify the places where they learn online. Ask your customers that very question: "Where do you go online to stay up-to-date?" You could also ask: "Who do you follow as a leader in your industry?" or "Which analysts or commentators do you rate most highly?" Then find those people online, subscribe to their blog (RSS feed), configure a Google Alert for their name, and follow them on Twitter. Now the information you need comes to you! Technology is now serving you and making you highly efficient for content sourcing and learning about the things your customers care about.

This is how you build a platform for sourcing and sharing content that will be of interest to your buyers. If your marketing team can help you with a corporate tool similar to Buffer, then use it, but do not share corporate propaganda. It will be perceived by your audience of potential customers as spam, and they will probably disconnect or ignore you. Your LinkedIn profile is your domain, not your employer's—you choose the content you share or publish. All of your content must be of value for your target audience.

Your goal is to be seen as an aggregator of high-quality, relevant content for those who are too busy to source it for themselves. If you were selling a cloud software solution for accounts payable automation, then your primary target audience is the CFO. You would investigate where they learn online about outsourcing and find the analysts and journalists who write about the latest trends and research for transforming the finance function within corporations. What are the major conferences? Who are the speakers? Which research has been published? Sharing this kind of content and associating yourself with credible brands is a smart thing to do. Therefore, seek to connect with the industry influencers and leaders who publish the best articles and papers.

Original articles or blogs require more effort, but they are massively powerful for proactively dealing with objections and setting the agenda on value and risk mitigation for customers. At a minimum, everyone should have three articles that they have published within their LinkedIn profile, and these articles should be 600 to 900 words, which is just over one page in a typical Word document.

The first topic to write about is proactive objection killers. This is a self-learning exercise that beats any sales training because it creates clarity of message with a narrative that has the power to avoid objections altogether! List the common objections you receive, and then adopt the positive counter position. As an example, I have worked with recruitment companies where salespeople commonly receive this objection from a hiring manager: "If I met with every headhunter that wanted my time, I'd never get anything done. I'm too busy to meet, so just send me a CV if you have a viable candidate."

To deal with this, I've helped recruiters write articles about why investing 20 minutes saves 12 hours and dramatically reduces hiring risk. In this example, you take the excuse for not wanting to meet and make it the reason to engage. The seller creates an article in LinkedIn Publisher that supports this narrative:

> It's because you're busy that we need to meet. It's not enough to screen based on skills, qualifications, and experience; you must also eliminate anyone early who is not a cultural fit. This is because that's where most of the risk is with a new hire. I define value by how few CVs I send, and I'll invest the time to understand how you personally define cultural fit to significantly de-risk your hiring process. That's why I need 20 minutes with you to understand how you personally define the culture of your team. Twenty minutes together will save you 12 hours and give you the right result. When can we get together for 20 minutes on Thursday?

Instead of leading with the product of supplying candidates for a role, the seller is leading with why a conversation matters. The reason for a conversation is that the seller can help the buyer save time and reduce risk; and that's what is being sold initially—a way for the buyer to save time, reduce risk, and protect the culture they have built into their team, so they can achieve the necessary results.

Writing an article and finding research to reference, even a funny video to embed, enables you to hone your narrative and deliver the conversation with relaxed authority. No script is necessary because you genuinely know your stuff. Start writing after hours; it will change your professional life! Find someone to be your editor before you publish, and always ensure that you are consistent with your employer's brand and values.

In addition to positive proactive objection killers, sellers should develop insights that hook the buyers' interest. Again, this is highly valuable sales training as it forces research into the customer's world. It should be done outside prime selling time and treated as homework in the evenings. What are the trends, risks, disruptive forces, innovations, or case studies that potential customers need to know? How are their customers or markets changing? Beyond information, what are the insights or lessons to be learned? What are their biggest risks concerning commoditization or disruption? The people you follow for creating posts are the sources for these articles you can write, and it is not a difficult task to create an article that quotes several experts. You can then add your own commentary before posing a question to your audience to create engagement.

Chris Beall believes salespeople are the smartest nonreaders on earth but that they need to become readers in order to write with strength. He says, "Listening, especially while driving (which provides a calming activity to absorb some of that native sales restlessness) lets them hear written language and begin to transform into a writer. Even if their writing ends up being spoken into Siri, cleaned up by Grammarly, and—if they're really smart—run through a friend. If something is worth writing, it is almost always worth a light editing pass."

Every seller needs to be a capable micro-marketer, and if you're serious about creating a stellar personal brand and embracing social selling, you must read David Meerman Scott's book *The New Rules of Marketing and PR*. As you build followers, who aren't necessarily connected to your profile, you can start to share insights such as short quotes, statistics, pithy phrases, and, especially, provocative questions. This will create threads of engagement where you can start building your network (again, outside prime selling time) with anyone relevant who views your profile, posts, or articles. These can become leads you can call, and it's a conversation starter to call out that they just looked at your profile.

When I first came across Jack Kosakowski, I noticed he had some amazing techniques for notifying prospects when a social action happened. One way he did this was to call them after they just added him if there was a number shared on their profile. There are other ways to connect to prospects, but first it's important to build a following. At one stage, the best way to build followers (audience and connections) was to be highly active in groups, and then it was about writing original long-form articles in Publisher, which would occasionally be picked up by the editors of Pulse Channels and pushed to a larger audience. Then LinkedIn almost killed the notification stream to first-degree connections, which created a big hole for many seeking to build a following. LinkedIn subsequently decided it needed more engagement in streams of content just like Facebook, so individual posts (previously called updates) became the key to attracting followers.

Let's review what needs to be done up to this point with your brand. You've created a professionally attractive profile within LinkedIn and enhanced it by showing insight and value in what you publish. You've identified the thought leaders who are relevant to your target market that you will begin to follow on LinkedIn and Twitter. Then you can curate their content and share it with your network. You can begin to be a "forager for the tribe," as Michael Hyatt describes it, which means being a content hub for relevant, quality information about a topic, domain, or industry. Then there is a reason for people to connect with you—because you provide insight and value relevant to those in your network.

Nurturing a Network That Enables You to Thrive

You cannot be successful on your own. Add to this the fact that a trusted referral is the shortest path to success, and you may begin to grasp the almost nuclear power of a high-quality network loaded with friendly human nodes of influence.

Yet I have heard it argued that we can only manage up to 70 meaningful relationships in our lives at any one time. Some people have told me that they only accept LinkedIn connection requests from people they would recognize on the street. You're reading this book because you're in sales, so forget that rubbish. You need an extensive and powerful network if you are to be successful. By all means reject connection requests from hookers, scammers, and competitors, but accept any connection request from any other credible professional. Reject competitor connection requests because you're opening up your relationships to them.

Accept connection requests from anyone who is a peer or above in your world. Especially seek to connect with potential customers and those they respect and admire. Associate yourself with the analysts, journalists, bloggers, and leaders in your target market. Praise their articles and blogs, share their content, comment within their posts. Quote them and include their Twitter handles. Type their names into your LinkedIn posts so they are notified of the post. Associate yourself with strong brands so that you have both quality and quantity within your network.

If you have fewer than 500 connections in LinkedIn, then your profile highlights that fact, and you look weak. Your first goal is to build more than 500 connections, but don't stop there. You need a minimum of 5,000 LinkedIn connections because networks are built on nodes, and sellers with 5,000+ connections on LinkedIn have a 98 percent likelihood of hitting quota.[4] The human brain can remember about 150 connections. This is something called the Dunbar number, and it pertains to the folds of the neocortex and is evident in chimpanzee societies. None of this matters to you, but what will matter is building out the nodes on a super-connected social network that rains down warm leads and gets you one or two degrees from every rock star you need to secure referrals. Buyers are five times more likely to engage if the outreach is through a mutual connection.[5]

There's been a ton of research written about the strength of weak ties. Basically, if you only network within your company for 20 years and then lose your job, those people are insular to that silo and are unlikely to help you be placed elsewhere. Therefore, to be antifragile (Taleb: stronger the more chaos there is in a system), you need to cultivate a vast array of strong and weak ties on LinkedIn. Five thousand strangers are more powerful than 500 power brokers in this case because of the millions of mutual connections they unlock in your prospect base.

In the early days of LinkedIn, I noticed a dashboard (no longer available unless you use Sales Navigator) that showed my 3,000 connections gave me access to 18,000,000 second- and third-degree contacts. Connections can be made like crazy, but here are some rules as you build your network.

Build your connections in your own time. Don't allow LinkedIn or other social platforms to take you away from hard-core prospecting and outreach in the prime-time selling hours. Turn the television off, and stop watching inane content on YouTube; instead, use the evenings to build your network and personal brand.

Never ask to connect using the generic message that LinkedIn generates. Always tailor your request by writing something like: "I was talking with Mary Jones recently, and she mentioned your name. Good to connect here on LinkedIn, and congratulations on your career!" Or: "I really enjoyed reading the article you published, and great to also connect with you here on LinkedIn." The golden rules for connecting are don't sell and don't ask for anything; just request to connect and provide context so they are likely to accept. Get yourself into their orbit so that when you call them in the future, it won't be a cold call.

Connect to everyone who can help you succeed. This includes the people above and around you within the hierarchy of your own organization. Also connect to your suppliers and anyone who can provide you with a referral. Go back through your records, and connect with past and present clients on LinkedIn. Later, you can give them a call and ask them for a referral. Build your network professionally by always providing context for a connection request, and then build value for the other person in any information you share. Always stay positive as you interact by commenting on posts, articles, or topics within groups.

Creating Effective Scripts and Templates

Salespeople need to be efficient and effective in everything they do. There is no point being brilliant at climbing a ladder if you lean it on the wrong wall. Quality and quantity both matter when it comes to social marketing and modernized selling, so templates for content are essential. Simply create a document in Evernote, Google Docs, or Word with your outreach scripts for every situation so you can quickly cut and paste, tailor, and then hit send.

Here are some script examples:

- Hi [name]. It was great meeting you at the conference earlier this week, and I was impressed to see what you've achieved when I looked at your LinkedIn profile. Good to connect here and looking forward to talking again at some stage.
- Hi [name]. I was speaking with [common contact] earlier this week and your name came up. After having a look at your profile, I thought it would be good for us to connect here on LinkedIn.
- Hi [name]. Thanks for sharing/commenting/liking [use as appropriate] my recent post, and great to also connect here on LinkedIn. Please let me know if there is ever anything I can do for you in sharing or promoting your content.

You can also create outreach templates to use in your emails. The value narrative you have already created should be used as the basis of emails that follow any voice mails you leave for potential new clients.

Later I will go into very specific detail about how to execute all this, but the key is to drive "youuuge" levels of effective activity with the right narrative through the best channels. You must use punchy COMBOs of tailored content that is relevant to the person with whom you are seeking a conversation. Phone, voice mail, email—do your triple in less than two minutes. Add a SMS message and LinkedIn InMail for first-time outreach. The key is to use templates for every channel so that you can make it fast.

The optimal voice mail message is between 8 and 14 seconds.[6] Eighty percent of calls go to voice mail, and 90 percent of first-time voice mails are never returned.[7] Voice mails need to be short and without any kind of pitch. Under no circumstances should you talk about your products, services, or solutions. Talk instead about the reason they should meet you and the value you can provide in a conversation.

You need your own scripts for these purposes:

- Phone narrative for requesting a meeting and that leads with why it matters rather than what you do or sell
- Voice mail message that is short and focuses on the reason to meet, which is in line with your phone narrative
- Email request for a meeting that is consistent with the voice mail message you leave
- Email confirmation of a meeting that anchors the reason to meet and sets the agenda on insights you can provide and what they will brief you about; this reduces the likelihood of them cancelling, not showing up, or delegating you down to someone else
- LinkedIn connection requests for every common situation, including: you met at a conference, met them today, talked on the phone, left them a voice mail, heard their name mentioned by someone in common, were referred to them by a common connection, work in the same industry, or admire what they publish on social
- Empathy email concerning excuses or objections, with links to your objection neutralizer article or evidence supporting the reason they should meet rather than push you away

It's not that you will read scripts to anyone, but if you cannot make the conversation look compelling on paper, you only worsen your odds of success. Just winging it will not work. In creating your templates, design your own process flow so that you are clear about when you will use your content. Think like an email engineer, and A/B test all that you do . . . then refine, refine, refine. Build decision trees with "if this, then that" logic. Salespeople must be innovators in how they manage various buyer personas and outreach channels to identify what works best. Then hone the message and the cadence for COMBO strategies that hit the mark with their target audience.

Once you identify a message that is "authentically you," hammer it relentlessly for maximum effect. Only change an approach or script when required by the market—not because you feel bored. Lee Bartlett in the United Kingdom crafted the world's most concise, efficient script ever:

Email Subject Line: Revenue Growth

Body: Lauren, I have a product that's very relevant to your work; do you mind if I tell you a bit about it? We help X, Y, and Z Companies achieve [insert amount]% (measurable) revenue growth. When's a good time to talk?[8]

This message, slightly tailored to your industry and existing clients, is lethal live on the phone or via voice mail, video mail, LinkedIn custom invite, or InMail.

Selecting the Right Enablement Tools

Tools will not make you techno-magically successful, and an idiot with a megaphone is just a more annoying idiot. Tools without the right strategy and professional use are of little value. To be successful, you must have the courage to move out of your comfort zone and face rejection. Fumbling and failing for a little while is okay as long as you learn quickly and become masterful.

Regardless of the tools you use, you need discipline to do the right things at the right time in the right way. You must use tools and platforms to show positive intent by relentlessly seeking to help your customers achieve a better state of affairs and always acting in their best interests. You must carry the right value narrative and technique for delivery, where you focus on client outcomes and lead with why a conversation matters. Finally, you must possess a positive attitude and have rock-solid values. This is all essential because you are the ultimate tool! Maybe I should phrase that differently . . . who you are is your most valuable instrument.

At minimum, and in order of importance, you need these tools:

- A smartphone for both talking and accessing the Internet and mobile apps
- LinkedIn Sales Navigator, best used on a laptop
- Sales intelligence tools that provide direct-dial phone numbers and email addresses

- Email and voice mail configured properly with a complete signature and upbeat, credible greeting
- CRM with integrated marketing automation for lead nurture
- A content curation and scheduling tool such as Buffer

If this were about managing existing qualified sales pipeline, then the list would be slightly different and CRM would be higher on the priority list. But this is about personal ownership of the vitally important task of consistently creating your own top-of-funnel sales pipeline.

Intelligent phone activity is the most powerful form of engagement because so many salespeople have stopped dialing and have become passive screen jockeys. It's not a good state of affairs in many sales organizations—spreadsheet jockey sales managers and screen jockey social sellers doing way too much research and digital connection and way too little actual H2H engagement.

If you want to set yourself apart today and drive the best results, combine social and the phone. It is also important to use technology wisely. These are some of the best specialist tools to support research, persuasion, data-driven email tracking, and lead nurturing:

- Social prospecting: Examples include LinkedIn Sales Navigator, KiteDesk, Nimble, Contactually, and Altify.
- Sales intelligence for direct phone numbers and trigger events: Examples include LinkedIn Sales Navigator, DiscoverOrg, RainKing, ZoomInfo, Data.com, Inside View, Avention, Seamless.ai, and Lusha.
- Artificial intelligence: Examples include Salesforce Einstein, Seamless.ai, Complexica, Troops.ai, x.ai, Nudge.ai, Node.io, and Slackbot. It's possible to automatically sync data to Salesforce and have a virtual sales assistant schedule meetings for you.
- Automation and sales productivity: Examples include Outreach.io, Groove, DataFox, Engagio, and SalesLoft, with outbound orchestration tools to keep SDR teams engaged.

- Email tracking and CRM sync: Examples include Cirrus Insight, YesWare, ToutApp, and ZynBit. See when prospects open your email, how many times, and on what device, which is lethal for the perfectly timed follow-up or customer service issue. There is a correlation and causation between opens and acceleration of stages in the funnel.
- Predictive modeling and sales intel: Examples include Lattice Engines, Node.io, InsideSales.com, and Salesforce Einstein. These identify which leads are most likely to convert and produce revenue based on AI that algorithmically crunches big data.
- Internal social collaboration: The best examples are Salesforce Chatter and Slack, which is the granddaddy of internal social productivity tools. I recommend you all use these and endeavor to move as many of your internal interactions as possible off email threads.

The most important thing about tools is that you must invest the time and energy in learning how to use them effectively. It amazes me that so many salespeople have virtually no understanding of how to construct a basic Boolean search to find the person or thing they are looking for. Equally, how can anyone call themselves a professional and not know how to configure their basic settings within LinkedIn? If a builder arrived to renovate your house and fumbled around setting up their workbench or power tools, you would begin to lose confidence. You would be terribly concerned if your doctor could not use the machine that measures your blood pressure or if your dentist was unable to adjust the chair in which you were sitting.

Be a professional by knowing your subject and knowing the tools of the trade. Configure all of them in a way that makes your brand shine. It staggers me when I call someone and their voice mail just goes "beep" or a telco-bot says, "Your message will be converted from voice to text." No confirmation I've called the right number, no voice of the actual person I want to talk to, and no professional image! When I tell people about my experience, they usually say, "Yeah, I can't seem to figure out how to change that." If that's you, you deserve to be fired! Imagine a carpenter saying, "Yeah, that bench I built for you could have been better but I can't seem to figure out how to sharpen my tools."

Just as annoying is when you want to call someone and they're not in your contacts, so you open a recent email from them thinking that their signature panel will have their contact details with a mobile phone number and . . . nothing, just their first name! Every email system should be set up with your email signature. By all means remove the signature block to reduce scrolling for people when sending a thread, but include your contact details as the default to make it easy for people to contact your cell or look at your LinkedIn profile. Your tailored LinkedIn URL should also be in your email signature and, unless you're a megastar, your phone number should be in your LinkedIn profile. You are in sales, so make it easy for people to contact you!

Every salesperson should know their way around their CRM and marketing automation platform. How can you possibly be productive if you don't embrace the tools provided for you at great expense by your employer? How will you inspire confidence from those above you if your data is always wrong? If you want your employer to invest in Sales Navigator, earn it by becoming masterful in the use of all the other tools they've already provided.

This leads to the next point, which is to use and contribute to your company's knowledge management systems. Marketing invests a huge amount of time, money, and resources in seeking to assist sales. Learn where to find content and contribute to the pool of case studies and market intelligence.

Nurturing the Machine That Feeds You Leads

Referrals are king, but no salesperson can make their numbers on referrals alone. Nor can you exceed sales target without the assistance of others. The passive-aggressive war between sales and marketing must end, and marketing departments must own sales targets for lower-value commodities within the portfolio. As a seller, you can lead the way by relinquishing the busy fool activities of selling cheap commodity offerings in highly competitive sectors. You can move to value with elevated relationships and a strong narrative and agenda. You can engineer value and own the relationship rather than merely winning a sale.

I've sat with salespeople and helped them do the math for their year ahead. Divide the sales target by the current average deal size, then divide that by 11 months (allow 1 month for annual vacation and public holidays). I see people go white with fear. Are there even enough hours in the day to do that many deals? The solution is: 1) proactively drive larger opportunities strategically by engaging early with senior people, based on trigger events or insights, and help them build a business case for change; and 2) work with "the machine" of your own organization to feed your pipeline with opportunities that can help you transact to keep the wolf from the door.

The elements of the machine are:

- Marketing generated leads from content publishing, websites, events, and alliances
- Sales development reps (SDRs) who are doing outbound like you but typically at a lower level in the target accounts and smaller-size prospects; they are sometimes called market development reps (MDRs) or inside sales reps (ISRs) and may seek to move leads from marketing qualified (MQL) to sales qualified (SQL)
- A formalized referral program with rewards for staff and customers
- Outsourced lead-generation and appointment-setting companies
- Your senior company executives or board members who have quality relationships and who can introduce you
- Partners and alliances who can provide you with referrals

Create a business plan for your own success. Analyze your territory, the suitability and market fit for what you sell, the competition, the resources available to you, and then create a plan in partnership with your sales manager and marketing team. Work the numbers backwards, from your sales target to average deal size to number of deals required to number of selling days available. This tells you how many deals you need to do in a week or month to achieve target. Then calculate the number of qualified pipeline opportunities required based on your proven conversation rate. You will need somewhere between two and five times the sales target in qualified opportunities. Then calculate how much prospecting activity is required per available day to achieve this in terms of emails sent, phone calls made and live conversations had with real decision-makers. Now you know how much prospecting activity you must do every day. If the number does not scare you, you botched the calculations.

Make sure the SDRs or outsourced lead-generation company can actually carry the conversation for proactive outbound by sitting with them and making calls together. Help them with their own COMBO strategy for blends that elevate the conversation and improve response rates so they can provide better quality leads for you and others.

What results should SDRs be generating? Luckily, we have some decent surveys to rely on, thanks to Trish Bertuzzi and The Bridge Group. These are the averages, blended across SaaS sales development teams, surveyed in 2016:

- Twenty-one meetings per month
- Sixty-two percent conversion rate from meeting-to-opportunity
- Thirteen opportunities per month[9]

How many social and email outreaches plus phone calls are needed to achieve these results? Again, do the math for your own business based on your own stats, and then discuss with your SDR team to agree on what's needed and what's acceptable to drive the necessary results. No one understands the metrics and disciplined process of predictable prospecting better than Marylou Tyler (co-author of the books *Predictable Revenue* and *Predictable Prospecting*), and you should follow her online. If your in-house SDR team cannot deliver the results, then consider outsourcing to meeting setters such as Frontline Selling. There are many others in your part of the world who will deploy software and sellers on your behalf to land qualified meetings. They are so worth it and they also bring powerful databases!

The leader in my opinion is ConnectAndSell, which operates at 1,000 dials a day and provides on-demand outbound with transparency. Every dial, conversation, and outcome is available online for inspection and listening. Chris Beall is a visionary for outsourced sales and deploys a team that sets 30 solid meetings a day for a client while also closing deals. The team uses four tools: ConnectAndSell, email, LinkedIn, and ZoomInfo. They embrace COMBO principles and underpin the activity with a research group. Can you see why you must become masterful yourself or face becoming redundant?

Let marketing know what resources and support you need to be successful, what events you need to attend, and what content will best attract early-stage leads. Be the fulcrum for sales and marketing actually working well together; treasure their MQL leads, and obsessively use the CRM and marketing automation platform. Sirius Decisions published research stating that salespeople speak with less than 9 percent of MQLs. This means that 91 percent of the marketing budget literally goes to waste. Not because the MQLs are bad but because they don't answer the phone or email in the limited number of attempts made by salespeople. I can't imagine giving up on trying to reach a legitimate MQL. Be the one to ferociously follow up and close the loop with marketing in the CRM.

The most fundamental marketing automation play for pipeline creation is web-to-lead programs based upon early funnel content initiatives. This is where sellers can play a role in working with their marketing teams to identify the topics that will attract the right kind of leads. The foundational element is incredibly difficult to create—content publishing. You should be researching your potential buyers and customers to identify the hot issues, so create a list of content topics for marketing to work with.

Truly appreciate those who can create high-value articles, papers, videos, and other content with which marketing teams can attract and nurture leads to keep your prospects swimming around the boat. Every business needs a platform that brings marketing, sales, service, support, and stakeholder engagement together. This is because customer experience (CX) is the single biggest point of differentiation, and it should be targeted as early in the buyer's journey as possible.

A lead called within five minutes of requesting information is over 10 times more likely to answer and 4 times more likely to qualify.[10] I once downloaded a state of sales report from the Salesforce website as part of my research for being a keynote speaker at one of their events. I was called within the hour, and they did it well—no hard sell. They simply asked what my interest was in the report and if there was anything else they could help me with. I am now in their sales and marketing database and being profiled for future contact as appropriate. Salesforce drinks their own champagne when it comes to sales and marketing automation.

The point here is that everything must work together: sales and marketing, insight and value, old-school content and new-school channels, humans and machines, and—dare I say it again—social and the phone.

The most important questions that marketers must ask when seeking to create high-quality sales pipeline are:

- What trigger events occur in the customer's world to start them on their buying journey?
- What do my buyers look for online before they know to look for me?
- Where do they go online to be educated about their problems and the opportunities?

These questions are important because they can create "blue ocean" leads, where buyers are motivated by their problems or opportunities but they are early in their journeys and you have little competition. "Red ocean" is where the competition is abundant like a dozen piranhas in a goldfish bowl. "Blue ocean" strategy requires you to identify topics for articles, papers, videos, and other content that your marketing team can create to attract leads. Reflect all of this in your own publishing within your LinkedIn profile, and be an industry thought leader. Have someone in marketing be your editor to make sure your content shines.

Also work with your sales operations team so they can help you with optimizing the way you use CRM and marketing automation for lead nurturing. Focus strongly on role-based trigger events from their social monitoring tools to go beyond what you are personally doing with Google Alerts, Twitter, and Sales Navigator. Remember, the most powerful trigger event for anyone in sales is when a buyer role changes in target organizations. Picture the scenario when your senior contact leaves and goes to another company:

- She can bring you into the new company where she now works, and she will have been hired there to effect change. You're in as a trusted adviser on the ground floor.
- Your current customer will hire a new person to back-fill, and you could influence who secures the role or you can win the heart and mind of the new person when they start. This is an opportunity to upsell and provide greater value.
- The new person joining your customer will have left their previous role at another company, which could be another opportunity for you at their old company.

Trigger events create a domino effect of opportunities. What you are looking for is what you see in life, and you must be wired to see opportunities every time there are role changes, mergers or acquisitions, changes in regulations or compliance obligations, economic shifts, changes in technology, and shifts in disruptive competition. Start to see the world through your customer's eyes, and use technology and the other resources in your own company to feed you with leads.

Account-Based Everything

The concept of account-based marketing is actually not new, but some nuances of it are. Key target accounts or named accounts have been a priority for sellers for ages, especially in the enterprise. You pick up your bag and get your book of business, let's say 25 to 50 accounts in a vertical like financial services, and off you go to make magic happen. The expectation has been: "We point you at the accounts, and you go close deals—easy, just like shelling peanuts."

Making your sales target is quite a mission impossible if you get a bad book or too few accounts to qualify the buying window. I had this happen when I worked at SAP back in 2000 when they gave the "white space" of the construction industry vertical. I had to fire my boss since he would not give me additional viable territory to sell into. I think all sellers should get a mix of 50 enterprise and 50 mid-market accounts and work to stack-rank prioritize the top 50 that they work on each quarter. This is what's best for the business. Skilled hunters can qualify-out quickly and pursue the opportunities in the pipe that are 1) suited for early strategic influence based upon the right triggers or 2) closest to decision, with the strongest compelling reason and alignment with value and ability to win.

Peter Strokhorb has coined the catchy term "smarketing," which is where sales and marketing extend an olive branch and declare a detente. They work together for account-based engagement incorporating marketing, sales development, and account management executives. They all hunt on a named set of accounts—that's the simplicity. Companies like Engagio automate this expertly as does Salesforce. Marketing can do targeted advertising to very specific accounts or types of accounts. SDRs can target only the right ideal client profiles (ICPs), and account executives can automate drip campaigns and follow-up. SalesLoft Cadence shows another great example of setting a finite set of targets and going after them.

What's remarkable about account-based engagement is that it's really just target prioritization. Can everything be automated and account-based? Probably not, as you would be lowering your hit rate if the prospect can sense you've created a template. I'd advocate for software like Outbound.io or SalesLoft, or even tasks in Google calendar or Salesforce, so you can keep track of where you are. It takes anywhere from 5 to 12 touches to unlock a meeting, and we know average salespeople typically follow up only twice, and when they follow up it's alarmingly single threaded. You must know who's who in the zoo, identified by advanced searches within Sales Navigator. Select only 50 names per quarter, find six to eight stakeholders per account (two must be C-level), and fire COMBOs on all of them five to eight times with phone, voice mail, email, text, LinkedIn, Twitter DM, likes, Comments, and shares.

The entire goal of account-based engagement is accurate pre-KPI forecasting. You can actually tell your boss: "Acme Corp is not looking at our minority report interface solution until quarter 3." This is game-changing when you take the attitude that you will be maximally rejected at machine-gun speed. Prospect every lead, situation, and opportunity. Get it embedded at your core that your entire goal is to hear the sublime word "no." If you push hard enough, dominate, and cut through the space at that level, some "yeses" will unlock. It's just like shaking the proverbial tree. You will not only rattle the low-hanging fruit, but also some prize apples peacefully sitting out of reach of predators in high branches waving in the breeze.

The book *Predictable Revenue* was written by Aaron Ross and Marylou Tyler and is a case study about the early scaling period at Salesforce. It articulates the problem that start-up revenues, nowadays based on recurring as-a-service models, are fundamentally tough. This is because when you sell "curve jumping, paradigm shifting technology,"[11] it's difficult to get traction. Sales cycles go long, pilots are inevitable, and strategic partnerships ultimately abound. But securing a beachhead to land and expand in time leads to a more mature, predictable company.

The theory in *Predictable Revenue* is a Henry Ford model for selling. Break your sales team into SDRs for landing meetings and AEs for closing. There's even a market development rep (MDR) concept of a rep that solely converts inbound interest as rapidly as possible, based on studies that show rapid response time creates exponential success at converting warm inbound leads to real opportunities.

Companies that try to contact potential customers within an hour of receiving queries are nearly seven times more likely to have meaningful conversations with key decision-makers than firms that try to contact prospects even an hour later. Yet only 37 percent of companies respond to queries within an hour.[12]

The problem is that junior sellers get fobbed off or delegated down, so the idea that appointment setters, who have never been on a phone or written unique value propositions, will land meetings with C-level decision-makers is high risk. The best person to carry the conversation with a customer C-level executive is an experienced salesperson or executive. No amount of training can create genuine gravitas. What I've seen more often is scorched earth with prospects writing back asking to be taken off your list. There are only so many accounts one can close, so your team has to be smarter.

Predictable Revenue talks about sending targeted B2B emails in massive blasts, and then, based on that format, a certain amount of prospects ask for meetings. But anyone who responds to a mass template email is probably a talker or blocker. *The Challenger Sale* breaks this down into talkers, blockers, and mobilizers, and it rightly points out that the folks most willing to talk to you in the account are often powerless. Skeptical C-level buyers are hard to coax out of the corner office, but they are the most powerful and rewarding to pursue.

So how do you do it right? Part of the answer is to hire fewer people, but they should be more senior and experienced—respect your elders. Go out and find folks who can create and deliver the value narrative. Position less-experienced sellers to run full sales cycles on lower-value transactional sales. SaaS is a great example because you can break the market into SMB and mid-market, more forgiving segments in which to hunt. I would rather hire fewer salespeople who carry higher quotas, deliver better results, and backchannel like crazy than hire 10 salespeople and cut 7. This is a Draconian yet surprisingly common corporate practice.

The argument of *Predictable Revenue* is that sales is like sport. Why bog down a home-run hitter with the pitching tasks? Just have that guy slug it out. The problem is this isn't actually *Moneyball.* Sales is the transference of belief and creation of value and trust between two people. You are the first impression of your company's brand. This is why you see the owner of the restaurant on the Champs-Élysées standing out front after 30 years and 3 Michelin stars. Because he is the opening; he is the entrance point to the experience. He's there throughout the meal. He remembers you when you bring in the grandkids.

As the trusted adviser, you are metaphorically the shepherd—perhaps even the ship's captain who will navigate the coming storm of self-disruption. Customers are looking for a single point of contact and continuity as a lifeline. This is why some successful start-ups are contrarian in their stance on role multitasking: The account executive lands the meeting, runs a full cycle, negotiates, closes, and then even upsells and cross-sells with some technical help from an account team. This is a move away from growth hacking, account-based marketing, and predictable revenue's "sales machines." Buyers are peripatetic and fickle, and the modern sales cycle looks more like a Jackson Pollack than a paint-by-numbers. It's very difficult to follow and needs intrepid sales detective skills like those of John Dougan.

Congratulations on reading to here. Now it's time to buckle up as we explore exactly how to execute your COMBO Prospecting strategies.

Executing Your COMBO Strategy

"To hell with circumstances, I create opportunities . . . The successful warrior is the average man, with laser-like focus."

—**BRUCE LEE**

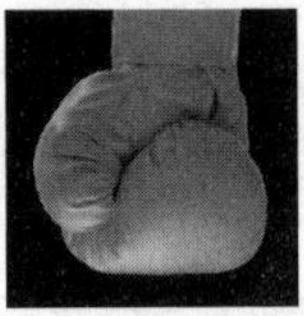

INSIGHT, CHALLENGER, AND SPIN CAN ALL BE APPLIED FOR top-of-funnel activities, but most people are focusing on deals already under way. The key to landing a meeting is the relevant insight that hooks the prospect into talking with you. Are you challenging how they see their business and reframing commonly held beliefs? You must ask the right provocative questions in outreach that uncover implications of unaddressed current-state status quo and the business case benefits of change versus the cost of inaction.

The devil is in the details, and the majority of human things fall down in the execution. In order for you to have resounding success in the application of the concepts in this book, you'll have to take my word for a few things on intelligent faith (not an oxymoron like "military intelligence").

There are laws of COMBO Prospecting that you must follow. If you social sell only, you will fail. If you wield the phone only, you will fail. If you blast away with email and InMail only, you will fail. Trainers will preach the contact rates you can achieve, but honestly you'll most likely reach 2 or 3 out of 100 with phone calls alone.

The bedazzling ingredient for dramatically increasing the rate of success is combinations. COMBOs unlock bizarre amounts of email response and enable you to break through and set meetings with the people who matter. Here are the essentials to effectively execute any form of COMBO:

- Your personal brand and value narrative must support the tone of outreach across every channel.
- You must dedicate yourself to being concise. Everything must resonate on a mobile device. Brevity is the soul of wit and cut-through.
- Commit to a minimum two-hour time-block (no distractions) every day for hard-core in-the-ring COMBO activity based on call lists you created before you left work the previous day.
- You are not running a COMBO if you have not included the phone at the heart of the strategy.
- You need powerful sales tools, including Sales Navigator and sales intelligence software that ethically sources cell phone numbers and direct dials.
- You must leverage time to complete every combination as fast as humanly possible to capture attention in this ADD-afflicted world.
- You quickly and pragmatically create context for outreach and phone calls so that they are warm rather than cold.
- Closing sales takes five to eight touches, so leverage best-of-breed marketing automation to score, nurture, and follow up.

These are hard lines I'm drawing in the sand. If you're not willing to shift your weight to the front foot or hold your leading hand up to prevent being punched in the face, you're going to get knocked out. The legendary fight in July 2017 between Manny Pacquiao (the only person to be a world champion in eight divisions) and the almost unknown Aussie battler Jeff

Horn, who defeated him, showed two people committed to always moving forward and keeping their hands up. You cannot be a winner unless you do, and it applies metaphorically in business and sales. I learned similar lessons in karate and also in flying—you must commit 100 percent to the takeoff and go full throttle.

The phone should always be prioritized. If your opportunity is warm, call. If they want to negotiate price, call. If you just got an email in response, call. If something happens in social, call. If you can't call, ask for a phone number and call. Always default to calling in every aspect of your sales process.

My own epiphany about COMBO came from watching a top-performing salesperson execute combinations in the morning before he went to the gym at lunch. It seemed like his three hours were more effective than the entire SDR team in North America that month. He inspired the theme of this book. Not only was he doing what others weren't, he was logging everything in the Salesforce CRM. He is a winner at every level and just eats rejection for breakfast with disciplined movement toward his goal every day. He was masterful with the platforms and technology, he trusted his competence and the numbers, and he executed in a disciplined manner. The CRM was not optional. It was a mandatory part of his process. Complete pro!

He showed the team what he did, but they showed little interest. Behind his back they were disparaging. They only emailed and lengthened the message, but they couldn't break through. They thought it was just his "magic." They didn't see the COMBOs in plain sight. They would go into the CRM and emulate him, sending the same exact message, and they still failed. But then the penny dropped for one of them—this person saw that it wasn't just the concise, confident blows, it was the sequence. The pro called, left a message, and sent an email—all in rapid succession. When he left a voice mail on a cell phone, he would also text. Then he would do this again, again, again, and again. By the fifth COMBO, there would be a response. Sacré bleu—impossible!

You can succeed at prospecting if you are consistent and concise and use triples—techniques honed to perfection. Simplicity can be like a laser. Call, voice mail, email. Send emails right out of the CRM so you don't even have to log it. Know the one message that is needed. Land punches at the C-level and never falter. It works in big and small companies. Those who followed the pro's lead won. He was the millionaire next door, now a VP of Sales. This could be you!

So it was upon observation of his behavior, along with the similar behavior of others, that I developed the core technique called COMBO—and it's lightning in a bottle! It's this simple. Pick some people who can actually buy. Call them. Leave them a message with why they should talk to you (do not talk about your company or products). Immediately email them referencing the message. That's it.

- COMBO triple: Once again, this is the core of call, email, and voice mail (in under two minutes).
- COMBO quads, quints, and sextets (not to be confused with sexting): Just add other channels such as text message, Twitter DM, and LinkedIn.
- COMBO custom: I'd call a video mail a super groundbreaking thing. I'd call adding a prospect on Facebook pretty out-of-the-box and dicey.

Virgil said, "Fortune favors the bold." There are many combinations a savvy seller could construct away from the core. If you think about how a fighter gets good, they hit a bag for 10,000 hours and pull heavy things through the snow. Repetition is the mother of skill, but the bursting effect of pattern interruption is what makes any technique lethal.

For the prospect, shortly after the phone stops ringing, a message light flashes or they receive a voice mail alert. Then they instantly receive an email, a text, and a notification in Twitter; when they open LinkedIn, there is a message from you. I think you could wake the dead with this strategy, and believe me, some C-level executives definitely remind me of the Crypt Keeper.

COMBO is not about multitasking. Instead, it requires dedicated focus. I honestly think it's fairly controversial to say this, but if you believe in science you shouldn't multitask at all. Efficient multitasking is a myth. The brain cannot do it; it's been proven. The female brain has the best shot, but the reason so few men die in their sleep is because the male brain definitely can't do two things at once. You might as well do one thing correctly and move on to the next rather than try to do two things poorly and have to do them again or, worse still, botch the engagement with an important person.

Social media takes your brain off your failures as you either admire artificially perfect profiles or simply judge others. The ability to check out mentally is a real detriment to work effectiveness. Your life isn't virtual; it's happening right now all around you. Carpe diem—seize this moment! Be willing to be uncomfortable and actually live your own life by embracing physical reality and the phone.

If you're spending the entire day on social networks, you're just not selling. Develop normal old-fashioned social skills, and interact with people. Remember, not everyone wants to be researched profusely, as it can be off-putting and creepy. If you absolutely have no need for a yacht, will getting a referral from your college buddy and realizing this seller researched your entire family tree really sway you? No compelling event, no trigger, no need.

Caveat emptor: Here are some tips to safely use the LinkedIn, Twitter, and Facebook platforms, which make a bazillion dollars serving ads to you: It's not necessarily helpful to be on social networks while working. It can be mesmerizing, and you're being paid to work, not socialize. If you were paying yourself, would you be happy with the lackadaisical way you're spending your billable hours? If your laptop screen were being broadcast in Times Square, what would you click on then? I would even argue that some flagrant uses of social media at work are a blatant time theft!

The argument for using these platforms during your day is that they can drive business success. To frame how crazy social can be, imagine if I encouraged you to watch a dozen concurrent sports games while doing discovery calls. Now imagine how many successful real-world touches you could achieve making a list of high-value prospects and then turning everything off, including your computer. You need to be focused on what you're doing. There's a rhythm to getting in the zone, a positive force that builds when you do a singular activity. It's called flow in positive psychology.

Effectively setting one to three qualified appointments with high-value prospects is more potent than a week of getting top executives to add you on social media and like your content. Even if you did get these likes, it's typically their executive assistant just powering their LinkedIn profile anyway. Why? CEOs are rarely on social media. They're doing business deals, which is why you can't get ahold of them.

Think of this as working out. If you're lifting a ton of weights and then eat a piece of cake, you're going to stumble. Social media is the Twinkie of life. You know you need to do the heavy lifting. If you delude yourself, you're not going to be successful. After work hours, go do whatever you want. What happens in Vegas ironically now lives on forever on social media, but I digress. It's probably healthier to allow your brain to relax. Are you allowing yourself to generally reset or are you half doing your life? Go exercise so the endorphins flow, and then get some high-quality sleep. Practice self-care. Wouldn't it be best to go 100 percent at work, and then have a hobby after hours? Or would you rather live your life halfway every waking hour of your day? I would personally rather interact with someone who is fully present.

In my first book, I set a cornerstone of full presence with my RSVPselling methodology, which manages large, complex deals already in play. I'll admit, I fall prey to time-wasters like everyone else, but it's important to spend as much time as possible proactively touching qualified prospects as much as you can during the business day. It's more fun to research your way down a deep rabbit hole, but remember to prioritize the phone over any other channel because you're going to resist it the most. You're human and don't want to be rejected.

We live in strange days where multitasking has reached epidemic proportions. Sales floors have become as quiet as churches and public libraries. So what should you do instead? Dead simple: Furiously protect your revenue-generating activities and selling time. Then go and actually drive the activities that create sales. Do research and make lists in off hours. Hit those lists whether you're in the field, in the office, or working from home. Do what you fear and hate the most, first thing in the morning before everyone's day goes out the window . . . call!

By doing that one thing you will double or triple outcomes because 25 calls turn into 50, which turn into 75. Never reaching prospects turns into setting multiple appointments. Consistency, persistency, and work ethic are not to be confused with massive amounts of social media. Many people want to eat candy all day, guzzle sugar drinks, and never brush their teeth. They haven't the foggiest idea why their teeth keep falling out. Catch my drift? If you're a manager reading this, get out from behind the computer and get out into the field to do deal reviews. Get into the fresh air to visit with clients and coach your people before and after key meetings so they can become better.

Be Your Own Sales Development Rep (SDR)

I fully respect SDRs, aka inside sales reps (ISRs) or lead development reps (LDRs), to the point of having a crush. They can use this book and become business development managers (BDMs) or account executives (AEs) and champions of new business sales in any company. We've all been influenced by "predictable revenue" with the concept that still works in many businesses where the Henry Ford model of selling is adopted and hunters abandon the idea that they should open and set meetings. The problem with the compartmentalization of sales is that it usually results in fewer people prospecting, and that's not healthy for any business because everyone needs to be opening opportunities and obtaining referrals.

Senior salespeople need to be their own SDRs, and here's why. If you have a multimillion-dollar quota, you're not going to be successful relying on someone junior to get you appointments with C-level executives. This is because they're bunkered behind a steel wall guarded by an impenetrable EA trained like a Doberman to eat not only the raw steak, but also your ego. The EA's main purpose in life is to prevent you from visiting the boss.

 No amount of marketing qualified leads (MQLs) being qualified to sales qualified leads (SQLs) is going to be enough for a senior salesperson to make their highly ambitious targets. This is especially true when the lunatic people at the top relentlessly halve your territory and uplift your quota by 30 percent.

Treat MQLs from the marketing folks and SQLs from SDRs as a bonus. Take control of your own success! If you have a finite list of target accounts that are highly matrixed, you'll need to be very surgical about how you multi-thread across multiple levels in a waterfall effect—this is the art of saturation. Military strategy comes into play as you try to flank, land and expand, change the rules, and eat the elephant. You'll risk the customer's entire IT organization or marketing team shutting you down, blocking your email address, or asking your company to stop calling. You may be asked to go fill out their vendor inquiry form on some website that is essentially a black hole. But that's more than okay because you gotta go poke the bear if you want to be truly successful.

I've watched the patterns of SDRs, and that's how I learned that even in the most well-respected companies, they get shut down when they try to set meetings with senior people. It's not because they lack skills or commitment. I also learned from SDRs the technique of screen-shotting a LinkedIn InMail and sending it as an email—simply brilliant. I saw them leverage things like SalesLoft Cadence to track and manage how frequently they contacted a prospect. Being able to carry the right narrative with gravitas is no mean feat. If you have a serious number to hit, you must own pipeline building as well as selling and closing.

You need to carve out a minimum of two hours per day to do COMBO Prospecting in a rock-solid prospecting block. The best time to do this is first thing in the morning once you've had a couple of cups of java but before your prospects have disappeared into their day.

Take a sheet of paper, fold it in half, and literally leave hatch marks for how many triples you've made in less than two minutes. A manual tracking mechanism rather than CRM is a critical component of success with this method. Ensuring that you are not multitasking in any way is crucial. That means locking a door, reserving a cubicle, or even calling from home if you're a remote operator out there in the field. Some salespeople have had to fight for approval to even make prospecting calls in a world gone socially crazy. A sales floor of churchlike silence is a scourge, a cancer in business. The boisterous chatter of salespeople connecting live with prospects and leaving voice messages is what should be regarded as sacrosanct.

Chris Beall came across a sales technology company in Silicon Valley that had two SDRs who were forbidden by the VP of Sales from making outbound prospecting calls! The rationale was that interrupting people is rude. Chris was shocked and so was I. Mark Hunter once wrote to me recounting another true story of an inside sales manager being told to remove the gong on the sales floor. Each time one of his team members made a sale they got to ring the gong, but HR instructed him to remove it because another sales manager said it was too noisy for his team. Mark's advice to HR: fire the other sales manager who complained. His advice to the CEO: fire HR!

Time-blocking is nothing new. University students do it, athletes do it, Arnie did it to become Mr. Universe. Effective time management and focus will get you where you need to be, which is 3X pipeline within a couple of quarters as a way to exceed your quota.

Now here's the kicker to being your own SDR. From the moment of reading this, you must become an SDR every day—forever. I know, that's a daunting task, and you really want to climb the ladder to SVP of Sales or even CEO someday. But the trickiest thing about leading in sales is that action bias reigns supreme. You can't be the heavyweight champion of the world and then never step into the ring again. It's like ancient tribes where the strongest warrior is also the leader of the pack. The strongest COMBO prospector is the leader of the company, and after reading many successful CEO interviews, I found that they are hustling the hardest. Even board members need to help generate revenue with their relationships.

Think of outbound calls like showering with caffeine soap, eating raw meat, or shaving with Crocodile Dundee's knife. You must do it every day to maintain hygiene, let alone keep up momentum. If you travel, make calls in airports. You can't ever miss a day. You can't ever delegate this core responsibility. The irony of the effective sales leader is that they wear every hat and still manage their time effectively. Sure, let your SDRs contribute and train them assiduously in these methods, but never for a second think you can let up on these daily COMBOs yourself. You must keep slogging, hitting the bag, and drilling into a finite list of 50 accounts, with six to eight contacts per account, until you hear that magical word, "no." Then cycle that prospect 90 to 180 days later. Calling is the top skill you should be developing to gain an edge, not just for prospecting and landing meetings with C-level decision-makers, but at every stage of the funnel.

Social selling is an epidemic. But it's not social to hide behind your computer, Neo. Reach out and touch someone! There's no doubt LinkedIn, Facebook, and Twitter are the most addictive, mind-numbingly fascinating voyeuristic paradises ever constructed since *The Matrix*. That being the case, I go into world-renowned technology companies to advise on new sales and can't help but witness the chilling silence. Digitally native millennials have embraced the digital-only approach while rocking to Spotify in their earbuds full blast, and lazy managers have also drunk the social selling–only Kool-Aid. I was interviewed on a London show in 2017, and the host told me that one of their clients had removed phones altogether from the sales floor, having gone "full bottle" on social. I was aghast and simply said, "That's insane."

Cell phone penetration will exceed world population. Multiple devices per human is coming, and with the Internet of Things (IOT), there will be 25 digital ways to reach a prospect—even through their refrigerator. Wouldn't you rather be the signal in all that meaningless noise? How can you miss communicating with an "always on" medium that's physically on every person? Within 10 years, one-third of the B2B global salesforce will be made obsolete by AI. Gerhard Gschwandtner made one of the boldest predictions about all sales being gone by a "not too distant future date," and we're seeing all sorts of doomsday prophecies emanating from the Gartners and Forresters of the world. Rest assured, trusted advisers are built to last and will not be affected. Conversely, they'll most likely be more in demand than ever.

Human beings lack discipline, and the fact that people check phones hundreds of times a day proves this flaw has never been more acute. If you can harness this and be excellent at interrupting prospects effectively out of the blue, you will always work. If you can do this at "sick levels of massive action," á la Grant Cardone, nobody who cares about Revenue with a capital *R* at your company will ever forget your full name (including middle) or let you leave the building to go to a competitor.

The best SVPs and GMs of Sales I've ever seen still pound the phone every day, leading with massive action from the front. Yes, don't you see this? Aren't your CEO and CFO always talking about that networking event where they saw the prospect CEO and they're going to make a warm introduction? When I personally met Mark Hawkins, the CFO of Salesforce, in the green room when we were both speaking at an event, I was impressed. When I heard him on stage in front of thousands, he blew me away with his sales and marketing savvy—all my accountant jokes were immediately redundant.

The masters of the universe are doing cold calls face-to-face all day. How about Zuckerberg and Parker raising the initial funding round for Facebook (an insane Matrix-like idea in its time) by going and cold-calling the office of Peter Thiel (of PayPal fame)? They got to the top of sales and entrepreneurship, then moved into the corner office as CEOs before matriculating to board members. They did it all with a philosophy of "let's take action and take no prisoners."

Artificial intelligence cannot make jokes, shoot the breeze, kibitz, and relate. Until AI has EQ, you will keep your job if you can create enough value to fund your role. The rapport step is everything. You can't respectfully Challenge or SPIN a person who dislikes you. You can't make someone like you because you comment on their white-water rafting photo above the desk. It's certainly off-putting when you stalk them on Facebook and let them know you'll be at the football game the same Saturday afternoon. There is no inflection in text mediums, so again the neuroscience-backed power of tone in the human voice is transcendent. This is why a simple call and voice mail slaughters 2030 level sales AI. It's elementary, my dear Watson!

Pre-revenue KPIs will protect you. If you are personally building 3X pipeline at a rapid rate while all the other snoozers are sitting with feet up on the desk swiping their Tinder, they are getting kicked off the island first. This means intelligently being on the phone. Chris Beall has listened to tens of thousands of sales conversations and classifies the way salespeople sound. He says there are three types: sincere/competent/confident (2 percent), the salesman (49 percent), and the deer in the headlights (49 percent).[1]

Chris tells the story of listening to John Legend singing some intentionally mundane lines about washing a sweater, and his voice makes it sound sexy, compelling, and memorable. "The voice speaks before the words are uttered, and I very rarely come across a rep who practices what they sound like. They don't sing—they bark, grunt, slur, chatter, fumble, or worse, they go for smooth because that worked on a girl in the 10th grade. If I could teach reps one thing it would be to "sing" like John Legend—not smooth, just pure and confident and competent sounding. Because buyers aren't looking—they are, unconsciously and brilliantly, listening for who they can trust."[2]

Being your own SDR and giving good phone builds confidence in every sphere of your life. You lose the awkward silences. It's therapeutic and life transforming to put yourself out there and become forged in the fires of rejection and the pressure to deliver results. You'll be a diamond, secure from within and admired by all those who matter in your career. Like Tom Cruise in *Jerry Maguire* and in person on *Oprah*, you'll jump on the couch radiating an aura of stupid-grin cool! People love to be around confident people; it sets them at ease emotionally. Calm executives like to buy things when they can open up their vulnerabilities and lower the veil. You will become as Abraham Maslow and Dr. Wayne Dyer opined: "Independent of the good opinion of others." That life state is self-actualized and near invincible for a seller or professional of any ilk.

It's unpopular to be a sanitation engineer, but plumbers can make a glorious living just going through the motions, and they don't give a crap about what people think. Sellers may not be held in the same regard as surgeons, but they can drive the same sports car and give their families similar life experiences. Plumbers don't like putting their hands up a sewer pipe just like nobody wants to do cold-calling, but they just embrace the task because it's what generates the results. Use warm techniques to never truly cold-call anyway. You'll soon be coaching the SDRs and have the CEO knocking on your cubicle. Trust me, I smell a promotion.

Shocking Paradoxes That Govern Prospecting

The average salesperson only makes two attempts to reach a prospect.[3] Eighty percent of sales require five follow-ups[4] yet 44 percent of salespeople give up after one follow-up.[5]

Mid-funnel and bottom-funnel closing depends entirely on prospecting skills. "If you can't gain the first commitment," as Anthony Iannarino says, "you're never going to gain subsequent commitments." Sales can be one of the most rewarding jobs in the world when you do it right, and it can be the brutally hardest when you fumble around in the dark.

My first book talked about finding your true North Star and the compass that guides you there being integrity of purpose. Tolkien summed it up best when he said: "Not all those who wander are lost." The most direct path is not always the best option, and the best sellers embrace the counterintuitive, sometimes contradictory wisdom in navigating the people and politics of the complex sale. Consider the following sales advice:

- "To be consultative, be assumptive."[6] You don't need to put yourself on a parity or equal playing field with powerful people. There's seldom been a deal for six or seven figures that wasn't between an average-paid rep and a titan in a corporation. Don't let it bruise your ego that you are not as powerful as the decision-maker. In their eyes, you being an expert in your technology, products, and services makes them admire and respect you as a trusted adviser. Sell with gravitas, assume the sale, and concentrate on what comes after the close. This is when they realize the benefits and embrace the win-win relationship that results from successful partnership.
- There are 6.8 decision-makers in the buying committee,[7] but you

don't need to close all of them to get a sale. The truth is, there is still one alpha sleigh dog, and she has the best view. Start very high with compelling insight to the bottom line and with a jargon-free value narrative, then let that player validate and vet you and give you the keys to the kingdom. Remember, there are so many people in a matrixed organization that only have the power of "no," not "yes"!

- Strategic planning and sharpening the axe for hours, days, or weeks does not allow you to cut the tree down faster. The great oddity of prospecting effectively is that a quick message in a blended set of channels will cut through and get you a meeting with your dream prospects worlds faster than obsessing over writing an email for hours.
- The most powerful people in the world want to engage with you only on the basis that you provide them with value and are worthy of trust in their eyes.
- Persistence and COMBOs are not just required lower in the funnel. Don't ever let up, keep delivering blows until you have closed mid-funnel and especially in procurement. You should be calling and emailing back and forth daily just before final signature.
- You'll achieve higher response with a blended channel than a better message. This means that a B-grade message delivered live on a phone call or left on a voice mail, then sent in an email or text in some omni-channel combination, will actually outperform the A+ message that is sent in only one channel, especially email. This one's easy to explain. CXOs are simply overloaded, so they don't check unsolicited emails of any kind. You could have the location of the Holy Grail or a winning lottery ticket, and they'd simply ignore it, or more likely, their executive assistant would be there blocking you.
- More personalized outreach does not bring about a higher conversion rate. Oddly, personalization often looks needy and repels. What to do: Laser focus with research based on business value and get straight to the point.

- You do not need to vary the message for each person to achieve cut-through. Mike Scher studied 1.4 million sales interactions and found that top-down strategies with identical messaging work better than changing the message each time. This is because it rattles the cage or tree and creates confusion, so everyone forwards it around, smoking out the actual buying committee. This is much like pouring smoke into an ant farm or beehive. CEB talks about this in *The Challenger Customer*. The more you challenge each stakeholder on the merits of your solution by reframing the problem, the more they each cement in a unique position. Then when they go to form a consensus, it's just gridlock and dysfunction.

Consider not varying your message much at all. Organizations are like waterfalls, and water moves down the chain of command; the underlings are always managing up so as not to be fired. When you send a powerful value message to one senior leader and neglect her colleague, they'll forward it to that colleague. If you send the same message to four people, they all compare notes, and suddenly it feels like the whole organization is talking about your unknown start-up by the watercooler.

My clients have experimented with sending thousands of emails into big companies, and they found several bizarre ways to create engagement:

- Start your outreach to someone with a single word related to revenue or ideas.
- Use "Your LinkedIn Profile" as a subject line. For some reason this gets astounding response rates.
- As explained above, if you write the exact same message to the C-level, SVP or VP, lateral VP, and operations folks, it cuts through better than tailoring each message.
- Be extremely assumptive in all communication by writing as if meeting with you is a given. Eliminate waffling words such as *maybe, perhaps*, or *with your permission*.

Sales is blocking and tackling, punting and kicking, rucking and mauling. There are many channels to leverage and pros and cons for all. I'd love to tell you that crafting a personalized, relevant, tailored message to every stakeholder will spark a consensus, but it won't. The more you challenge each individual stakeholder, the more individual ossification and peer dysfunction will grow, until you're knee deep in the boggy morass of the status quo.

The reason I share all this is the most basic sales paradox of all: You don't have all the answers, you are often lost, or maybe you fell into your profession. Yet your job is to be the guide and shepherd of the world's largest customers. There are approximately 3 million global sellers who have to service, in many cases, just 1,000 global accounts with the highest revenues. Breaking through requires different levels of thinking and disciplined execution of innovative methods.

Time-Blocking—Discipline Within the Hours

Discipline beats motivation every time. Who cares whether you feel like doing it? I brush my teeth morning and night whether I feel like it or not. Dedicate two hours every day to 30 triples: 30 calls, voice mails, and emails (feel free to add text message and InMail). The idea is that you do 30 COMBO touches (triples at a minimum) to your prospects in key target accounts per day. At a minimum, that's five accounts, six contacts in each, with two to three being C-level decision-makers, VP and up.

Apportion your workday according to Mike Weinberg's 33/33/33 rule. Once you've built your pipeline, you spend a third of your time in top, middle, and bottom.

Then apply the Single Lever Rule—focus on the one thing that scares you the most, and knock that out first. The truth is that showing up to work and just reactively answering email to get to in-box zero is probably the biggest waste of time in the history of mankind. Jeb Blount calls the work hours the golden hours and the outside of work hours the platinum hours. The point is that moving the needle on revenue is a Sisyphean task if you're moving the wrong levers. The Single Lever Rule is to find that one key lever that moves your day forward to any key performance indicator (KPI) you need to drive.

If you're looking to break into new accounts and have those crucial conversations that matter, it may be a certain type of call or outreach with a certain method done a certain amount of times. What we do know for sure from Jason Jordan's work in *Cracking the Sales Management Code* is that revenue is a lagging indicator. Merely looking at it cannot influence it. You need to back into all the smart activities that lead from an action, to an objective, to an ultimate result.

Trigger Events and Social Listening

We've discussed the power of trigger events throughout this book, and they are massively important for pipeline generation. At any given time, only 3 percent of your market is actively buying. Fifty-six percent is not ready, and 41 percent is poised to begin.[8] The most powerful trigger event is a job change, where someone has switched companies or been promoted. In this case, you can't sell on features or a solution anymore; you must go to the next level and be a political seller. This means thinking consistently about making your customer a hero and helping them advance politically within their organization. According to Craig Elias and Tibor Shanto in their book *Shift!* the other two triggers are "awareness" (news, events or press coverage, etc.) and "bad suppliers" (competitors stumbling in the market or dropping the ball with the client). LinkedIn Sales Navigator along with RainKing, DiscoverOrg, and Cognism even have "scoops" that give you real-time actionable business intel on prospects and triggers. Funding is a powerful trigger, so CrunchBase should be monitored daily for funding rounds and mergers and acquisitions (M&A) that could make a prospect suddenly flush with cash. Configure Google Alerts, and don't be afraid to brazenly mention relevant news in your candid outreach. Marketing software or technology upgrades are immediate ways to deploy funds to fuel profitable revenue growth for potential clients.

Monitor for events that trigger awareness or need within your market and with specific potential customers. Also, identify the best way to automate the monitoring and listening. Social platforms are not for narcissistic blasting but instead for social listening! Follow key people, companies, and Twitter hashtags. Triggers give you context for outreach and a reason to call. Trigger events and referrals are hugely important because they provide you with the highest probability of engagement and the fastest path to a sale.

Referrals—The Path of Highest Probability

Referrals create a head start with trust, a prerequisite in any sale, and buyers are five times more likely to engage with a salesperson when there is a trusted common connection and warm introduction.[9] Programmatically leveraging warm personal introductions and referrals, both internal and external, is an intelligent way to build sales pipeline. When I say programmatic, I mean that you invest time specifically focused on doing this each week, ideally every day. Here's why you must make it a priority. Referrals are 69 percent faster to close, referrals convert to revenue at a higher rate than any other lead source, and referred clients have a higher lifetime value.[10]

According to Joanne Black, America's leading authority on referral selling, a referral enables you to secure a meeting with just one call because you open with immediate credibility and context. She makes the valid point that the sales process shortens and the cost of sale plummets. Joanne's own surveys with clients, conducted over two decades, reveal that competition diminishes greatly with referral selling and conversion rates increase to be greater than 50 percent![11]

The smartest and most successful salespeople embrace referral selling. Here are more compelling statistics: A referred customer provides 25 percent higher profit margins, is 18 percent less likely to leave, and provides a lifetime value 16 percent higher than a nonreferred customer.[12] Eighty-four percent of decision-makers begin their buying process with a referral.[13] Ninety-two percent of consumers trust referrals from people they know and are four times more likely to buy when referred by someone they know and trust.[14] Seventy-three percent of buyers prefer to work with a salesperson referred by a trusted common connection.[15] Eighty-four percent of executives grant a meeting to a salesperson who is recommended internally.[16]

LinkedIn allows you to immediately see connections in common by first or second degree. Who do you know who knows someone in the account? You can easily just filter connections in common and click under the profiles to surface patterns and themes. Typically, you'll start to see some of the same super-connectors or nodes showing up over and over again as you're prospecting into a specific industry vertical.

I'm a huge proponent of making a phone call to the connection in common and being willing to ghostwrite the warm introduction. Send them a paragraph on why the intro matters, and write it from their viewpoint to make it easier for them to introduce you. These warm referrals convert at an astoundingly higher rate than a direct selling approach.

A powerful channel is alumni, even if you don't have any connections in common. Common jobs or schools are a huge point of empathy and connectivity. I've seen amazing doors get opened by sharing a story about the school you have in common. Sports teams in common also convert well. But beware too much personalized communication because it can be seen as a "used car salesman" approach, or overly needy and hungry.

There are those who purport to generate all of their business with pure referrals, but the reality of modern selling is that it's a world of named accounts or defined territories. Aggressive sales targets mean that no one can make their sales number on referrals alone. Nor can they make their number from inbound leads, SDRs, and outsourced demand generation providers. All of these tools must be used to achieve the best outcomes.

Here is how to drive your own targeted referrals: Take each key account, look in the How You're Connected panel in LinkedIn Sales Navigator, and mine your first- and second-degree connectivity. Identify those you actually know within your social network who can make a personal introduction to anyone in that prospective account. Any first-degree connectivity at any echelon will get you light-years into the account. It's a Trojan horse. Even if you went to school with someone in their HR department or on the sales team, it's still worlds warmer than an unsolicited cold call. Inside coaching and intelligence is gold.

You may be in a big enough company to have Sales Navigator Enterprise Edition, which shows with the TeamLink feature whether anyone in your entire company overlaps into the prospect base. It's even better if the connection is an engineer. Imagine the credibility of your VP of IT having worked with someone at the prospect company. What if your entire C-suite was thinking this way? What if you institutionalized the process of looking for common connections between your entire company and the most coveted dream accounts?

They key to referrals is simply being in the habit of asking! If you've completed a project for a client, you can say: "Hey John, I really enjoyed working with your team on that project! The feedback on the job we've done has been great. Whom else in the company should I be talking to?" If you've built a good relationship in one area of the client's business, you can say: "Hey Mary, what's going on inside the business where we could potentially help, and whom should I be speaking with?"

There are hundreds of ways of asking, but so few do it. You see what you are looking for, and every happy customer should be seen as a source of referrals, internally within their organization and externally within their extended network. Be in the habit of asking.

Advanced Technique Playbook

I've touched on how to use technology throughout this book to break through, but let's go deeper with how to interweave technology and platforms into your COMBO strategy. First, these are the possible types of social platforms relevant in business-to-business sales:

- **Personal social:** You should be open to adding prospects on Facebook and then messaging them. Weird, awkward, controversial? Yes, and don't invade their personal life, but Facebook is an integral part of the social graph.

- **Picture-based social:** Instagram and Pinterest are winners here, and this is the interest graph.
- **Professional social:** LinkedIn is the giant gorilla, and it combines the social graph and interest graph with the economic graph.
- **Messaging social:** Twitter is super powerful for monitoring triggers and understanding what interests the people you seek to meet. It's also a powerful notification engine, and direct messaging in Twitter or a phone text message can achieve amazing response rates.

The most powerful platform of all for B2B sellers is LinkedIn Sales Navigator coupled with CRM and marketing automation such as the Salesforce suite. Use Sales Navigator for creating sales funnel and CRM with integrated marketing automation for every account and contact that shows any sign of life. Here is my approach for leveraging LinkedIn Sales Navigator:

Step 1: Take an account list of no greater than 50 accounts, and add it on Sales Navigator.

Step 2: Save five to seven prospects per account as leads because you are going to monitor the content they share and where they are mentioned plus interact with this content.

Step 3: Build a robust Sales Navigator feed that you'll utilize in both web and mobile streams. This is a Custom Feed.

Step 4: Here's the kicker. Sort by Lead Shares, and start to comment on what they're sharing in a thoughtful way. Remember, you're not connected to these people, so it's a wow factor for CXOs to have some total stranger commenting in a relevant way out of the blue! Contacts that share based on the 90, 9, and 1 Internet theory of presumption are massively valuable. Basically, only 1 percent write, 9 percent share, and the other 90 percent are really more voyeurs on the web.[17] If someone is sharing, call them. Use a service like Data.com, ZoomInfo, DiscoverOrg, Lusha or RainKing to directly call them and intelligently comment (with context and relevance) on what they've shared on social (as evidenced by Navigator).

Step 5: You need to set aside time to mine your potential referrals per account. Your goal is to call colleagues who are connected into prospect companies. All of these connections should be exploited so you never cold-call again. If you sell software to CMOs, you can still leverage a connection to the HR or legal department. All connections are golden, and these weak ties between your company and the prospect organization are powerful for intelligence and coaching.

Step 6: Set aside time to explore all your first- and second-degree referral sources into prospect organizations. These are represented in Navigator, and you can click to expand them and look for patterns that emerge in the common connections. This will reveal competitive salespeople in other vendor companies or nodes on the network. Nodes can be industry thought leaders or well-connected influencers. Mapping the connections to the power base is a heat-seeking-missile way to reach the right decision-maker.

Call up sellers in affiliated vendors that are harmonious to what you sell, and cohost networking events with them to overlap your networks. The cardinal rule of referral selling on LinkedIn is not to do it digitally. When you identify the connection in common, call that connection and offer to ghostwrite a message they can pass along to make the warm introduction. Make it frictionless. B2B buyers are five times more likely to engage when the outreach is through a mutual connection.[18]

Step 7: Watch the daily email digest from Navigator for job changes. When you are going after a calling list, start to call down the Navigator Newsfeed, which shows news mentions, job changes, lead recommendations, and other triggers like funding or innovation projects. Use the Navigator real-time feed as the bedrock for your triples. You'll remember the basis of COMBO is a call, voice mail, and email—back-to-back and in less than two minutes. Jab, jab, jab!

Step 8: Don't exceed 50 target accounts and up to seven contacts per account. This means you should only ever be monitoring 300 objects, which is double the Dunbar number of 150. The neocortex can hold only 150 connections. Sales Navigator actually gets unwieldy, and you start to miss information if you follow too many people or accounts. Even if you change your stream by sorting by "recent" instead of "most important," it's cumbersome. You should have 50 key target accounts per quarter max, five to seven leads per prospect, and at least one C-level per account. Remember, you can easily purge out accounts and leads if you track too many. Work clean and keep it organized and tight. Move the contacts into CRM, and leverage LinkedIn integration with CRM market leaders such as Salesforce and Microsoft.

There are a bunch of platforms like SalesLoft and Groove to keep your blended prospecting touches consistent. Build a simple Excel or Google spreadsheet with your top 50 account names, stack rank them as 1, 2, or 3 for hot, warm, or cold. Put a column next to them for VITO (Very Important Top Officers) and then a column for the additional decision-makers. Then add a column for strategy and notes. As your main column to the left of every name and the rank, add Last Contacted. When you're doing a two-hour or three-hour COMBO block, you want to cycle through at least 3 triples on 10 accounts for 30 triples in total. Keep track of every account you covered that day. If at all possible, do all of this in your CRM or dialing software platform.

If you've got a list of 50, you can cycle through the entire list this way each week or every other week. Basically, you can start to cover all the contacts in all 50 accounts five to seven times in a two- to three-month period over the course of a quarter. This thoroughness is how the breakthrough comes, and it's okay if there are no signs of life on the first call, voice mail, or email. You can track opens by device type and geographically via Cirrus Insight, ToutApp, or YesWare.

Pull each key account in Navigator and see the leads attributed. Read their profile and check their activity stream to understand relevant context. Reading their profile is not enough. Find a common connection who can introduce you, and by all means Google their name before contacting them and hit the News button to pull memorable quotes. Tie this back to your product or services. You'd think this advice is Sales 101, but so few SDRs, AEs, or BDMs actually do the 30 seconds of research, which can increase engagement. I would recommend putting a + sign in the subject line and combining things that seem random like: University of Michigan + fly fishing. Business context is best, but think outside the box.

"From an email perspective, we normally hit a 12 percent open rate off a cold list, which is exceptionally good. With LinkedIn InMail, we hit 48 percent open rate. We have never seen open rates like this for a long time,"[19] says Brett Chester, vice president of online marketing and demand generation at Replicon. Don't let people tell you that InMail is spam or a waste of time—it's a vitally important channel for your COMBO outreach. Exhaust all of your InMails every month no matter what; even a disinterested response gives you a credit back on the InMail counter.

Nobody ever calls presidents, CEOs, or board members. You should call VCs who back the companies if you are going after earlier-stage ventures. Where do you get the phone number? Many times, by simply becoming a first-degree connection (always write a customized LinkedIn request)—their phone number will be freely available on their profile in the Contact area. Otherwise, Lusha, RainKing, DiscoverOrg, ZoomInfo, Inside View, Avention, Data.com, and others can provide this seamlessly. Subscribe—it's essential for your success.

I talk to CXOs, and they say they get very little InMail compared with email. They get one phone call or voice mail compared with 500+ emails. Stop—read that again. What does this tell you? It's not even the quality of a cold call, voice mail, or InMail—it's just doing it at all that makes the lion's share of the difference. This massive uplift in action alone completely stands out in the all-digital social selling cacophony. Pretty much everyone I add now (and I've tested this) immediately spams me back selling products or services. Social selling fail! No value is being created. The vast majority of sellers are lazily only emailing and adding without a custom invite, only to immediately send spam (once). No follow-up. The golden secret of sales, Grant Cardone will tell you, is: "Follow-up, follow-up, follow-up!"

The relevancy paradox is the idea that adding value and changing up the message every time will yield a better result than never varying. The problem is that it can make you look needy. Over-researching can cripple an outreach campaign. You've developed your scripts and a hypothesis of value for their industry, so just create some relevance in the preamble. Don't overthink it and go into analysis paralysis. Get on the blower and set the appointment!

But for this to work, you need a relevant target who is similar to existing prospects or who leverages a direct competitor's solution. They've bought before; they get it. Some percentage will be dissatisfied and buy again. Be there when the buying cycle is embryonic, and capture them into your CRM for lead nurturing and insight content marketing campaigns. Provide value in the education phase, but move fast and identify prospects who will soon enter the buying phase. Your pipeline must have nice shape and balance; it must be strategic and tactical, short-term and long-term, with some rats and mice plus some elephants or whales.

Seeking to engage based on work anniversaries or birthdays is pretty spammy. Congratulating people incessantly on a new role, funding, or a school in common is wildly overplayed. One senior executive with whom I have a good relationship told me he updated his LinkedIn profile to "looking for new opportunities" after he was let go. He received 17 InMails congratulating him on the new role. He had been unfairly pushed out after nearly two decades of excellent leadership performance and service. I laughed, he went silent. I apologized, and then he laughed, too.

The best messaging is focused on the results you provide for a similar company, and quantifying this with hard dollars is best. It's really that simple and cut-and-dried. The Cialdini concept of social proof is very powerful. If you talk to the CMO of Pepsi about something you're doing for Coke, you'll get a callback. It's fiercely competitive to innovate at the top, but be careful about divulging your customer's competitive IP because you'll have a personal integrity issue if you do, and you can destroy trust before you begin. They'll simply suck you dry of information and spit you out into the reception area.

I've tested every type of messaging under the sun and found that repetition is the key. Sending a very similar message to the top of the food chain and down through the ranks, only slightly varying it if at all, as you blitz triples every 72 hours will get your emails circulated. Some call this "the art of confusion." Don't be linear in your approach because it's too slow, and someone will inevitably seek to block you from talking with others. Go after the 13 people who are relevant in the account, all at the same time! Obsessively focus on the chief executive office and the company's internal and even external customers. You need to both push and pull in your strategy.

I'd be remiss not to mention the mid-funnel practice of multi-threading contacts as well as communication avenues. Remember there are now almost seven stakeholders in every buying committee in a complex sale according to CEB, so if you're single-threaded you're "deaded"! Okay, it rhymes. But take the time midstream, once you've opened the opportunity, to get connectivity with your contact's boss, lateral VPs, and operational players. These are the victims of the problem, aka the users of the solution. This is priceless for mobilizing consensus, and it increases close rates and accelerates deals.

Insider Secrets of Savvy Sellers

As you create your own strategy utilizing a tailored playbook, technology stack, templates, and processes, recognize that the devil is in the details, or perhaps it's the angel depending on how you look at it. Here are 13 nuances to give you the inside track:

1. Referrals and warm introductions are exponentially more powerful than any other channel. So the first step in pursuing any account is to study connections in common and actually reach out to those people to ask how strong their connection is and if they can help you. Connecting with a prospect based on context and trust is almost magical in its power to help you outsell anyone in your company.
2. The size of your social network will determine the strength of your weak ties. Google "strength of weak ties" for background on this concept. In plain English, you are more likely to tap into more warm introductions (see point #1), and the network effects are much more powerful. Therefore, courageously cultivate a large, diverse global network of connections. You should also add everyone you ever meet, shake hands with at a networking event, or connect with at a conference. Start to harvest as many accurate email addresses and cell phone numbers you can, and build your LinkedIn profile to 5,000 first-degree connections ASAP, as this dramatically increases the likelihood of hitting quota!
3. A LinkedIn view of your profile is a lead, unless it's a spam profile or frenemy (easy to detect). I'd controversially encourage you to always connect. It works . . . I became the most-read person on LinkedIn globally on B2B selling, and this was part of the strategy to build a following. Everyone in sales needs an extensive and powerful network.
4. Prospect organizations are pyramidal as much as they'd like to be flat and meritocratic. Therefore, it is an everlasting imperative to drive conversations at the C-suite, VP, and operational management level for any complex sale—all levels, all the time. Consensus is essential for anything to happen. Go for them all at the same time rather than at the snail's pace approach of just one person at a time.

5. Leverage LinkedIn for social engineering or social conquesting. This is the practice of divining the exact prospects within an incumbent competitor's installed base. Connect with thought leaders in your space, influential CMOs or SVPs of Sales of competitive vendors, when you look at your second-degree connections in Navigator. The connections in common results are ranked by some sort of propensity algorithm. Simply click under each contact in Connections in Common, and look for patterns. You'll see the same people emerging over and over. Bingo! Unfortunately, even if you block your connections, the enemy can also see the second-degree connections of your network, but most people are ignorant of the potential here. Therefore, in ultra-competitive markets, I'd advise new business sellers not to connect by first degree on LinkedIn with prospective client leaders. Note: Generally speaking, you don't want to open with a LinkedIn connection request, but perhaps you have a referral or strong context for doing so. Maybe you're wanting to establish a first-degree node within the account to open up the database if you don't have Sales Navigator.
6. Pattern interruption is why COMBO Prospecting works. The channels don't matter as much as something unexpected that arrests the prospect's attention. I've still never met a seller who's not a beast on the phone on any continent, even in the heart of Silicon Valley. People fall into ruts or habits, so break yours by crowdsourcing a template file of sales verbiage and tactics that are getting responses. Using the collective wisdom is the best way to create your own templates.
7. Your own venture capitalists, CEO, board members, and angel investors can accelerate deals by miles even in the current quarter. If they're not onboard to make these intros and communicate from the top to the bottom of the organizations they back, then you have the wrong support system in place. Sit down with your CEO, and open that channel immediately.

8. Military strategy is Napoleonic when it's constantly changing in real time. Such is guerrilla warfare. Exhaust any warm introduction you know within the target organization at any level. You'll be shocked by the one degree of separation between a random assistant in a mail room and the CFO's husband.
9. You have not completed prospecting a company until you receive a "no" at all the right levels. Always prospect every lead to a "no" because it is the most magical word in sales—no more false hope, no more wasted time. Let it thicken your skin. Selling is a rejection-based business, and you must become antifragile. You'd rather get a "no" decision on 50 key target accounts and close 5 to smash your quota than be wishy-washy and have happy ears, with a tidal wave of ambivalent blowback and skinny kids.
10. Conferences and networking events are filled with C-levels. Book a hotel across the street and schedule a wave of meetings there. The conference floor, exhibition hall, and parties are noise—eschew the hot wings! Private dinners at Michelin restaurants work.
11. Every sales leader should be publishing on LinkedIn, sharing use-cases, subject-matter expertise, and genuine insights. Pull prospects toward you inbound with compelling content. Set your value agenda, and proactively kill potential objections. Challenge the conventional wisdom and status quo. Brainstorm with your solutions consultant for ideas nobody's heard before that only your solution can address.
12. Productivity is a myth. Like a keystone holds a medieval arch above the doors, massive persistent and smart activity in one key area will yield the greatest results. It is just as much about quality as it is quantity, so develop scalable systems. You as an individual are a brand, and the one thing you should always be doing is prospecting intelligently and wholeheartedly. "The power of a brand is inversely proportional to its scope," says Al Ries.
13. The grass is rarely greener. I almost never see a seller leave a company for a better scenario. From one frying pan into another tow-

ering inferno they leap like Mario and Luigi. Ramp to consistent brilliant results and put a ding in the universe. President's Club winners are seldom managers but make much more money and have infinitely better work/life balance.

The Importance of Multi-Threading

To close a significant deal, you need the line of business, IT team, stakeholders, C-suite, and procurement—it takes a village to close a deal in this modern age. You need to establish multiple bridges to span the moat into the castle. These are called threads, and the number-one reason deals don't close is because the seller is working single-threaded or is dependent on one stakeholder. Even the most senior of people won't sign off unless they are convinced that there is consensus for the business case and change management.

When I'm doing deal reviews, any time I notice that someone has only one contact record in the CRM, I know that the deal has a low propensity of actually closing. Go multi-thread the account is my advice. If one stakeholder says "no," go attack the account from another angle. If the CIO says "no," go try other IT folks lower on the food chain. Maybe this is too technical for the CIO to care about now. Maybe the CFO cares about how it's impacting the top or bottom line. Perhaps there are friendlies in nontechnical strategic areas who will benefit from what you offer. I've even seen a prospector who got in through procurement itself, ensuring that his solution was on their supplier preference sheet to get shortlisted.

I typically start any pursuit campaign at the very top of the marketing or sales organization. I work with that executive's personal assistant and ask, "What if I really wanted to set a meeting with Mrs. Big—how would I actually do it?" They always love to provide an email address from which they'll then vet you or send your stuff to the right internal division. Do this one time, then bypass the EA even though it's risky. I do that by sending an InMail to the C-level on a separate day.

I can't tell you how many initial calls to the top of the org got me to an EA that pipelined me right to the Center of Excellence for my product or service. Gold calls are the ones to an EA, and they can champion you because they run that C-level's life. Give them complete respect and the benefit of the doubt to set up a time for you.

Now if I start to get crickets from C-levels, I'll work down the organizational chart. I always get asked what the right cadence is. Think of the organization like a pyramid, and move slower toward the top. COMBO the C-suite on a biweekly basis, maybe even bimonthly. COMBO the VP layer weekly. COMBO the operational layer or approvers every 72 hours until you get a genuine "no." Start high and seek to get yourself sponsored down, but quickly move to driving multi-threaded outreach concurrently. Linear prospecting is for losers because each month rolls into the next as you wait and wait. Before you know it, it's a new quarter, and then you try for the next person in the account; then the year is almost gone, and you've missed your sales target . . . if you've survived that long. A huge piece of this method is that you're actually trying to prospect to the "no" because nature abhors a vacuum.

COMBO hinges on concurrent multi-threading. If you do this properly, you can open 20 opportunities in 100 named accounts in a six-month period. You should pick 50 dream accounts, the logos you'd put in a trophy case, and then multi-thread COMBOs to the six to nine decision-makers in each account, going 5 to 12 touches deep.

A strategy I love is keeping a subset of the top 25 decision-makers in your book and putting them on perma-call. This means you're going to call them around the clock without any COMBOs at all until someone picks up. When I think of an auto-magical hot-switching technology like ConnectAndSell, I think of the sheer luxury of having this done for you in real time. Thank you to the genius Chris Beall for his thought leadership in this area; interactive feedback with him definitely contributed to the solidification of ideas in this book.

Not all of you will be able to convince your boss to buy DiscoverOrg (email tracking software), have the right CRM like Salesforce, or invest in Sales Navigator. I'd require the best sales tools if I were you after diving headlong into this book. Maybe the best strategy is to buy them a copy of this book, hand it to them, and say that they need to read it because you'll be testing them at an upcoming sales meeting on which sales tools matter the most.

If you have only a phone and a free LinkedIn and email account, you can still drive a COMBO strategy with multi-threading. Work the account proactively, early, up high, and across several stakeholder groups or divisions.

COMBOs to Conquer Executive ADD

Neuroscience has revealed that the average human brain can remember about 20 to 30 seconds. I think it's more like 5 seconds. Try to remember a friend's phone number with 9 or 10 digits. Now add the country code. Now add a 4-digit extension. It becomes near impossible once you exceed 5 seconds.

In a world where an executive has hundreds of tasks to achieve with tight budgets, and needs a full-time executive assistant who is also completely overworked, it's unlikely you're ever going to make it into the executive's priority sub-list. Mike Bosworth put it plainly: "The human brain only has seven slots and so as sellers, we must fight to make it into one of them."[20]

Repetition alone won't cut it. The research that says you have to have between 5 and 12 personalized touches to educate and then you will suddenly land a meeting is no longer true. Two thousand other emails were sent to that target this month, and the average is about 225 per day. This executive, or their EA, checks their in-box/phone 250 times per day, typically marking spam and clearing. No, no, no.

What I've isolated with COMBO is that the combinations themselves become the signal in the noise. The act of fast sequencing of blended touches sticks out because it conveys a kind of pattern-interrupt that makes the prospect think, "Wow, Jane is persistent." In fact, it creates such a bee swarm that the prospect will sometimes seek to hire that seller rather than be perturbed at the interruption.

Why so fast on the receipt point? It's neuroscience. Prospects are like Dory the Fish—they have short-term memory loss. You must bash in:

phone rings, message alert sounds, email chimes, Twitter DM alerts. Bam-bam-bam-bam! The closer together the better. Exasperated, they may actually snap out of the malaise of midday pre-caffeine fog and, hallelujah, read your outreach.

The rule of COMBO is a universal law that is in part based on the power of the human voice. Your voice affects the COMBO just like the physical shockwave effect that happens when an adult sees a baby. Your voice must be the heart of any COMBO strategy. So it's never a COMBO if you're not using an H2H channel. Remember the five-second rule, and you must execute this punchy COMBO outreach in under two minutes. Ninety seconds would be ideal. Build your list the night before, and manually track your progress. Outside the hours of 9–5, there is no executive assistant blocking the executive's phone or killing InMail messages. It's a golden opportunity to break through first thing in the morning while they're driving to work or having their coffee.

Another crucial set of prospecting laws for COMBO is about brevity. Email subject lines should be two to three words max and contain a + sign. The weirder the subject line, the better: Growth + Notre Dame. Revenue + Bilbo Baggins. The email body should never exceed four sentences. Remember, they're going to check Outlook or Gmail on a smartphone. You need to show them how a similar client or competitor made or saved money. Show me the money!

You must have a powerful call to action (CTA). You can suggest two specific dates to make scheduling flawless. You can also use the Weinberg terms: *visit, fit*, and *value*. "When would be a good time to visit to see if there's a fit for creating value for Acme Corp?"

What I'll tell you is that to even the most blue-blooded, formal bank CXOs, colloquial English is better than looking like a robot or unsolicited drip email campaign. Design all your communication for high-level prospects to look natural, spontaneous, and massively relevant. You want your prospect to think: "Wow! If this person can be this helpful and organic, imagine the kind of trusted advice and insights she can bring if I let her onto the premises."

Remember the vampire rule of prospecting: Once they let you in, it's over. Being on-site dramatically increases the probability of revenue. That's why there are less on-sites than ever. That also reminds me of the rule of interactivity: When the prospect starts to drive the deal from the front, it's going to close. When you're chasing shadows and trying to hound a prospect to the next step, it has an ultra-low probability of closing.

Breaking Through to CXOs and Board Members

One of the greatest hidden paths to strategically creating an opportunity is reaching out to a board member, even through social media. Respond to their tweet, engage with content they've published on LinkedIn, send a targeted InMail, even hook in with Facebook if there is business context.

The truth is that almost no one is trying to sell at the very top. If they want to sell HR solutions, they sell to the VP of HR. Or many others sell to the same small number of CIOs. It's a recipe for disaster to hunt the same obvious contacts in the account. Think about the internal or external customer and how they can create pull and a compelling business case for change. You have to think chief executive officer, venture capitalists, or board members. Those people are easily revealed online and within LinkedIn.

One of the most lethal Sales Navigator techniques is to view the decision-maker themselves; maybe it's the CMO. Once you save them as a lead against an account, look at the lead recommendations, which suggest those within the company who are similar. My estimation is that this is an algorithm that predicts who this person interfaces with the most on the back end, so it's like peering into a crystal ball of data.

Maybe it's a random VP of Financial Planning and Analysis, some actuary who de-risks executive decisions. Maybe it's a general counsel or a random person they just happen to hang out with because they were in the same sorority or book club. The point is that establishing multiple contacts to gather information and support, using the multi-threading strategy, is often the best way to obtain personal cell numbers. There have been deals opened up and won using this strategy. In LinkedIn, go beyond just looking down the list of people "also viewed" in someone's profile. Live in Sales Navigator to find the real sales clues for identifying the executive power base and its linkages.

Of course, the easiest way to get to a C-level or board member is through someone they know and trust. In Sales Navigator, you can see connections in common and connections within one's own company. How many times does your own CTO know a prospect's CXO (CIO, CFO, CEO, VP of Engineering, etc.), but you as a seller feel too disconnected internally to leverage that connection? Be up front with your sales manager and country head that you will be asking for pertinent internal referrals when you start your new job, and ensure that they sign you up for Sales Navigator Enterprise Edition. This will allow you to see how your entire company, not just licensed Navigator users, connects into the prospect's employee base.

Who do you work with or know who knows someone in this dream account? That's the most important path to revenue that I show you. Fortune favors the bold, so you have to reach very high immediately, go upstream of the dreaded RFP or purchasing cycle, and start generating value with the right group of people. Start sparking them with your content, and start showing them what's possible.

Anatomy of Giving Good Social Phone

Again, kudos to Kenny Madden for coining the term the *social phone*. COMBO Prospecting is the idea that multiple contacts and blended channels are more powerful. A cold call is bold but quite dumb because you are simply taking a shot in the dark. Now it's really a quick search to find the kind of intel on a prospect that used to take months. I liken this to sending letters back to the British Empire by boat versus Skype today. With a simple Sales Navigator profile skim, a Google search, or a look into your CRM system history, you can glean a strong reference point to begin creating trust and position yourself as an expert. Some people call this the ledge of a call.

Always do pragmatic research on their industry, their company, and the individual. Then make the approach all about them rather than about you.

You will notice that many a calling template looks exactly the same, saying "how are you today?" and asking for the "appropriate person" or "just 15 minutes of your time." Don't use them! Friending approaches and sales speak simply paint you as a low-level seller. When following up, never use phrases such as "checking in" and "touching base." Never, ever remind them of your failed past attempts to reach them. Finally, never show any form of frustration with them ignoring you; just remain politely determined to break through.

Jill Konrath's *SNAP Selling* does a phenomenal job of breaking down the clichés. Her first book, *Selling to Big Companies*, is highly recommended reading about how to nail the "what to say and how to say it" part of prospecting.

Everything hinges on the phone because email alerts, text messages, Facebook Messenger updates, Twitter direct messages or mentions, LinkedIn InMails, and more all take place on smartphone apps. What you really have to conceptualize is that you get an unprotected clear shot to the prospect if you communicate outside of EA hours, which is when a direct message could actually reach a VP.

LinkedIn is the world's first self-healing database or social CRM. When you build out a custom stream in Sales Navigator by saving all your best leads and accounts, you suddenly have a fertile calling bed from which to make prospecting calls the next day. For example, you could call just people mentioned in the news or just contacts who have shared an article or update. You could interact with the update by liking or commenting and then pick up the phone and mention something you read. This already puts you ahead of 99 percent of lazy salespeople.

There is no excuse for giving bad phone because there is no need for any call to be cold, and you should now have a value narrative that never mentions your products or solutions. Anyone can find context for engagement by leveraging the power of social and then, rather than friending, lead with value. Stay calm and just have a normal conversation. It's not astrophysics.

You don't need elaborate social selling systems or scripts. Simply be human and create value in the conversation for the person on the other end.

Some other versions of the social phone for mid- and lower-funnel include Skype, GoToMeeting, LogMeIn, BlueJeans, Webex, Join.Me, and Zoom. Video conferencing is ubiquitous, so do all you can to get face-to-face this way as the next best thing to being on-site.

Technologies tend to diverge not converge. Despite the massive convergence of the smartphone, you'll notice the plethora of apps and the fact that humans still do call each other, still have tablets, laptops, desktops, TVs, and keep adding to their tech stack just about every widget and doodad conceivable. But when you take the train or bus, what do you see? Everyone is glued to their smartphone and has their earbuds in. Texting is the next event horizon, and Mark Hunter has written brilliantly about ways to leverage text for prospecting properly today.

Pick up the social phone. The social phone means that you've used LinkedIn Sales Navigator or Premium to identify your best prospects. You've then used something like Data.com or DiscoverOrg to get direct dials. You've then called (and texted them) about what they're sharing on social media and left a message about the relevant bits they have showed they care about. Now you're blending, and you're not shackled by analysis paralysis. You've done less than a minute of pre-call targeting to get a quick topic to pivot on once you connect live. It's really devilishly simple. Use whatever LinkedIn feed you have access to for visibility into what prospects care about so you can call them with relevant conversation starters.

COMBO selling is designed to get you 1–3X pipeline within two quarters. While the social sellers are connecting and helping, you've already gotten your triple or quad returned and you're in discovery mode. Those who embrace the social phone get into the sales cycle much faster than the pure social sellers. Sometimes social sellers miss the boat entirely, feeling proud that they now have 50 more CFO connections even though it's probably their EA or virtual assistant who managed it for them.

Getting pumped to go make 30 triples is a matter of mindset. I love that scene in *Caddyshack* where Chevy Chase is getting into the zone by "being the ball." You're reaching out and touching someone, but you're wired at the reptilian brain level to abhor rejection. So how can you buck the trend and do it anyway? Mindset and discipline: This is the idea that the more hits you take, the more fired up you get. It reminds me of an MMA fighter taking blows and just smiling and begging for more, dancing around the ring trash talking. The best fighters know they're going to take a few hits on the chin, so they're mentally prepared.

Remaining calm and being real are critical components of successful calling psychology. Speaking from the heart, being honest, and not having the movie phone voice are crucial. You're better off dialing through 10 or 20 numbers and just having conversations than overthinking it.

The number-one rule of prospecting by phone is "make it a game and have fun!" You may say, "But Tony, I fear it worse than death and dismemberment!" I know . . . what's wild about calling is how long it can take to make 50 dials if you don't time-block. It's crucial to shut everything off, keep a manual log, and keep your triples short. Lock yourself in a room and throw away the key! You should be able to bang out 30 to 50 calls and send immediate email follow-ups in under two hours.

You may be thinking right now, This guy is repetitive . . . time-blocking, 30 triples—how many times is going to say this? Yep, but will you actually do it? Very few actually do.

Decide you're going to enjoy getting a "no" because it means no more false hope. Every one of them takes you closer to a "yes," and every one of them stops you wasting any more time or energy with someone who will not buy from you.

When you connect, calmly explain the reason you are calling as if you were calling a friend or relative with good advice. Exert calm, confident, and positive control. "I am calling because . . ." Then focus on the business value you offer rather than droning on about your company and products. Explain why they should talk with you—what's in it for them. Give proof of your value by telling them about other clients for whom you've delivered bottom-line results in terms of dollars, percentage improvements, and also gains in KPIs or metrics that they care about. Do you actually understand how your customers measure progress and results in their business? What are their industry benchmarks for customer retention, and what is their rate of churn? If they use net promoter score (NPS), what is the industry benchmark, and how do they rank comparatively? If they measure debtors, do they use daily sales outstanding (DSO), and what is best practice in their industry?

Make sure you have a preset list of direct dials, or even switchboard numbers if that's all you can source, and the "who's who in the zoo" you're going to reach out to beforehand. Here's a huge secret: Call directly out of your Sales Navigator feed. Use a clear phone line, not a scratchy cell phone in a back boiler room. Never use hands-free because you sound like you're in the bottom of a well, and you may cause distrust if they wonder who else is listening. Some people like a landline and some use headsets, but the risk with headsets is that they can be scratchy if Bluetooth batteries go low. VoIP over a lousy network is worse, as packet loss creates chop—the most distracting of the telephone audio problems. Cell phones are, interestingly, often the highest fidelity, lowest latency option, depending on where you are relative to towers and congestion.

A great noise-cancelling microphone can do wonders and lets you talk with your hands, which, for most people, directly affects how natural they sound. I am always amused when I see people walking down a crowded street, gesturing like crazy to make a point to the person on the other end of their hands-free cell calls. Anyone who won't invest $100 or so in great gear is not taking the phone or their career seriously. Test your signal by calling a friend or loved one. Again, unless you're The Donald, never make business calls using a hands-free phone!

When you call into organizations, call the top dog first, the CEO of the problem you solve. Call the C-level executive who reigns supreme over all the domains to which you can deliver benefits. The CFO will refer you to the CIO, and the CIO can't refuse the CFO. There's a pecking order; you all know this. The board member regulates the CEO because that leader has to answer to the board's whims. The first-biggest mistake is trying to start with a bottom-up groundswell.

Call in high and ask the executive assistant for guidance after you've treated her like she is actually the CEO rather than a gatekeeper. Mike Scher suggests treating the EA as a tour guide. Whatever you do, you must push beyond their trigger response to ask you for an email or your capabilities deck, which they plan to file away in the trash email folder.

Leverage fear to your advantage. If you're not scared to talk to the person you're about to call first in that account, you're calling too low. Without butterflies in your stomach, just like the ones you had before you asked your significant other on that first date or to marry you, you're not reaching your full potential in prospecting. Face the fear and do it anyway. Discomfort is the price of success.

You've got to stay psyched throughout the calling block because you're going to have streaks where all you get are sterile machines. If you follow the COMBO core method, you will start to get some immediate email pings back. So have faith and don't lose heart!

Everyone is trying to get your email out of their in-box or your request off their desk. They will push it down and sideways around the organizational chart ad infinitum. Your emails and voice mails are going to get forwarded all around in a massive game of telephone until you get the lantern fish to come forward. Stay on message knowing that you must be able to pitch your technology in a way that a two-year-old could understand. Practice with your spouse, who is already putting up with your sales mumbo jumbo! At the end of the day, all prospects care about is making or saving money.

To paraphrase the late, great David Sandler, "You can't derive your satisfaction from selling." You can't define your self-worth or happiness by whether or not you succeed or fail on the phone that day. You must be bigger than that and take the high road. Keep yourself whole inside, and be the prime mover committed to making a positive difference for your customers. Don't be shaken by any negative feedback. Keep pushing through the morass that is the slog of outbound prospecting. Build a tremendous daily cadence and be rigorous. Massive discipline is how you hit that same list day after day after day. After a while, opportunities unlock like a series of gates in the Panama Canal.

Positive mental attitude (PMA) is everything. You've got to be curious and get a kick out of making the dials and hearing the voice of the one you seek to help. Directly address the prospect by name, and super briefly explain why you're calling. Don't ask: "Is this a good time?" Don't ask: "How are you today?" Just provide brief context, and then go right into the reason you're calling and the way you quantifiably helped a similar company. Selling is the transference of belief, so show you believe you can help them. Confidence is king, and content of your conversation is queen.

Sell the appointment, not the product. Brian Tracy is a huge proponent of this. Sometimes disarming them with blatant appointment setting makes them say, "You've got three minutes right now—hit me."

Be blunt. Ask outright for a meeting, no circumlocution or beating around the bush. Be honest about your motives to set an appointment. Tell them it's important, and then ask: "When is the best time to meet?"

After making 10,000 hours of prospecting calls over three decades, I've found a bizarre inertia that plays out. When I resist making the calls, it feels like a Sisyphean task (pushing a boulder up a hill) to get back on the horn. When I start pounding away on the blower with reckless abandon, it gets easier and easier, and hark . . . I connect. That's the beauty of a focused two hours of phone prospecting—it pays dividends.

While you're calling, visualize connecting with key prospects. Set an intention to make contact at the highest practical level, and you'll be surprised how often you get someone amazingly high up the food chain that you never believed you could talk to.

You really should read Jill Konrath, as she is brilliant about the phone. Here also are some tips from my good friend Steve Hall:

- Spend a lot of time on a generic message, and then tailor it to every individual to hit their hot spots. (Caveat from me: Sometimes there is a relevance paradox where too much tailoring could look needy, so it's a fine line.)
- Be prepared. You will be asked to send emails, you'll get voice

mail, you'll get EAs, and very occasionally you'll get the CEO. Have a plan prepared with template content for each eventuality.

- In your message, use curiosity and tell them as little as possible commensurate with getting a meeting. Your value proposition isn't about why they should buy from you; it's about why they should talk with you.
- Be confident and develop rapport with the EA, and remember everything they say to you. You'll use it next time because often you'll have to make multiple calls to build familiarity.[21]

Giving good phone is ultimately about preparing and then being courageous and relentlessly disciplined, just like Jeff Horn, who won a world title in a massive upset by endlessly moving forward, hitting Manny Pacquiao's fists with his face to get close and battle on his own terms. Beyond relentless courage you also need the right narrative, and you must feel passionately worthy to become the trusted adviser who engineers consensus and a winning business case for the customer. Self-belief, passion, cunning, determination. You need all this to execute COMBO with the phone. You must also have the ability to eat rejection for breakfast and spit it into the bucket in the corner while they shove smelling salts up your nose . . . bring it on!

Growth Hacks—Thinking like a Marketer

Each day when you get to work, be data driven and see who opened your previous outreach the most by using tools such as Cirrus, ToutApp, or YesWare. Follow up again if you see a number greater than three. Many times, you'll send outreach to a CXO and see 25 shares, and you can see from which device and region of the country as well. You should be sending out all your presentations in ClearSlide so you can track which page they stick on the longest; yes, it's often the pricing page. Ensure that all outreach and attachments can be tracked for engagement.

You want to be a micro-marketer and create some thought leadership pieces in LinkedIn Publisher. These should talk about the top three to five pain points you solve for clients, along with anonymized case studies and Challenger-style content. When you rattle the cages and shake up the trees, 85 percent of prospects are going to go assess who you are on social, specifically LinkedIn, and view your profile. You should have built a strong brand there, with compelling articles posted. This sets the tone and establishes you as a high-caliber subject-matter expert who is trusted by others in the field.

If you're at the pinnacle of your sales career journey, you'll have a very specific named account list or you'll work regionally in specific target prospect companies. You'll have three to five arch competitors, and the pressure of commoditization will be bearing down, causing buyers to focus on price and wait as long as possible before dealing with the likes of you, the self-described "trusted adviser" salesperson. I don't know about you, but I'd engage only with people who exhibit the brass cajones to phone me up and convince me that I could be making a lot more money if I intelligently considered changing from my crumbling status quo!

Interruption only works when it's relevant, so having intel on the decision-makers is essential. The likelihood of landing a meeting with a powerful decision-maker—who can fast track you into an active evaluation or smoke out the actual buying committee—increases 10 times when you are using Sales Navigator, your own CRM data, Google, and a sales intelligence suite. Are you mixing LinkedIn Sales Navigator custom streams to do advanced searches, saving the right people in each account, and finding linchpin content to reach out with over the phone with your sales intelligence tools?

Here's how to penetrate any account. Let's say you're selling Salesforce to Acme Widget Company. You would first search your own CRM (Salesforce integrates with Sales Navigator and everything else that matters), and then look up the account in DiscoverOrg. It would instantly give you the direct dials and emails of the head of sales, head of marketing, and executive leadership. You would cross-reference this to Sales Navigator's view of that prospect (they won't even know you're viewing them if you use Navigator). You read their profiles and study the last 10 posts they have shared. Now Google their names + the company name and filter results in News to see quotes from an individual at a recent conference, interview, or press release.

Now call the direct lines and reference what they've said, and then leap into your value narrative: "In working with others in your industry, I'm seeing XYZ as a key issue. Is that something you're grappling with as you seek to acquire and retain more of the right customers? I'd like to share some ideas on this; when can you clear some space in your calendar for 40 minutes?" If you get voice mail, mention their quote and that you have relevant ideas based on it. Say that you want to discuss how they could better drive top-line revenue.

Once you've identified any level of heartbeat within the prospect organization, you need to think like a marketer seeking to nurture the buyer throughout their journey. There are systems such as Marketo, Pardot, and HubSpot, which effectively execute lead nurturing where high-value prospects go into a drip sequence. You can retarget these prospects with white papers on LinkedIn. You can go remarket to these folks across Facebook. You'd typically partner up with marketing to pull off these latter scenarios, but the mere act of proactively collaborating with the marketing team will set you apart and favor you for driving leads within your own company.

Secure buy-in internally to fund a Very Important Top Officer campaign; here is how VITO (Parinello) works for me. I've never met a C-level who doesn't accept courier mail or a FedEx envelope. Inside is a plain manila envelope with just their name and then inside a single page with no company logo on it. The letter states the bottom-line business case of increased revenue, efficiency, cost savings, innovation to carve out a competitive advantage, and a very specific time you'll call or would like to meet. Then you've got a shot. The CEOs I've spoken to say they aren't looking to make friends or talk about their kids and fishing trip. You've got to be relevant and to-the-point without being arrogant or bragging about your clientele. All they care about is what you can prove you can do for them to transform results.

One last growth hack is around closing deals by discussing money up front to build constructive tension. But you also want to gate the deal by always putting up a high price tag and then understanding if there's a threshold that avoids a request for proposal (RFP). You can always restrict the contract terms to a certain cap or ceiling, but this will allow you to strike early to take the deal off the table for competition. It relates to prospecting because you have to operate like the most venomous snake in the Australian outback—it developed that lethal injection because prey is scarce. For those disruptive sellers or entrepreneurs, this is sound advice in any market.

Ghost Your Own CEO's Profile

This one is hard to believe, but CEOs will often allow a senior salesperson to ghost-drive their LinkedIn profile and work with preapproved content and template messages. What's really wild about ghost-driving is that even being the CEO of a hot start-up company doesn't guarantee you a meeting.

Most CEOs are consumed by delivering for their company, and many neglect their personal life and brand. Burnout is common. Why don't you offer personal education and assistance to the CEO on how to build their personal brand in B2B social? In doing so, you can personally help them while also driving revenue for the company. Here is why it works. Senior customer executives are more likely to meet a peer from the potential supplier organization. This is because it strokes their egos, and they believe there will be industry or competitor insights rather than a sales pitch.

You can differentiate and outmaneuver your competition by ghost-driving for CEOs. Analysis on the social presence of every Fortune 500 CEO was published on CEO.com.[22] Here are some of the findings, which showed little change in behavior from the previous survey:

- Sixty-one percent of CEOs have no social presence on any of the top six social platforms.
- Of those who are on social, 70 percent are solely on LinkedIn.

- Forty percent of CEOs on Twitter don't tweet at all.
- Almost none understand social strategy and the interconnectedness of all the platforms.

Become the trusted expert your own CXO can rely upon. Don't be intimidated. It's not as scary as you think, and here is how to execute once you have the keys to their LinkedIn. Focus outreach around events where your CEO can appear. It reduces friction when a CEO is inviting a prospect to Dreamforce or another relevant conference or thought leadership dinner. This is infinitely better than trying to land discovery calls where the prospect, another C-level, knows they're going to get cornered or guilted into moving forward with an evaluation they may not want. They also just don't want to disappoint someone they respect.

A powerful strategy here is to get your CEO, president, or cofounder to start sharing thought leadership articles on LinkedIn. I've seen trusted senior salespeople gain access to their CEO's LinkedIn profile and start to land event invites this way. I've done it myself for my clients. You could conceivably utilize this idea for prospecting, but you need to have the necessary level of trust with your CEO. Especially powerful is to ghost-drive your CEO's LinkedIn account around a specific event that they are going to attend. Here is why it makes sense.

An outside sales call costs up to six times more than an inside sales call.[23] On this note, many a start-up heeds the siren song of hiring guys in suits to go close enterprise deals ASAP. They increase their cash burn but not the commensurate revenue, and they start hemorrhaging money. Typically, they then fire the squadron before the first red ink dries on the MSA for a mere trial or pilot. You can make yourself the indispensable salesperson if you are the CEO's ghost-driver; you'll fireproof yourself and be the very last to be booted off the island!

It works this way: You use LinkedIn InMails and emails to set up neighborhood meetings for your CEO with you in attendance. These focus on a conference that's coming up or a planned trip to a particular city. Ideally, you and your CEO go and team-sell at the meeting. If the CEO can't attend, then you, acting as the CEO, simply hand off the meeting to yourself "due to unforeseen circumstances" just before the scheduled date.

There is even software to help you triangulate a large swath of potential clients in a geographical area! Data.com can be searched by city and state for a relevant list of prospects. RainKing also has a GPS-like heat map element that you can use to schedule a bunch of meetings around a nominated city with similar prospects. Even Sales Navigator, with its friendly Boolean search interface, enables you to identify the executives in a particular region.

Call the executive assistants of a targeted list, and be the EA of your own CEO. Ask if they can find 30 minutes for your boss and theirs to chew the fat. "Hi Daisy. My boss, the CEO, is in town Thursday speaking at a conference, and he asked me to tee up a meeting with your boss because he has some research he thought would be of interest to Bill. How is his calendar for dinner or breakfast on Wednesday? If that's no good, how about 20 minutes for them to talk over coffee?" Simply being in their area dramatically ups the probability of a meeting. They can just open a conference room and meet with you and your boss. You're already there, so they don't have to feel guilty about committing you to travel costs.

Neighborhood techniques work flawlessly for conferences, too. Special thanks to Scott Britton, who came up with the best conference idea: Call every single prospect attending or on the speakers' list. Then, either for yourself or your CXO, book a meeting room across the street at a premium hotel and secure back-to-back meetings there. In general, neighborhooding and setting meetings with like-minded people attending events is a good strategy. Throwing events while at conferences is also very powerful. Put together a VIP dinner with extra seats, and as C-levels roll through your booth that day, get 50 business cards and then text them all about the dinner. You should be able to fill out a dinner party of 20 that way.

Use your own CEO and CXO team to help you elevate everything you do. Be known internally as the stately honey badger that can build pipeline like no other in the history of the world. But also be known as someone who operates with intelligent stealth, finesse, gravitas, and business acumen. Be seen as someone who talks the language of customers and who understands the language of business, achieving important outcomes, managing risk, and delivering on a rock-solid business case.

In short, you are the one and only person worthy of the log-in and password of the CXO's LinkedIn account. This is because you are intelligent, well-read, and have command of the English language. You humbly enhance their brand, work with prearranged templates and scripts, build out their network with high-quality contacts, and leverage their own time to drive growth in their business.

Sales Coaching from a CEO Buyer

Six months before finalizing content for this book, I delivered a two-day sales training workshop in Singapore. We had more than 80 salespeople and managers in attendance from seven countries, and the primary purpose was to enable everyone to personally create sales pipeline.

I was told: "The number-one problem salespeople have is not having enough pipeline." Yet lack of pipeline is a symptom rather than a root cause. The real issues are typically a lack of disciplined daily activity in working referrals and prospecting. More root issues are:

- Not enough know-how in driving sales success through old-school high levels of effective activity combined with new-school digital engagement
- Lack of customer industry knowledge or poor understanding of the client
- Inability to leverage personal networks and technologies to find the right path for connection with decision-makers
- Inadequate insight and value narrative needed for senior engagement

The VP of Sales who engaged me for the workshop with his team is a sales master in every sense of the term. He and I were in harmony from the beginning. He maintained a laser-like focus on helping his sellers create an industry-specific point of view that they could take to potential clients. As part of the agenda, he invited Hari Krishnan, CEO at Property Guru Group, to join for a one-hour interview. Property Guru is the market leader in its industry in Asia and, prior to this CEO role, Hari held board of director positions and was head of LinkedIn in the Asia-Pacific region and Japan. As such, he is impeccably credentialed to provide the most senior buyer perspective.

He was asked this powerful question: "On what basis do you as the CEO of a market leader engage directly with sellers?" Everyone at the workshop was riveted, and here is my paraphrase of this sage CEO's advice for sellers (with my own advice added occasionally within brackets):

> If you want to get to me then it's going to happen only through a warm introduction from someone I know and trust. Understanding the nature of my relationship with the introducer will give you some context into how I am likely to receive your introduction.
>
> Cultivate multiple stakeholders in my organization and educate them on your solution, too. I don't make unilateral decisions or try to push decisions down the organization, so you need to build multiple relationships.
>
> Don't be creepy personal. Stick to business early in the relationship. Don't stalk on personal social platforms such as Facebook. I'm not seeking a new friend or looking for someone to buy me a meal or host me at an event. [Senior successful people are incredibly busy and would rather invest their time with family or where they have strong personal relationships.]
>
> Do your research. Seeking a conversation with me without doing your homework is unprofessional and shows a lack of respect. Don't drop names of competitors or reference industry trends that are not relevant to my region or business. The examples you use need to be

from within my geography and relate to what is happening in my markets.

Know my industry. As the market leader, I am not chasing disruptors, but I am interested in what relevant companies are doing. Know whom I define as my competition (current and emerging), and bring me insights about them, their strategies and initiatives. I am not seeking confidential information or trade secrets, nor should you offer them, but you must bring a perspective that is of value to me. [The VP of Sales doing the interview later commented that sellers should always seek to be a customer of their prospective client, or talk to some of their customers, as part of their own research. They should then take a perspective on how that experience could be improved.]

Don't appear arrogant. Assuming that your brand alone is the reason I should buy from you is a mistake. [If you're the market leader, don't tell the customer that you are dominant. Instead use the term *leader*, and earn their interest and trust rather than assume it.]

Take the time to understand how I define success. Know what motivates our organization and how we measure improvement and success. Focus on how you can help me achieve our KPIs and performance measures.

Aspire to be a trusted adviser. Not in a clichéd way, but differentiate yourself in the way you engage our organization by acting in our best interests rather than your own. Resist the urge to push and close when we are not ready. Trusted adviser status for a seller is achieved over time through alignment with my organization's success and me. "Your focus should be on my success as the customer rather than on your sales goal."[24]

According to Hari Krishnan, the three levels of relationship are:

1. **Trusted adviser:** I collaborate with you and involve you deeply in my planning process, and there is emotional, personal connection and trust.

2. **Partner:** I regard you as being strategic to my business, and I solicit your thoughts in the planning process.
3. **Vendor:** I transact with you and focus on price as the primary way of defining greater value.

This dispels the myth that trusted adviser is unachievable for sellers. Here is more important advice from me:

- Don't use LinkedIn as a spamming platform; instead, use it to research and find the best path for a warm introduction.
- Referrals are the fastest and highest probability for acquiring a new customer. This is why you must cultivate your networks and nurture your own brand.
- Once you've secured your path for an introduction, you need the right narrative to form the basis of the conversation, and it should set the agenda on insight and value.
- Treat the EA with respect, and have empathy for his need to protect the boss. Seek guidance and coaching.
- You must be wildly persistent across multiple channels if you are to break through.

In reading all this, you now have enough information to be the number-one performer in your company. Let's now look at supercharging lead flow and then turning up the heat deeper in the funnel. Then you can close predictably based on how you open a relationship, with the agenda firmly set on value and trust.

Supercharge Lead Flow—Pulling It All Together

If you're lucky, you have the ultimate sales machine: a crack team of SDRs firing on all cylinders, marketing driving a high-value content strategy, industry events, and a lead-nurturing machine, augmented with a third-party appointment-setting company like Frontline Selling. On top of that, you obsessively create quality opportunities yourself. All this means you have the healthiest pipeline in the known universe and exude nonhunger. You no longer need to pressure anyone to buy but rather work based on alignment of timing and priorities within your customer base. Your competitors entice you to move to them every month, and you just say, "No thanks, I'm happy here."

You know that compartmentalizing the business development roles isn't necessarily as powerful as having everyone in the organization, up to your own CEO, accountable to opening qualified conversations. In essence, everyone is responsible for setting meetings with qualified prospects, and you're seen as the lead dog. It's the most important responsibility of every employee in the company because the best product in the world is of little consequence without new clientele to benefit from its transformative results.

Regardless of the level of support, even if there's almost none, you drive your own marketing and pipeline creation. You obsessively focus on trigger events and referrals as the fastest path and highest probability of a sale. You are keenly aware that being strategic, by definition, means injecting yourself during the customer's "ignorant and unaware" phase to educate and inspire them to consider a far better state of affairs. You artfully spring from the bushes on social and grab the prospective customer's attention on the phone by delighting them with your surprising insights and business acumen. You guide them to their happy place of better results and a more secure career.

Your personal hallmark is disciplined, intelligent determination as you engineer value and the customer's buying process to eliminate competition. Most of your time is invested in building high-quality opportunity pipeline. Then you are qualifying whether a prospect is in a window where you can influence and build a business case with a future-state vision that drags them away from status quo apathy. A typical day in your work life as a masterful COMBO prospector looks like this. It's late afternoon, so you block all distractions and then:

- You take a plain piece of paper and pen that writes fast. You date it. Beside the clean plain sheet is your messy COMBO action sheet from the last 24 hours with tally marks. You now create your fresh call sheet for tomorrow.
- You get to work and check Cirrus, ToutApp, or YesWare for your analytics: Who clicked, who opened, who forwarded your emails?
- You open your shared spreadsheet called Key Target Accounts that lists your top 50 target names in alphabetical order. Each name has the date of last contact next to it, and you've memorized the "who's who of the zoo."
- You study the organizational chart in DiscoverOrg or RainKing, looking for triggers there and also in the Sales Navigator feed.
- It's approaching knock-off time for your prospects, and they are emerging from meetings. The perfect time to strike with high-intensity COMBO outreach! You first look each one up on LinkedIn, then you go to COMBO—basic triples at first.
- You're running hot and in the flow, so you adopt sextets: phone, voice mail, InMail, email, text, Twitter DM. Where possible, you call and email directly out of the CRM.
- You leave concise value narrative messages on voice mail, plus leave your phone number twice and say, "I'll follow up with a note."
- As rapidly as possible, you send an email to the prospect that opens by referencing that you just tried their line, or write "as per my voice mail . . ."
- You operate with confidence and know in your heart, soul, and every fiber of your being that you can help them, that they will want to talk to you once they understand how you can transform their business results. Your tone conveys the confidence that they will take your meeting.
- On a high, you stop, and your updated list is now the call sheet for tomorrow morning. It has an added column for you to track the number of COMBOs executed with new tally marks. Most everyone else has left for the day, but you leave knowing you've

earned success and that you're ready to be hyper-effective the next morning.

The next morning, you wake and shower with caffeine soap. On the way into the office, you consume a triple-shot coffee with a Red Bull chaser. You arrived before everyone else and, standing at your Varidesk so you're ergonomically poised with your headset, you take the updated list you created the previous evening. Then:

- You smile and immediately jump into COMBO outreach with all those folks, again after first looking them up on LinkedIn. You limit yourself to 90 seconds of research on each prospect before dialing. Where you can, you go the extra mile and adopt sextets: phone, voice mail, InMail, email, text, Twitter DM. Again, where possible, you call and email directly out of CRM.
- You follow the exact same COMBO process as the day before.
- As you finish your calls, the bewildered "sheeple" meander onto the sales floor like lambs to the slaughter to fire up their computers. Then they head out for java to complain about how the compensation plan is unfair, the marketing leads are poor, the SDRs aren't booking enough meetings for them, and no one answers the phone (when they themselves don't bother calling).
- It's 9:30 a.m. and you decline the invitation for coffee so you can instead update the CRM for the next hour or so, and then jump into dedicated activity on the opportunities already qualified and well into the sales funnel.
- You go to lunch having done more than a full day's work.
- Before you go home that day, around 4:30 p.m., you go again. Like Rocky, you bounce out of your corner ready to hit your prospects. Bam! Rejection—you just grin and move forward, ever forward, COMBO after COMBO.
- Then victory! Engagement with the right people based upon the right narrative and your persistence.

Call it whatever you choose: Sowing and reaping, attracting what you radiate, karma, God's blessing, the universe's favor—the harder you intelligently work, sincerely wanting the best for your customers, the more successful you will be. Luck has very little to do with it.

Turning Up the Heat Deeper in the Funnel

I could write another entire book on the subject of leveraging COMBO for things like negotiation and closing. What I have learned is that once the marlin is on the line, you must strip line (let it run) at times—but in the enterprise battleground, wild persistence is how you reel the fish into the boat. Once you've opened an opportunity, you cannot rest on your laurels. You must continue to educate, enable, and reach out via all manner of channels, even mid-funnel.

Once you've had the first on-site, bring some solutions experts and go meet again. Pre-wire each meeting with personal calls to understand agendas. Go in and cross-sell to the account while closing the first sale. Multi-thread and meet with more senior, more junior, and lateral contacts. If you are single-threaded in a deal, you're at high risk.

In her phenomenal book *SNAP Selling*, Jill Konrath talks about raising priorities as the *P* in SNAP. The book talks about counterintuitive ways to break into big accounts. The power of creating a sense of urgency and harnessing FOMO (fear of missing out) cannot be underestimated.

Deals go to the grave 90 days out, even on an 18-month sales cycle. You want to engage early, up high, and thread the account to as many friendly stakeholders as possible who will talk to you and "conduct the symphony" for both sides. The top seller closing Fortune 10 accounts is bringing in their own CTO, CMO, and CEO. This seller is bringing in multiple teams on both sides, both tactical and strategic, to craft a custom solution that is complex enough to maintain a value differential and box out competitors selling on features alone.

Jim Holden talks about this in his Four Stage Model. The key takeaway is to make a customer look like a hero by choosing you, as measured in cost savings, efficiency, revenue generated, innovation, and competitive advantage. These are the primary reasons that deals get done. Massive ROI happens, and people get promoted or leverage that breakthrough to switch companies into an even more influential role. Salespeople who embrace COMBO cultivate success at every level. Over the years, they focus on a vertical where they develop a massive network and subject-matter expertise that allows them to freely consult and advise on a range of issues. They may even recommend other harmonic vendors.

Imagine pulling a marlin into a deep-sea fishing boat. It takes one hell of an effort. In boxing, it's that final knockout punch after you've done rope a dope. This is a boxing strategy of pretending to be trapped against the ropes, enticing the opponent to throw tiring, ineffective punches. Muhammad Ali coined the term in the 1970s when he referred to a tactic he employed against George Foreman. Look how tactical Ali was, thinking on his feet, appearing weak when he was strong. Lying in wait, you must be patient and fiercely disciplined so as not to reveal too many cards and lose the fight.

You've got to have explosive cunning to knock out your opponent, and you've got to have the same to clinch a massively competitive strategic sale. You're waiting for your moment when the stars align and you have the perfect shot. Make no mistake, it's going to take massive action to steal business away from entrenched competitors who out-resource you in the knife fight of modern sales. The extra mile is a lonely place, and the vendor who gives their all in the process gains the richest reward as prospects take notice. Trusted adviser status is granted based on intent, value, effort, and collaboration. Teamwork unleashes the sword in the stone.

Dispelling Myths of the Serial Closer

The way you open a relationship and set the agenda is indeed far more important than how you seek to close. Thrashing around desperately pushing for the order is for amateurs. As stated earlier, the closing

COMBO depends on 1) coverage, 2) trust and confidence, and 3) commitment and partnership.

Asking for the customer's business must be earned and attempted only after the buyer has signaled they are ready to take that next step. The seller should never attempt to close until these three bases are covered:

1. Establish trust and rapport by being authentic, insightful, and a domain expert.
2. Agree on the compelling business value, as defined by them and with a future-state vision and rock-solid business case.
3. Understand their timing and priorities, as well as their process for evaluation, selection, and procurement.

Many salespeople make the mistake of pressuring their potential client when the buyer isn't in a position to commit to the purchase. Managers often push their sales team to offer discounts on one hand and threats of a price increase on the other if the buyer fails to meet the seller's deadline. Chris Beall says, "Pressure-filled closing is often a symptom of a weak, thin pipeline which creates rational desperation." I've had crazy bosses over the years instruct my teams and me to go sit in the reception areas of client offices until we have the order. Threatening customers, withdrawing discounts, and acting desperate is the worst way to attempt a close.

Difficulty in closing is almost always a symptom of not opening the relationship properly or not managing the sales process effectively. This is why having the right value narrative and executing COMBO masterfully at the opening phase is critical. Objections are usually evidence of the fact that the seller has made mistakes by pushing before trust and value have been established and without the necessary understanding of the customer's timing, priorities, and processes.

All managers need to know that they cannot manage by results and must instead focus on driving activities and actions while coaching strategy and skills. Read *Cracking the Sales Management Code* by Jason Jordan and Michelle Vazzana to go deep on this topic. Ask the right questions at the beginning of the quarter, and help identify and execute the right actions that create progression of the sale. Firing up the blowtorch with just days to go for hitting sales targets, after neglecting the inputs that create success, is a surefire way to damage relationships, undermine credibility, and drive down price and margin.

A deal, once properly qualified and quantified, will naturally follow an organic progression to a close—but not on its own. Maintain intensity and momentum using COMBO to touch everyone who represents risk and who can provide support. Objections are signs that you've made a blunder or you're misaligned with the buyer. If you sell technology, you'll have two sides to every deal, the strategic and the technical. You should be smart enough to be the conductor of the symphony and bring in your sharpest stakeholders on either side. The buyer has a supporting cast and so should you.

So much has been written about the art of closing, and all the *Glengarry Glen Ross* "coffee is for closers" style high-pressure techniques are stale as a cracker. What you need to do is build synergy in collaboration on a solution worth more than the sum of its parts. You need to foster interactivity around solving a problem or unlocking an opportunity. You need to mutually quantify a business case based on the relevant use-cases that prove economic value as seen in cost savings or revenue uptick. By communicating this intention and sitting on their side of the table from the start, you've got a shot.

The myth is that a close is something that you do to the prospect, not with the customer. In fact, if you focus intently on the delivery phase of customer execution, you can build out a logical sequence of events that includes a "go live" date. By focusing the customer's attention on the product or service going live within their organization and beginning to deliver the value from day one of the effective date, they've already pre-closed in their mind. You work backward from that positive outcome, saying something like, "I don't consider myself successful until this is delivering for you and your company." That's being a transparent trusted adviser because it's not about a fat commission and handoff to others; instead, you convey that you're sticking around and seeing the implementation through. Some forward-thinking companies have instituted blended compensation plans to ensure that this happens, as there's a vested interest in success and renewals.

There are a couple of critical gauges for understanding whether a deal is going to close and move forward. The first is whether the prospect is pulling from the front rather than the seller relentlessly pushing from behind. The second is the level of interactivity in the cycle. If you're constantly chasing prospects down for their time, it's unlikely to be a sizable agreement if it is one at all. So how can you influence this?

Savvy COMBO salespeople are focused on fostering interactivity at many levels in the organization: top-down, bottom-up, middle-out, C-suite, board of directors, and warm referrals in network. They leave no stone unturned, building groundswell and connectivity into the account as they accelerate the deal to a close.

The tipping point is once the deal goes from brainstorming with the client to the client starting to push you to reach climax. Since "opening is the new closing" (according to Anthony Iannarino), you should start conversations with the main decision-makers, lateral stakeholders, IT head (if you sell technology), and other stakeholders. Any group that your solution touches, who could be brought in early to build even more consensus, is worth reaching out to with blended COMBO methods to build an army of support.

At the end of the day, there is no ability to close or even propose a solution, unless you are masterfully effective at prospecting and opening. SPIN, solution selling, value selling, Challenger, Miller Heiman, strategic selling, Sandler, and all the qualification frameworks—they are all moot unless you have an actual live and kicking prospect. If you can't gain access to the buyer, if you're incapable of carrying the right value narrative, if you cannot secure simple commitments for time and access at the beginning, then you're knocked out before even stepping into the ring.

Yet closing is everything because nothing happens until someone creates a customer. The only measure of a man is his deeds. Deeds become legacy. The only measure of a seller is revenue. Revenue becomes growth and companies rise and fall on it.

You've probably read many articles about how closing is not important, and if you open properly, the deal will automatically close. Do you really think you can land a date that way or do a seven-figure deal? Do you really think you can succeed just by opening and never needing to ask the big question or handle objections? Winning a new client requires the COMBO of opening with value, building relationships of trust, building consensus and a business case, and then closing with confidence. It should never be a white-knuckle adventure; instead, it must be a logical and agreeable next step for the customer.

Humans are mostly fear-based, and C-levels are risk-averse. There is a paradox with "opening as the new closing" because a worthwhile deal will not close itself. Although first impressions can be everything and you must tee up the deal, set the tone, and psychologically anchor the C-level prospect, you also need to engineer a decision to secure the contract. Sure, they can break off a paid pilot, but that's probably the only exception you should ever allow. The answer is: You drive the close, every day. You've gotta drive the vision, which is the "art of the possible." Sell today but sell the future, too. Sell the dream of transformational, spine-tingling future-state results.

I recently watched a deal go into legal contract review phase, and I was shocked to see the buyer go into redline review with two other vendors. Can you imagine that? Russian Roulette! Another classic Bake-Off with three bullets in the chamber where they could literally just sign any of the vendors. My client was backed into the corner, up against the ropes.

My advice: Don't play the game; instead, phone the customer CEO. "This is not how to build a relationship of trust and partnership. If you'd like to negotiate, then we're happy to do that. Otherwise we're out."

If they think they're the hottest one at the bar and you walk away, they can't stand it! This is because no one ever walked on Heather

Locklear, Cleopatra, Alexander the Great, or Brad Pitt. No one ever walked on a telco with $50 billion in revenue. But you have the sheer hubris to actually do it, and that's refreshing to the powerful. They love it when you lock horns—game on! Only the strong will survive. Never panic or sweat. When the piranha swarm, establish ethical presence and let them get focused on the negative selling tactics of the other two or three late entrants to the game. Let the client hear them hissing in despair, dropping price, caving in on terms, bending and twisting in the wind.

To recap, here's how you close: Open the relationship with value, build trust and engineer consensus, collaborate on a compelling business case and align with their process. Then drive the sale every day as hard as you can. When you receive a verbal, consider it just getting started. Call every single day. Leave a message of resounding confidence. Send an email. Be persistent and strong. When you get the contract in redlines, call procurement every day. Get your C-levels aligned with theirs. When they say they're going to sign on Monday and it's Tuesday night, call in again. It's at risk. As Brian Burns says: "What is not overtly positive is covertly negative." Your competitor and their allies are always undermining you.

And here's the final play: Save the CEO bullet for the end game. Do not play your CEO card until you're in the final round. Sure, the CEO can open the first piece of an initial meeting when all members are present. Later, it's better to let your executives grab some wine and clink a glass, to let them shoot you a text to "get it done" while they are behind the scenes where the power brokers break bread. In many situations, the important moments are known about in advance, and the CEO can be in reserve. On occasion, that moment can arise in the course of something else—even an integration discussion—and the CEO must be available. It's like a straight right knockout punch: You better have it cocked and know how and when to fire it when the opening is there—and in some fights, that could be at an unexpected moment.

This is the way of captains and kings of industry. This is the way real business deals are getting done. This is closing. It's not weak, and it's not collaborative—a euphemism and excuse when you're in a deadly waiting game. Customers want to buy, but they'll never let you sell them. They buy on emotion and close on logic. They actually crave leadership, and they want you to take charge of the room and find a shared vision as the impresario of the theater. They don't know how to talk to each other, collaborate, ideate, or see their businesses through the right lens. They're afraid and insecure in many respects.

The piece that *The Challenger Sale* got right is that you must teach, tailor, and take control with key insight. In regard to closing, the piece you need to hear is about the inner game. You must be able to own a room, standing or relaxed at the head of a conference table, with Fortune 1000 executives. You must be able to radiate confidence in every interaction from pitch to proposal, to negotiation, to close, to legal redlines, to DocuSign. You fight like hell to open and to move through the mid-funnel, but you hammer full throttle like a bat out of hell, racing the daylight for that photo finish.

Know that Google has changed the game, and I never see a solo run. The minute prospects sense the end game, they panic and hit Search. They call two or three of your competitors and shop the bid. It's instantaneous cutting at your knees. The top dogs I know are cool as ice. When the "alternative facts" roll in to poke holes in their solution, they laugh because they anticipated it.

I'm not going to give you 27 classic closes out of the ABC almanac. I'm going to tell the truth. Humans smell fear. All sales methodologies and processes succeed or fail for you based on one thing: your supreme confidence in yourself. The experience with the seller is 53 percent of why organizations buy (CEB Research). They need a powerful leader to hold their hand while they walk over fire coals to the promised land.

Remember, always to start the bidding at seven figures. Always walk. Always drive the sale until it's inked, until the system is installed, until the commission check cashes in your investment account. Period. Then you can sleep. My final tip here: Be the hottest one at the bar. It's your turn to be the one who got away. I've closed many a sale on a boomerang. It's not about arrogance, but be willing to cash your chips and walk out of the casino. Pipeline cures all ills, and you'll want for nothing—you've always got another bullet in the chamber.

The Act of Personal Sales Leadership

"The world is full of people who want to play it safe, people who have tremendous potential but never use it. Somewhere deep inside them, they know that they could do more in life, be more, and have more—if only they were willing to take a few risks."

—GEORGE FOREMAN

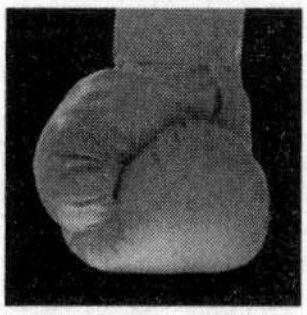

I'M GOING TO TELL YOU A HARD TRUTH. *YOU* ARE THE VERY reason that you don't have the success you think you deserve. Stop blaming your boss, your parents, circumstance, the product, the market, competition, God, the universe, or plain bad luck. We all attract what we radiate, we harvest what we sow, and we deserve what we get. Embrace it. Life was never intended to be easy. The value of what we pursue is in who we become, not what we attain. Adversity makes us stronger, and all lessons in life are repeated until they are learned.

If you want success in selling, think like a Marine—it's a privilege to serve, no matter how much crap is thrown your way. Choose to feel grateful rather than entitled. You're on a mission to change the lives of your customers and those you love. Do whatever it takes rather than merely your best. Embrace the difficulties because you will be one of the few who does, and this makes you more valuable in the market. If succeeding in professional selling were easy, it would not be very rewarding. Choose to personally be the biggest point of difference for your employer and customers as they make decisions and strive for success.

This is your time to rise above the pack. The way you sell is more important than what you sell. Leadership is the name of the game, if you're an individual contributor or otherwise. You've got to believe you are worthy of breaking through and being trusted. The sellers who became champions all questioned their ability. They all had peaks and troughs but raised themselves up through positive affirmation, belief, and massive action. A bias toward action will dissipate any negativity. Keep drinking cups of coffee; keep getting back up to get knocked down again. Always make one last call at the end of the day, and be the first in the office and on the phone every morning.

Eliminate all negative self-talk and instead visualize the goal, germinate the seed, and then plan for success. I've always been amazed when I set my heart on a particular client at the beginning of a sales calendar year, and later that year I end up meeting and then closing a sizable engagement with them. Goals and dreams are the cosmic rudder, so you must breathe life into your prayers to bring about high performance.

There are so many examples I could provide about the importance of integrity in professional selling, but lawyers won't allow this because it involves real negative examples. I've seen obscene greed, lies, knives in the back as footholds to climb higher, robbery using the corporate expense card, and customer and staff welfare being flagrantly disregarded. I'd like to say that bad behavior is always punished, but many times the corporate psychopaths and snakes rise higher and higher as they play politics and manage perceptions. Please just know this: Your personal integrity and reputation is your most precious asset—period. Stay true to yourself, and hold on to positive, timeless values.

Integrity is about telling the truth, warts and all, even if it makes your solution look a little weaker. I guarantee you that your cutthroat competitors are talking trash about you and your product and falsely positioning themselves as superior in every way. That's disconcerting on a subconscious level to prospects. I remember one of the top performers I ever saw delivering good news and bad news, exactly what the solution could and couldn't do. He was candid and trusted, just as you should be with your customers. The best salespeople aspire to trusted adviser status and treat prospective customers as if they were a part of their own extended family, looking out for their financial best interests.

Fight, Fight, Fight to Earn the Right

I mentor a stunningly brilliant salesperson who sells marketing technology across the United States. He's been living COMBO Prospecting for the last 12 months and has been achieving amazing results. Here is his true story:

> Breakthrough! Three months of COMBOs on three continents. It started with a dead account in the CRM and progressed to the dialer. The company had been contacting this lead for six years via drip campaigns in marketing automation to no avail. The response was, "Please stop calling. I told you we are cool—we're good!" I was amused. Bring it!
>
> I kept going . . . I saw an article in *WIRED Magazine* in which the CMO of that company was talking about innovation, and it gave me context, a use case and the business value angle. It hit me like a bolt out of the blue. So I wrote her an InMail. Then I wrote her an email with her best quote from the magazine article in the header. I then called her direct line. Amazingly, there was no EA, and it rang right to her voice mail. I left a concise message about her article and the result I could help her achieve. Then I tracked the email in Cirrus Insight and noticed she forwarded it umpteen times: to Britain, to the West Coast of the States, to the East Coast.
>
> Two days later, driven by the opens and forwards analytics, I called her office and left a message again. I sent another email. It was

opened six times. Forwarded to some more far-off destinations.

At last, on a Friday night, a response came via email: "My team has informed me that we're already using a solution like yours, but you'd have to talk to my colleague in the UK who vets everything like this. The UK person had been copied." I thanked the CMO and felt pretty jazzed that I broke through with a COMBO after our company had failed to engage this Fortune 1000 for the last six years.

Next step was to start dialing the UK. I finally pinned down a response using triples: call, voice mail, email. The problem was that UK confirmed that the incumbent was already deep in there; in fact, it was just installed plus the company was very satisfied. But it didn't matter because I sold a complex solution, so I pivoted to another niche pillar in our offering. I found the CEO of the problem in the Midwest and referenced the vetter in UK and the CMO. I called them for three weeks straight, and used five COMBOs each time: call, voice mail, email, as well as text and InMail, but I never got a response.

But then, out of the blue, he responded and agreed to a meeting. We demoed and he vetted the stack. He loved it and figured we could replace the incumbent due to better value and stronger alignment with where they were going. In time (once contracts expired), we could provide a single holistic view of the data. This was a bonanza—David versus Goliath.

Was it 27 touches, or was it 63? Maybe it was 100. It was COMBOs all the way. It was grit, tenacity, vision, and a relevant business case. The person who asked to stop being called left the business, and that's a good thing because they were the blocker. I didn't give up. I saw that departure as a trigger. I got in the air, and I pitched to the team and gained consensus to help them create the business case with all of the complex funding issues covered. I got a niche deal in the door.

I got punched in the face from day one. I heard crickets. The account was radio silent. The competitor was embedded. But I got in

> high at the C-level and made the case for a solution sale where I could plug in my technology as a turbocharger for a multi-vendor approach. The ultimate outcome I offered was of far greater value with fewer supplier relationships—and their CFO loved it. We offered the best of breed initially, and, over time, we integrated everything they needed into one single place and with one system.

This is what it takes to break through and succeed in selling. A CMO gets 1,700 emails a month. They get 200 InMails a week. They have a full-time EA blocking the pesky salespeople and time wasters. But like Dale Carnegie said, "Nothing in the English language is as beautiful as the sound of the prospect's own name."[1] And nothing is more relevant than their own quotes in leading publications or the annual shareholder call. They're putting themselves on the world stage to build their brand. The apex predator's competitive instinct is to kill or be killed. That's how they got into the corner office. Can you? Apply COMBO and you will. Many CEOs rose through the ranks as top sellers.

Visualize the goal, germinate the seed, and plan for success. Create a strong personal brand to leverage Cialdini's law of social proof.[2] You don't have to bite their ear off with rudeness or bluntness, but be the honey badger and cultivate finesse while being wildly persistent. This is how you fight for the meeting. Once you open, you're in with a shot. Assemble the A-team: your CTO, your CEO, and your solutions consultants. Scramble a jet on the tarmac, parachute in, and make sure it's a brainstorming or whiteboarding session where they're talking 80 percent of the time. Sell a multiplier not a "rip and replace." Build consensus in a place that used to be broken. Harmonize. Sell in. Land and expand. If you create value, they will come, and you can close to open a lifelong relationship.

The leader defines the culture, and you lead the individual sales cycle as the face of your company's brand. Leadership comes in many forms, but you'll need to lead as the conductor of a symphony to bring harmony where there is discord; you'll need to bring utility to the dysfunction. You deserve to lead because you've faced your fears and embraced the phone, poked the bear, spat in the face of rejection, embraced the difficult, and loved your customer.

Avoiding the Roller-Coaster Performance Ride

Consistent, intelligent hard work always wins, but sales is one of the hardest jobs in the history of the world. You can run for 18 months and exhaust every resource and still lose. It's extremely repetitive and tactical but also demands masterful strategy. You've got quotas, deadlines, reporting, admin, expenses, travel, and management breathing down your neck. It's a 50 hour a week job of rejection and disappointment if you suck, and it can be a 70 hour a week obsession if you're great.

The point here is that you must first inculcate yourself to just how difficult high performance is in professional selling and in life in general. It's going to be painful and you're going to want to quit if you don't know why you're doing what you do. Once you pass through the trough of disillusionment and out the other side, you can gain a determined, conscious competence. But it really all starts with overcoming your fear, and that fear is always, always, always . . . the telephone. This is because when you're not using the phone, you aren't really being fully rejected—aka punched in the mouth. The phone is becoming more important because your competitors are abandoning it in droves, but the smartest people are not where the competition is. They are where the customers are present. Everyone you want to sell to has a social phone.

Disciplined, intelligent activity is what sets the great apart from those who are merely talented. At the end of the day, Dwayne "The Rock" Johnson's success isn't a fluke; he worked out six hours a day for 20 years. Arnie was the same, and so are all the greats. Without being desperate, you still need to be hungry and driven to wildly exceed your quota. The harder I work, the luckier I get. Daily smart activity builds the mental muscle and grit you need to break through. Abs are made in the kitchen and the gym; but the first discipline is usually the hardest. Analogies abound, but at the end of the day you have to be tenacious beyond belief.

You can't just send the same stale template over and over. You need to keep a consistent message but one that is smart, well researched, and with an edge for cut-through. You need to take that one extra step to make each task just a bit better. Reverse look-up their email address in Discover.ly or Rapportive. Double-check your common connections for a warm introduction. Check their LinkedIn profile to see if they publicly share their email address or cell phone. Ask, who on my team knows this person or used to work with them at a company in common? What are the internal and external referrals I can garner? What are the trigger events I can monitor and pounce upon? We've already covered all this and more . . . but will you actually do what needs to be done every workday?

The world is filled with busy fools who feel justified in their failure. One failing senior salesperson looked me in the eye and said, "There's nothing else I could be doing; our brand is just not strong enough, and I'm not getting enough leads." His qualified pipeline was less than 70 percent of his target. He needed to make it 3X, but he ignored COMBO principles and persisted with tiny deals that made it impossible to succeed because there were not enough hours in the day to transact the necessary volume. I explained the CEB Research that revealed that 53 percent of the buyer's decision is due to how the salesperson and their team engage. Brand and capabilities contribute 19 percent each, and price accounts for a mere 9 percent of decision weighting. Yet he chose to lead with price and sought to be the cheapest as a way of entering an account. His strategy was madness—he was fired.

You can also sit on a silent sales floor and work 12 hours a day blasting out emails and socializing on LinkedIn but never making a deal. Massive dumb action, at any level, is just plain stupid. It's even dumb to do the right activity but inconsistently. I see it everywhere I consult—salespeople lurching into action once they realize, too late, that they don't have enough pipeline. Prodded into action, they thrash around and create barely enough opportunities before stopping. They stop on the basis that they are now too busy "selling and closing."

Imagine a timeline going left to right in a spreadsheet. Two key metrics are tracked for each month: prospecting calls and revenue. Tracking the number of calls is the only key pipeline metric needed because all social and email activity is designed to result in a phone call for a real H2H connection. My experience is that, over time, 98 percent of sellers have wild cross-overs in the two tracking lines of prospecting activity and revenue achieved. Here is how the story goes: "I'm so busy responding to web leads, updating the CRM, following up on existing deals, doing proposals, and closing that I just don't have time for prospecting . . . no one answers the phone anyway. I do what I can each week and push updates on LinkedIn and social—that's outbound isn't it?"

Note: The idea that "no one answers the phone" is one of the strangest and most powerfully destructive beliefs in sales! It's 100 percent wrong, so don't buy the lie! Chris Beall, Mike Scher, Kyle Porter, Steve Richard, Anthony Iannarino, Jeb Blount, Mike Weinberg, Jill Konrath, and Mark Hunter are just a few who can prove incontrovertibly that senior people answer the phone to then become customers.

For those who don't consistently do the required prospecting activity, sales results fall well below target within 60 to 90 days: "Holy crap, marketing and the SDR team have failed to deliver leads—again! I've gotta prospect to fill my pipe!" A few weeks of furious activity ensues to create enough qualified pipeline to keep the wolf from the door . . . but then the cycle repeats. The lag between prospecting activity and revenue creates a false impression that they are disconnected. The same happens with our weight. We diet and don't seem to lose any weight after a week, so we give up and binge only to see weight fall off. *Wow, dieting doesn't work! I do the right thing and don't lose weight, yet when I eat crap (carbs and sugar) I don't get fat!* Wrong. It's just a lag between inputs and results. Selling is exactly the same.

Intelligent targeting + the right value narrative + disciplined COMBO with good phone = appointments = prospects = sales = referrals = more appointments = overachievement. The key is having consistent inputs every day of every week of every month. That is the only way to smooth and align revenue and activity to deliver consistent high performance results.

How many COMBOs do you need to execute on a daily basis to create 3–5X your quota or sales target? Do the math yourself. You need to back into your own number based on the results goal you set. If a day goes by and you have no appointments set, you're just snoozing or marketing. You're not hunting and it's not sales; it's almost like you're a human banner advertisement to build ambient awareness of the brand. You will be cut from the roster because that's the most expensive billboard ever and a quarter-million cars aren't passing you every day.

Work ethic is important but, make no mistake, it's real quality sales pipeline that cures all ills—even if you're missing your revenue targets. What gets measured, gets managed, gets done (according to Peter Drucker). Track all that you do, even if it has to be manually on a sheet of paper or spreadsheet. You'll find yourself cycling through the 50 accounts, mining for warm intros, nodes in your network, and pattern recognition. You'll be running fresh COMBO plays on each. You'll do a pass with more personalized outreach referencing profile data, then a pass with stats, then a pass with questions. The seller who uses COMBO with B content but is rigorous in adhering to cadence (even uses SalesLoft Cadence software) will achieve much better results than a strategic seller who communicates like a powerful A+ but doesn't have the magical skill of consistent follow-up.

Selling is not rocket science; it's far more difficult than that. Consistent COMBO outreach and follow-up is the secret of everything. You'll COMBO top-funnel just to land the meeting. You'll COMBO mid-funnel just to progress to next steps. You'll COMBO in the bottom-funnel to close, negotiate with procurement, and drive the deal over the line. Pay attention to your children and how they hound you for candy, gaming, and television time. You could sell jet engines, and you still need to hound with COMBO—it's just the nature of the beast.

But you're not a machine, and it's very hard to Six Sigma your way into optimal productivity. You could call 50 prospects and get nothing from it—it would be just like going through the motions. You could spend the entire day commenting in LinkedIn groups and have a few other interesting narcissists poke you back. You could research the perfect business case to high heaven! If a bear researches in the woods . . . you get my point! For many, selling truly is an exercise in futility.

We are all allotted the same cosmic clock, so why then do some optimize this time for better results? This has been dogging management consultants—thinkers such as W. Edwards Deming and Peter F. Drucker—throughout the ages since the days of Aristotle and Plato. We live in deeds, not years; in thoughts, not days; in feelings, not in figures on a dial. We should count time by heartbeats. Read Matthew Michalewicz's book *Life in Half a Second*—it will change your life if you act on his advice.

You can have the perfect dashboard pulling your Salesforce CRM data. You can use predictive intelligence to decide whom you should prospect next with your auto-dialer featuring local presence and optimal time of day. You can use marketing automation lead scoring to see which prospect is hot based on rules. But it's truly a mystery sandwich to actually know what to do tomorrow that will be most effective.

Peter F. Drucker was right when he said, "There is nothing so useless as doing efficiently that which should not be done at all." Here are some areas where I would look to find the answer for sales effectiveness:

- **Leading vs. lagging indicators:** Very little has been written about proactive sales management, but it's an important science to understand from rep level all the way to the corner office. There are myriad KPIs to measure but precious few smart actions that actually move the needle on revenue. Revenue itself is a lagging (rearview) metric, and not one that can be moved by the SVP of Sales barking at the team to walk through the pipeline strategy again each week. The book *Cracking the Sales Management Code* by Jason Jordan and Michelle Vazzana is essential reading in this area.
- **WIGs (wildly important goals):** These are literally daily goals you set that are massive. By focusing on them, they gradually lever the boulder toward overarching objectives. *The 4 Disciplines of Execution* by Chris McChesney, Sean Covey, and Jim Huling is a stellar book that looks at execution as a management science for confronting the whirlwind of your day. For most sellers, just handling their email and getting to in-box zero is unfathomable.

- **Pick a major action to do before lunch that scares you:** Look at your pipe and think from the gut—who is the one person you could call today to truly move the needle? Who can sign? Who can say "yes"? Who can only say "no"? Who do you really need to phone in that account that you're petrified to call? Board member? Time to go to the CEO, CTO, or CIO?
- **Make strategic lists of prospects that are "similar to your best customers" (Mike Weinberg's idea):** COMBO with these lists daily like there is no next week, and then do it every week. Prioritize interactivity as the highest leading indicator of success. Who is returning your call, replying to email, responding on LinkedIn, interfacing with your LinkedIn Publisher post, willing to have subsequent calls with you, inviting you on-site, and asking provocative questions? Interactivity is the litmus test for prioritizing a book of business. When the prospect starts to drive the sales cycle from the front, you know it's going to close.

Thinking about doing it and talking about doing it are not the same as actually doing it. "The number-one trait of successful people is a bias toward action," says Dan Forbes. "Have a bias toward action—let's see something happen now. You can break that big plan into small steps and take the first step right away," says Indira Gandhi.

The bottom line is few people furiously protect their calendar to make 30 targeted prospecting calls happen in a two hour block every day, followed by a voice mail, email, InMail, and text message. Most salespeople enjoy the coffee catch-up with colleagues and like to check email and their LinkedIn and Facebook accounts throughout the day. Most salespeople have fewer than three on-site meetings in their territory per week.

If you're willing to take 30 to 50 smart actions per day, every day, you'll kill it. This is like a commitment to brushing and flossing. If you have a beautiful smile and no cavities late in life, you get it! Make a commitment to A/B test everything: email length, message delivery medium, script, unique value proposition (UVP), subject line, time of day, cadence, length, message style, tone, relevant clients, social, SlideShare, networking events, even how you dress in meetings. Be teachable and determined, and you'll crush it.

I can't make you stop being a two- or three-toed sloth. It will take your own commitment to understanding what the smart actions are that lever deals forward and truly produce leading indicators. You've got to drive progression with prospects rather than accept continuation. Let me give you a pro tip: Next time management jubilantly dumps a carcass of an RFP on your desk, push back with gusto! Even flat out reject it. As Lee Bartlett mentions in his fabulous book *No. 1 Best Seller*, "Furiously protect revenue-generating activities." This means you have to be willing to check out of the glad-handing and internal corporate politics of your sales organization. Let the other yes-men and yes-women go get coffee with your GM. Trust me, you're better off getting one more discovery or on-site in that week. Commissions are worlds better than backslapping and a hangover.

These tactics won't make you well-liked, but they'll make you consistently successful, without the stressful troughs after a peak. Once you're incredibly successful, you'll be untouchable as long as you stay true to ethical values and conduct. Your actions protect you and so do revenue and the trusted relationships you have with valuable customers.

To pull off all of the above will take a tremendous amount of focus. Simply shut out the noise of all the social networks, mobile phone blips and beeps, and intra-office spam email and collaboration messaging. Make no mistake, 80 percent of most people's workday is actually wasted, with only 20 percent being productive. This is the Pareto Principle, which is an inexorable universal power distribution law. I don't care how aggressively you sell, time will defeat you before you slay the dragon. You must prioritize executing COMBOS every day and become addicted to the hustle, flow, and grind. You've got to move from wasting 80 percent of the day to driving 80 percent of the output to a reverse power curve.

80/20 Power Laws and Personal Effectiveness

I'm a big fan of Richard Koch and the 80/20 rule based on the Pareto Principle. In many respects, this inspired Tim Ferriss to write *The 4-Hour Workweek*. The truth is that waste is rampant in all human and natural systems. Eighty percent of your effective output is generated by 20 percent of your actions. This is why the tale of the jar with rocks and sand is everything from a prioritization and time management standpoint. I discovered the analogy of rocks and sand from Dr. Stephen R. Covey's book, *First Things First*. If you fill the jar with the sand, the rocks never fit. In contrast, if you put the big rocks in first and then pour in the sand, it all fits. Big rocks, then pebbles, then sand . . . in that order. Prioritize the important rather than have your chain jerked by someone else's "urgent."

We all feel that there is never enough time in the day. You must therefore use time-blocking and focus on the 20 percent of the opportunities that will drive 80 percent of the revenue. But how do you choose? Each day when you get to your desk, don't even open your email. Write down the top three things you need to accomplish by lunch on a pad, and execute on those in the optimal sequence. Better still, write that list the evening before. These are the big rocks to fit into the jar of your life. These are the proactive lead measures you can effect to lever the Sisyphean boulder of your day up the proverbial hill. The pebbles are the reactive prospect emails. The sand is the training video you had started to watch, social media notifications, the news of the day, sports scores, etc.

What's important is that you take the time to clearly define what the rocks and sand are for you. If you put the sand into the jar first, you'll never fit the rocks that matter into your schedule. You'll struggle just to play catch-up. Social media is just one tool in your arsenal. It's very powerful when you leverage batch processing. Utilize a social listening platform to track your greatest prospects in target companies first. Prioritize them. Companies like Avention, InsideView, and Nimble can help you do this. Watch what's trending with CXOs, and take the time to comment on it. First, listen to the stream and pick out the people with whom you'd like to engage. Then make it meaningful. Ten touches trump 100 when you make them count. Setting Google Alerts or a daily LinkedIn digest of group activity can give you an edge to find the signal in the noise. Batch process by having the discipline to take just 30 minutes when you wake up and 30 minutes before bed on this exercise. You'd be amazed how far you can get with a concerted mono-tasking effort on the target. The secret is scheduling time just like you would with COMBOs, and don't forget to still do that, too. Yes, it can be rocks or sand. The choice is yours based on the due diligence and time you put in to picking the right targets.

LinkedIn Navigator is a powerful weapon for frontline sales managers and salespeople alike. It enables the monitoring of targets you wish to pursue and then engagement at precisely the right moment. It allows you to receive a blended digest of these updates without needing to glue your eyes to the feed like a stock ticker. The myth of social media is that you have to spend all your time on it. Just as with using a tool such as the telephone, if you schedule your time, have an objective in mind, and execute your plan in a concerted way, you can produce dramatic results. There's a major compulsion to always be on because you fear missing something. But control this impulse, and realize you can always catch up at scheduled intervals.

Do at least one thing that scares you before lunch. If that means contacting Mr. Big in your book, do it! You'll get his executive assistant anyway. Does that mean calling the cell phone of your warmest opportunity and moving it to the next step, demo, on-site, or proposal phase? What really scares you this week, this month, or today? Do it now! By starting to prioritize the WIG, or wildly important goal, you'll be able to create a true lever. If you identify the 20 percent of actions that make the biggest difference, and then do them as a priority, you can tip the scales of efficiency in your favor.

You need every possible advantage in selling. Make your calls warm instead of cold; have an awesome personal brand on LinkedIn, stand up straight with great posture, have a great headset with fully charged batteries, use practiced scripts that you drilled with friends, kill objections with finesse—every single thing makes you more effective. The fact that you're prioritizing the COMBO outreach method means you can buck the 80/20 rule and create your own 70/30 or 60/40 rule.

If you want to change the rules altogether, you can make your output massively more efficient by embracing technology. If you're serious about achieving live conversations, use hot switch-dialing software such as ConenctAndSell that can increase your conversations 20-fold. They integrate with your CRM and dial in the background to techno-magically connect you only when there is a live person on the other end of the phone. No dialing courage required, no call fatigue; just fit your headset, strap yourself in front of the screen, and hit the start button.

Why You Must Become a Mentor and Coach

Guard your attitude and your time. Revenue protects but it is also good to align with winning agendas and the powerful people internally, within your channel and inside your customer base. If you don't know how to manage the internal politics in your organization or those within the prospect base, you could be euthanized and be DOA. Dissing competitors, gossiping, and rumor-mongering are never the way to go. Take the high road and be stately in how you operate. Your hallmarks should be a warm and friendly persona tempered with thoughtfulness, good manners, and deliberate language. You are on a mission to make a difference, and you know why you invest your time in any project or pursuit. Be seen as the one who rises above the negativity and noise to create strategy and then execute without a fuss.

Be under no illusion: You will make enemies if you are committed to COMBO Prospecting because others will look bad. They will accuse you of all manner of nonsense, from harassing customers to damaging the company's brand by calling people on the phone, spamming prospects with too much outreach, working too hard, being too provocative, failing to push the corporate message of product and solution superiority, and much more. My advice: Stay laser focused on a business value narrative, and keep a low profile as you execute your COMBO time-blocks—in a meeting room if you can. Stay humble and be Switzerland. Smile and simply say, "I can see why you'd think that. Have you read *COMBO Prospecting*?"

Your enemies are driven by envy, jealousy, and fear of being found out for being lazy, cowardly, and unimaginative. It's just like the old days of unions when the young, enthusiastic new worker would be pulled aside and dressed down by the shop floor steward for making everyone look bad: "If ya wanna last here, slow down and stop makin' the rest of us look bad. Ya get my meaning?" For you it's all just water off a duck's back.

One of the people I mentor worked for a company that was full-bottle social selling and frowned upon anyone prospecting on the phone. He had to get in early and stay late plus book meeting rooms to make his calls. This was so that he was not labeled a nonbeliever in the new passive silent sales floor approach to nonselling. The head of global sales had flown in from HQ and walked onto the floor—my mentee literally terminated a prospecting call mid sentence because he did not want to get fired. You can find insanity in every business. He called the prospect back 15 minutes later, apologizing for the call dropping out.

If you want to succeed with COMBO, you better wear a headset every day and light up the keypad on an honest-to-goodness phone. You also need to infect your organization with truth and the presence of the social phone. Spread the word with this book and my articles on LinkedIn. At the end of the day, it's undeniable that a seller actually interacting live with a prospect is infinitely more power than anything digital. We all know this, and we know that the best things in life are still messy—love, business, growth, learning, and sales. Watch kids play in the dirt and convince their mother to get them a lollipop, playing one parent against the other. This stuff is so innate and hardwired to our neuropsychology that it's more of an internal awakening than an esoteric ivory-tower epiphany.

Your success is not a game, and it's certainly not optional. You could be the VP of Sales within five years if you lead the way with spectacular revenue and stupendous customer acquisition. What you learn and who you become, by overcoming your fear of the phone and becoming masterful with your voice and attitude, make you worthy of becoming a CEO. Every entrepreneur needs to be brilliant at setting a vision and winning the support of investors, partners, and customers. It's all selling and leading. Everyone needs to make a living, but most also really want to make a difference. What will be the legacy of your work life, and how will you help others achieve theirs?

It's a fitting end to the book to make one last point. Readers are leaders, but legacy comes from deeds. What will you do now? Really, what will you change in your life? Is this all too hard? Are you not up to it? Too much hassle and hard work? Jonathan Farrington says it best:

> Perhaps of all the temptations we meet in life, the subtlest of all is the comfort zone, that invitation to settle for less, to go for contentment when the stresses of over achievement beckon. The way that takes you out of the comfort zone is the route less travelled. Most of us when we come to that place where the two paths divide prefer the one that leads to safety, to warmth and to comfort.

Before you finally decide on the blue pill or the red pill (from *The Matrix*), settle in for an evening and watch two movies back-to-back: *Jerry Maguire* and *The Pursuit of Happyness*. Then go outside and look into the night sky and ponder your future. I think you can be so much better and make a far greater difference in the lives of others. Professional selling could be the ideal vehicle for you to do just that. What do you think?

Success is about achieving your goals and living the life you want. There is nothing wrong with stepping back into an account management role or maybe abandoning sales altogether. Do what is best for you and your family. All I ask is that you are honest with yourself—if you claim to be a business development person, then actually do what it takes to claim that title.

If you accept that challenge, as swamped as you may be, take the time to pass on the knowledge. You can pay it forward and make a difference in other people's lives. You'll be enriched and learn by helping others, and you'll create your own unique selling style. The infinitely curious seller can never become bored because, however hard the grind in the coal mine, you will see more diamonds than anyone else.

Zig Ziglar was a man of genuine faith and integrity, and early in my sales career he said to me, "You can have anything you want in life if you help enough people get what they want." Success is not about grasping and greed, nor about dominance and power. It's not about bluster and bravado or crushing and closing. It's about courage, values, leadership, and service.

This book may seem over the top and the metaphors a little violent, but you really are fighting your own fears and the apathy of the people who need your help. Be the person worthy of the success you seek. Love and respect yourself and others as you strive to make a difference by giving everything you've got. Most important, have the courage to believe you are capable of achieving anything you intelligently and passionately commit to do. Carpe diem!

RESOURCES

More information and free resources from Tony are available here:

- Speaker website: www.TonyHughes.com.au
- Sales methodology website: www.RSVPselling.com
- YouTube channel: www.youtube.com/user/RSVPselling/playlists
- Interviews & podcasts: www.TonyHughes.com.au/interviews-podcasts-webinars
- LinkedIn profile: www.linkedin.com/today/posts/hughestony
- LinkedIn blog: www.linkedin.com/today/posts/hughestony

The following referenced books are recommended and listed in alphabetical order:

- *Cracking the Sales Management Code*, Jason Jordan and Michelle Vazzana
- *Fanatical Prospecting*, Jeb Blount
- *High-Profit Prospecting*, Mark Hunter
- *How to Get a Meeting with Anyone*, Stu Heinecke and Jay Conrad Levinson
- *Life in Half a Second*, Matthew Michalewicz
- *Never Split the Difference*, Chris Voss
- *New Sales. Simplified.*, Mike Weinberg
- *No More Cold Calling*, Joanne S. Black
- *Platform*, Michael Hyatt

- *Predictable Prospecting*, Marylou Tyler and Jeremey Donovan
- *Predictable Revenue*, Aaron Ross and Marylou Tyler
- *Pre-Suasion*, Robert Cialdini
- *Selling to Big Companies*, Jill Konrath
- *Selling to VITO*, Anthony Parinello
- *Shift!*, Craig Elias and Tibor Shanto
- *SNAP Selling*, Jill Konrath
- *Solution Selling*, Michael Bosworth
- *SPIN Selling*, Neil Rackham
- *Strategic Selling*, Robert Miller and Stephen Heiman
- *The Challenger Customer*, Brent Adamson, Matt Dixon, Pat Spenner, and Nick Toman
- *The Challenger Sale*, Brent Adamson and Matt Dixon
- *The 80/20 Principle*, Richard Koch
- *The 4 Disciplines of Execution*, Chris McChesney, Sean Covey, and Jim Huling
- *The 4-Hour Workweek*, Tim Ferriss
- *The Future of the Sales Profession*, Graham Hawkins
- *The Joshua Principle: Leadership Secrets of Selling*, Tony Hughes
- The *New Power Base Selling*, Jim Holden and Ryan Kubacki
- The *New Rules of Marketing and PR*, David Meerman Scott
- The *New Solution Selling*, Keith Eades
- *The No. 1 Best Seller*, Lee Bartlett
- *The Only Sales Guide You'll Ever Need*, Anthony Iannarino
- *The Speed of Trust*, Stephen Covey
- *Trust-Based Selling*, Charles H. Green

ENDNOTES

INTRODUCTION

1 www.linkedin.com/in/kennymadden.

2 CSO Insights, Miller Heiman Group, *Sales Performance Optimization Study*, 2015.

3 The Bridge Group, *Sales Development, Metrics and Compensation Report*, 2016.

4 Jack Canfield, *The Key to Living the Law of Attraction*. HCI, 2007.

5 Anthony Parinello, *Selling to VITO*. Adams Media, 1999. www.vitoselling.com.

6 Kyle Porter, CEO SalesLoft. www.salesloft.com.

7 Charles H. Green, *Trust-Based Selling*. McGraw-Hill, 2006.

8 Dr. Chester Karrass, *In Business as in Life, You Don't Get What You Deserve, You Get What You Negotiate*. Stanford Street Press, 1996.

CHAPTER ONE

1 Anthony Iannarino, www.thesalesblog.com.

2 Jill Rowley, www.jillrowley.com.

3 Jason Jordan and Michelle Vazzana, *Cracking the Sales Management Code*. McGraw-Hill, 2011.

4 Anthony Iannarino, *The Only Sales Guide You'll Ever Need*. Portfolio, 2016.

5 TOPO Research, "2016 Strategic Sales Development Report." http://topohq.com.

6 Jeb Blount, *Fanatical Prospecting*. Wiley, 2015.

7 Mike Weinberg, *New Sales. Simplified.* AMACOM, 2012.

8 Grant Cardone, *The 10X Rule: The Only Difference Between Success and Failure*. Wiley, 2011.

9 Grant Cardone, *Sell to Survive*. Card1 Publications, 2008.

10 CSO Insights, Miller Heiman Group, *Sales Performance Optimization Study*, 2015.

11 McKinsey Global Institute, "The Social Economy—Unlocking Value and Productivity Through Social Technologies." www.mckinsey.com/industries/high-tech/our-insights/the-social-economy.

12 Tamara Schenk and Jim Dickie, CSO Insights, *Sales Enablement Optimization Study*, 2016.

13 Lynette Ryals and Iain Davies, "The 8 Types of Salespeople," *Harvard Business Review*, January 2016.

14 Dan Lyons, "Sales Reps Have Little to No Idea What They're Doing," *Huffington Post*, 2014. http://www.huffingtonpost.com/dan-lyons/sales-reps-business_b_4949207.html.

15 Chris Beall, ConnectAndSell, *Analysis of 50 Million Outbound Sales Calls in 2017.*

16 Dale Lampertz, Baylor University, "Has Cold Calling Gone Cold?" www.baylor.edu/content/services/document.php/183060.pdf.

17 LinkedIn and C9 Research, https://business.linkedin.com/sales-solutions/blog/s/sales-navigahttpssales-linkedin-comblogwp-adminpost-phppost4579actionedittor-users-net-11x-more-revenue-growth.

18 Matthew Dixon and Brent Adamson, CEB Research, *The Challenger Sale*. Portfolio, 2011.

19 Andy Hoar, Forrester Research, *Death of a (B2B) Salesman*, April 2015.

20 David Ogilvy, *Ogilvy on Advertising*. Vintage, 1985.

21 Michael Bosworth, *What Great Salespeople Do: The Science of Selling Through Emotional Connection and the Power of Story*. McGraw-Hill, 2012.

22 Matthew Dixon and Brent Adamson, CEB Research, *The Challenger Sale*. Portfolio, 2011.

23 Conrad Bayer, Tellwise, "An Ultimate Guide to Conversion Rates," 2016. https://tellwise.com/blog/ultimate-guide-conversion-rates.

24 Brian Carroll, "The B2B Lead." www.b2bleadblog.com.

25 RingDNA, "The Complete Guide to Inside Sales Analytics," 2017. http://www.ringdna.com/whitepapers/the-complete-guide-to-inside-sales-analytics-2017.

26 ContactMonkey, www.contactmonkey.com/blog.

27 ContactMonkey, www.contactmonkey.com/blog/category/email-subject-lines.

28 Jake Atwood, Ovation Sales Group. www.ovationsales.com.

29 SalesLoft, Research presented at Rainmaker 2016 conference. www.salesloft.com.

30 Lee Bartlett, *The No. 1 Best Seller*. Lee Bartlett, 2016.

31 Velocify, "The Ultimate Contact Strategy, How to Use Phone and Email for Conversion Success." http://pages.velocify.com/rs/leads360/images/Ultimate-Contact-Strategy.pdf.

32 Scott Britton, "How to Close More Deals with the Neighborhood Technique," 2016. www.troops.ai/blog/how-to-close-more-deals-with-the-neighborhood-technique.

33 Michael Bosworth, *Solution Selling*. McGraw-Hill, 1994.

34 Jeb Blount, *Fanatical Prospecting*. Wiley, 2015.

35 Lee Bartlett, *The No.1 Best Seller*. Lee Bartlett, 2016.

36 Jeffrey Gitomer and Jennifer Gluckow, "Sell or Die." www.linkedin.com/pulse/funny-thing-sales-pipeline-tony-j-hughes.

37 Brynne Tillman, "The New Formula for Connecting with B2B Buyers." www.business.linkedin.com/sales-solutions/blog/t/the-new-formula-for-connecting-with-b2b-buyers-infographic.

38 Chris McChesney, Sean Covey, and Jim Huling, *The 4 Disciplines of Execution*. Simon & Schuster, 2012.

39 Jeb Blount, *Fanatical Prospecting*. Wiley, 2015.

CHAPTER TWO

1 Kristen Bell, Drexel University in partnership with Fenman Limited.

2 Albert Mehrabian, Stephen Covey, Wharton Business School.

3 Matthew Dixon and Brent Adamson, CEB Research, *The Challenger Sale*. Portfolio, 2011.

4 Nic Dennis, www.linkedin.com/in/nicdennis.

5 CEB Research, www.cebglobal.com.

6 Matthew Dixon and Brent Adamson, CEB Research, *The Challenger Sale*. Portfolio, 2011.

7 Jill Rowley, www.linkedin.com/in/jillrowley.

8 CSO Insights, "2016 Sales Performance Optimization Study." www.csoinsights.com/blog/overcoming-the-no-decision-sales-challenge-and-more.

9 Matthew Dixon and Brent Adamson, CEB Research, *The Challenger Sale*. Portfolio, 2011. Matthew Dixon, Brent Adamson, Pat Spencer, and Nick Toman, *The Challenger Customer*. Penguin, 2015.

CHAPTER THREE

1 LinkedIn, *Sales Benchmark Index (SBI) Report*, 2015.

2 Kathleen Schaub, IDC Research, "Social Buying Meets Social Selling: How Trusted Networks Improve the Purchase Experience," 2014. https://business.linkedin.com/content/dam/business/sales-solutions/global/en_US/c/pdfs/idc-wp-247829.pdf.

3 Mark Lindwall, Forrester Research, "To Win Against Increasing Competition, Equip Your Salespeople with a Deeper Understanding of Your Buyers," 2014. http://blogs.forrester.com/mark_lindwall/14-01-27-to_win_against_increasing_competition_equip_your_salespeople_with_a_deeper_understanding_of_your_buy. Corporate Visions, www.corporatevisions.com.

4 LinkedIn, *Sales Benchmark Index (SBI) Report*, 2015.

5 Brynne Tillman, "The New Formula for Connecting with B2B Buyers." www.business.linkedin.com/sales-solutions/blog/t/the-new-formula-for-connecting-with-b2b-buyers-infographic.

6 Mark Hunter, *High-Profit Prospecting.* AMACOM, 2016.

7 RingLead, "9 Voicemail Tips to Dramatically Improve Return Calls." www.ringlead.com/voicemail-tips-to-improve-return-calls/#.WVUnLtPyuRs.

8 Lee Bartlett, *The No. 1 Best Seller.* Lee Bartlett, 2016.

9 The Bridge Group, "Sales Development 2016, Metrics and Compensation Report." http://blog.bridgegroupinc.com/sales-development-metrics.

10 InsideSales.com, "Top Challenges of the Inside Sales Industry 2016." www.insidesales.com/research-paper/top-challenges-inside-sales-industry-2016.

11 Guy Kawasaki, *The Art of the Start 2.0.* Portfolio, 2015.

12 *Harvard Business Review* with data originally from a study of 2,241 U.S. firms led by a researcher at South Korea's Sungkyunkwan University. hbr.org/2011/03/the-short-life-of-online-sales-leads.

CHAPTER FOUR

1 Chris Beall, CEO ConnectAndSell. www.connectandsell.com/blog.

2 Ibid.

3 Megan Heuer, SiriusDecisions, www.siriusdecisions.com/resources.

4 Robert Clay, Marketing Donut, "Why 8% of Sales People Get 80% of the Sales." www.marketingdonut.co.uk/sales/sales-techniques-and-negotiations/why-8-of-sales-people-get-80-of-the-sales.

5 Puranjay S., Scripted, "5 Statistics to Motivate You to Make Sales Calls." www.scripted.com/writing-samples/5-statistics-to-motivate-you-to-make-sales-calls.

6 Jill Konrath, *SNAP Selling.* Portfolio, 2010.

7 CEB Research, "2016 Sales and Marketing Summit." www.cebglobal.com/sales-service/sales-marketing-summit.html.

8 Chet Holmes, *The Ultimate Sales Machine.* Portfolio, 2007.

9 Kathleen Schaub, IDC Research, "Social Buying Meets Social Selling: How Trusted Networks Improve the Purchase Experience," 2014. https://business.linkedin.com/content/dam/business/sales-solutions/global/en_US/c/pdfs/idc-wp-247829.pdf.

10 Matt Heinz, Influitive, "What You Should Know About B2B Referrals (But Probably Don't)," 2015. http://www.heinzmarketing.com/2015/12/new-research-formal-referral-programs-lead-to-higher-sales-faster-deals.

11 Joanne Black, *No More Cold Calling.* Warner Business Books, 2006.

12 Phillipp Schmitt, Bernd Skiera, Christopher Van den Bulte, Goethe University and Wharton Business School, "Referral Programs and Customer Value," 2010. www.slideshare.net/pooya-rajamand/jm-referral-programsandcustomervalue.

13 Koka Sexton, LinkedIn, *Social Selling Report*, 2014.

14 Nielsen.com, "Global Trust in Advertising and Brand Messages Report," 2013. www.nielsen.com/us/en/insights/reports/2013/global-trust-in-advertising-and-brand-messages.html.

15 LinkedIn and IDC, *Sales Connect Report*, 2014.

16 Nicholas Read and Stephen Bistritz, *Selling to the C-Suite*. McGraw-Hill, 2009.

17 Wikipedia, *Power Law Distribution.*

18 LinkedIn, *Sales Benchmark Index (SBI) Report*, 2015.

19 Brett Chester (while VP at Replicon), www.linkedin.com/in/brettchester.

20 Michael Bosworth, *What Great Salespeople Do: The Science of Selling Through Emotional Connection and the Power of Story.* McGraw-Hill, 2012.

21 Steve Hall, www.linkedin.com/in/stevehallsydney.

22 CEO.com, "2015 Social CEO Report." www.ceo.com/social-ceo-report-2015.

23 Jesse Davis, RingDNA and PointClear, "What Is Inside Sales and How Is It Changing?" 2015. www.ringdna.com/blog/what-is-inside-sales.

24 Originally published: www.linkedin.com/pulse/sales-coaching-from-actual-ceo-buyer-tony-j-hughes. Reprinted with permission of Hari Krishnan.

CHAPTER FIVE

1 Dale Carnegie, *How to Win Friends and Influence People*. Simon & Schuster, 1936.

2 Dr. Robert Cialdini, *Pre-Suasion.* Random House, 2016.

INDEX

Note: Page numbers in italics indicate figures.